READINGS IN CONTEMPORARY BUSINESS

Second Edition — Grainger and Hodge

READINGS IN CONTEMPORARY BUSINESS

Second Edition

EDITED BY

DAVID E. GRAINGER
Oakland Community College

MARIE R. HODGE
Bowling Green State University

THE DRYDEN PRESS
Hinsdale, Illinois

Library of Congress Catalog Card Number 75-21318
ISBN: 0-03-015526-6
Printed in the United States of America
67890 039 987654321

FOREWORD

This volume contains 39 exciting articles designed to supplement *Contemporary Business*. The contents are divided according to the major section headings of the parent text. Each section is preceded by a brief introduction and followed by discussion questions.

These selections were chosen on the basis of their relevancy to students in the introductory business course. They can be a useful adjunct to the study of business by providing fresh viewpoints on critical matters affecting executive decisions.

We are delighted that Professors Grainger and Hodge were able to lend their considerable talents to improving the *Contemporary Business* project. Both are experienced, well-qualified instructors whose genuine concern for students is reflected in the anthology they have prepared. After reviewing this book, we think you will agree that Professors Grainger and Hodge have done an excellent job in developing a truly teachable readings collection.

Louis E. Boone
The University of Tulsa

David L. Kurtz
Eastern Michigan University

CONTENTS

READINGS IN CONTEMPORARY BUSINESS

Second Edition — Grainger and Hodge

BUSINESS AND ITS ENVIRONMENT

The United States is not the only country in the world with a business system; every country has some sort. Business exists to solve the basic economic problem of humanity—nearly unlimited wants but limited resources to satisfy all of them. The business system is an agent by which scarce resources are rationed to the people.

Throughout the history of our society, the U.S. private enterprise system has produced more goods and services for its citizens than any other type of business system. Of course, the U.S. system has some faults—unjust pricing, commercial bribery, excessive size and discriminatory hiring practices to name a few. However, in spite of its faults, the U.S. system is the most productive business system in the world; it maintains the world's highest standard of living; and it has the highest degree of technology ever known to humanity.

Today the business system faces its greatest challenge ever. Some of its basic concepts are facing inquiry by consumers, government, and even its own employees. For example, in the 1950s business firms felt that they had unlimited markets for goods. The goal seemed to be two cars in every garage and color TV in every room. Then came the rude awakening that resources were running out, energy was limited, and the environment could not take all of the abuse that we had inflicted on it over the past centuries.

The following articles represent various points of view concerning the possible changes to the U.S. business system. The one thread of consistency is that some changes are coming. The main question seems to be "What kind of changes?" rather than "Will there be changes?"

1

CAN PRIVATE OWNERSHIP OF ENTERPRISE SURVIVE IN AMERICA?

CHARLES H. SMITH, JR.

I'm sure you all remember King Pyrrhus from Military History I. But I'd like to review a little of that history to make a point. The time was roughly 280 BC, the scene Tarentum, a Greek colony on the heel of the Italian boot.

The people of Tarentum had dealt cavalierly with some quaint barbarians from the North and—not being very warlike themselves—they began to worry about the possible consequences.

In the name of Hellenistic unity and brotherhood, they appealed for help to Pyrrhus of Epirus.

Pyrrus, in the name of Hellenistic unity and brotherhood, had conquered half of Macedon. He was one of the best generals of his time. And he was itching for something else to conquer, but he realized that he'd gone about as far as he could safely go in his immediate neighborhood. So he welcomed the invitation from Tarentum.

In the spring of 280 he arrived on the Italian peninsula with an army of 25,000.

The barbarians from the North called themselves Romans. Pyrrhus fought them three times.

He won the first battle, in 280, after a hard fight—largely by use of his secret weapon, elephants. The Romans lost a total of 9,000 men to Pyrrhus's 4,000.

At Asculum, in 278, they met again. And again, Pyrrhus won. The Romans lost 6,000 men, Pyrrhus lost 3,500. But among the 3,500 were most of his generals and his best troops.

It was at Asculum that he made the remark by which his name enters our language: "One more such victory and I am undone."

And he was right.

They met a third and final time at Beneventum, in 275. The Romans won that battle decisively. Pyrrhus returned home with only 8,500 of the 25,000 men he had when he started.

He died three years later, when an old woman on a rooftop in Argos threw a chamber pot at him. Which proves, I guess, that not all old generals just fade away.

In terms of tactical ability, Pyrrhus and his Roman opponents were closely matched. What

SOURCE: *Vital Speeches of the Day,* published by City News Publishing Co. Reprinted by permission.

Pyrrhus could not match was the total Roman system; the combination of high morale, administration, organization and economics that enabled the Romans to keep coming back for more.

Pyrrhus and his army were wholly exposed. They could not recover from a single major defeat. The Roman armies, like the tail of a lizard, were expendable extensions of a system able to regrow what it had lost.

King Pyrrhus's Roman campaign may not be the first example in history of the essential link between military strength and socio-economic strength, but it is probably the most famous.

After the fall of Rome, as you know, the Western world experienced a long era of feudal economics and personal generalship.

I believe many historians cite the defeat of Napoleon Bonaparte to mark the end of this period; the end of the time when the ruler of a country could personally direct the details of major battles. Ever since, war has become an increasingly complex matter of transportation, communication, coordination, supply and technology.

It's interesting to note, in passing, that economics was one of Napoleon's major weaknesses as a ruler.

In his biography of Napoleon, Vincent Cronin comments on the technological and economic backwardness of the French Empire, in contrast to Great Britain.

Napoleon, he says, "considered economic sacrifices a small price to pay for equality and the rights of man. He who thought in terms of honor believed that others must think in those terms also. It was not true. The ordinary people of the Empire thought of their comforts and of attractive novelties in the shops."

Napoleon had other faults, of course. I understand the British considered him a little weak on naval strategy.

In any case, the point is that we have now reached a stage in history where the military forces of a nation can be worse than its socio-economic system, but they cannot be better.

It is our technological capacity that limits our ability to forestall a nuclear war as well as our ability to win one, if "win" is an applicable term. It is our economic strength that determines the amount of national resources that can be devoted to lesser wars at an acceptable cost to civilian morale. And of course, it is our economic strength that determines our technological capacity.

So the resources, morale and technology in support of a modern military effort are determined by a nation's economic base.

Before we get into the current state of our economic base, let's review some fundamental economic principles.

The really important economic principles are quite simple. Complexity enters into it only in arguing over the details.

The fundamental principle was discovered by the advisors of an ancient king.

This king had become interested in the subject, but he feared its complexity. So he called in his three wise men and told them: "I want to learn everything of importance about economics. Present it to me in a form that I can easily understand."

Several months later the wise men returned. They said they had condensed all of economics into a single book of 500 pages.

That's too long," said the king, "I don't have time for that." He had the chairman beheaded and said to the other two: "Get back to work and boil it down further."

They returned in one month with a single chapter of 20 pages. "It's still too long," said the king, and he beheaded the chairman. "When I say 'boil it down,' I *mean* boil it down," he said to the remaining wise man. "Now get busy!"

The last wise man returned in only three days: "Your Majesty," he said, "I have reduced the principles of economics to only one sentence, of just eight words."

"That's more like it," said the King. "I have time for that. What is it?"

"There's no such thing as a free lunch."

That pretty well sums it all up. At any given time, we have a finite amount of resources available to devote to the satisfaction of our needs and desires. We may shift resources from one sector of the economy, or one industry, or one government program to another. But the total of claims on our resources cannot exceed the total of those resources.

I realize that that statement sounds so simple and so obvious you may well wonder why I make it.

I make it because, simple and obvious though it is, we have been running the country lately in a fashion that suggests either ignorance of this fundamental truth or a willful decision to ignore it.

The virulent inflation we suffer from today got its start when Lyndon Johnson tried to pay for both the Great Society and the Vietnamese War without shifting the necessary resources away from other sectors of the economy.

He could have taken these resources by a tax increase. He eventually did, but he waited too long to do it.

In attempting to avoid a tax increase, he borrowed. Borrowing, of course, shifts resources from the lender to the borrower—at least temporarily. But there is a great hidden danger in government borrowing.

When the economy is producing close to capacity—as it was in those years—there is a big demand for credit. When the Federal Government competes with borrowers in the private sector for credit, existing credit shortages are worsened and the price of money— its interest rate—goes up.

For some time now, business has been facing these disruptive effects of inflation in the capital markets. Current tax levels amount in effect to a levy on assets, thus depressing the equity capital markets and constituting a disincentive to investment.

Profits—a possible internal source of investment funds—have been calculated largely on the basis of original costs for inventories and depreciated plant and equipment, and hence have been much overstated.

The inability of business firms to generate enough capital funds internally to finance new plant and equipment at inflated prices leads business to scramble for borrowed funds, while the shortage is aggravated and interest rates are bid up as government expands its borrowing.

Higher interest rates raise costs and discourage expansion in the private sector. Initially, some industries are harder hit than others. Housing, for instance, is especially sensitive to changes in the interest rate and the availability of credit.

At this point, the Federal Reserve System usually steps in to save the economy from the credit crunch. It effects the rescue by increasing the supply of money, so there is enough available to satisfy the credit needs of both the Federal Government and the private sector.

The trouble is, the result of these "rescues" by the Fed is that the money supply increases faster than the supply of goods and services.

In other words, people have more money to spend, but they don't have more to spend it on. So they bid up prices in competition for goods.

The inevitable outcome is a rise in the general level of prices. That is, money becomes worth less in terms of goods and services. Its purchasing power declines.

Knowing this, it's easy to see that a cure for inflation must involve either an increase in the production of goods and services, or a decrease in the money supply, or some combination of the two.

Now the plot thickens. A decrease in the money supply—or, more realistically, a decrease in the rate of increase—requires a cut in borrowing by the Federal Government and a willingness to continue to suffer temporarily the pains of high interest rates. But after we balance the budget and ease the present heavy government demand for borrowed funds, interest rates will be free to start downward as investment funds become more available for business expansion.

The government can decrease its borrowing in either of two ways, or, once again, in some combination of the two.

It can·raise taxes to fund programs instead of borrowing to fund them.

Or it can trim its budget to live within its existing income.

Now keep those two alternatives in mind—raise taxes or lower expenditures—while we look at the other anti-inflationary measure: Increasing the production of goods and services at least as fast as the money supply.

An increase in the production of goods and services requires greater investment in productive facilities: New machines for old factories and new factories for new machines. It also requires new technology so we can produce more at less relative expense.

New technology, in turn, requires greater investment in research and development.

A company can get the necessary investment capital by saving it from its income, by selling new stock to the public, by selling bonds to the public, or by negotiating loans from a bank.

The ability of a business to exercise any or all of these options will depend on both its general health—its profitability—and on the availability of credit and the prevailing interest rate.

Obviously, people will be more inclined to lend money to a profitable business. And, a profitable business can more easily accumulate capital from its income.

But the interest rate is an important factor, too. If interest rates are high, the business will have to use more of its profit to pay dividends to keep its stock competitive with other securities.This will reduce its ability to accumulate capital from income. It also makes sales of new stock issues more difficult. And of course, it makes other forms of borrowing more expensive and therefore less attractive.

So we have come full circle: An increase in productivity can help cure inflation caused by government borrowing, but government borrowing makes an increase in productivity more difficult to attain by disrupting capital markets and impending the flow of investment funds, and therefore capital formation.

There are other government policies hampering productivity increases today. In a moment, we'll examine some of them.

But first, I'd like to dispose of another "cure" for inflation that's being bandied about in some circles; an entirely spurious cure.

This purported cure is a cut in the personal income tax. The reasoning being advanced for a tax cut is that it would help make up for the loss in purchasing power suffered by the consumer as a result of inflation.

That argument has a certain surface plausibility. It has if you're willing to overlook the fact that a tax cut under present conditions would worsen the very inflation it is supposed to compensate for.

Cutting the personal income tax is worth trying when there is plenty of spare industrial capacity and business is sluggish because the consumer just isn't buying. Given such conditions, the cut may stimulate new purchases and an upturn in business activity.

But the problem today is undercapacity and technological obsolescence, not over-capacity. People already have the money to buy more goods and services than business can produce. Many of our basic industries are running at top speed. The economy is plagued with shortages.

A tax cut without a corresponding cut in the federal budget would increase the government's need to borrow, thus decreasing still further the funds available for business expansion. And the extra money in the hands of consumers—if it stimulated demand—would not bring forth more goods and services. Only new plant capacity can do that. What the extra money would do is further bid up the prices of those goods and services that are available. In other words, it would worsen inflation.

So a tax cut—at this time—is definitely not the answer.

However, please don't conclude from that statement that I think our present tax system is ideal. It is far from ideal. Indeed, it is one of the major contributors to our economic problems.

Government—at all levels—is claiming and disposing of an ever larger share of our national income. Total government spending has grown from about 10 percent of national income prior to 1929 to about 40 percent today. If present trends continue, the distinguished economist Milton Friedman calculates that government will be disposing of over half the national income by 1988.

Our tax system combines with inflation and anticompetitive regulatory practices to hinder capital formation, and thus, productivity improvement.

The income tax is biased against effort compared to leisure, against saving in favor of current consumption, against independent and innovative investment and business under-takings in favor of cautious and low productivity processes, and against capital-intensive and in favor of labor-intensive production.

We tax capital more heavily than any other major industrial nation.

Our tax policy is one of the major reasons we are becoming less efficient, less productive. But it is far from being the only reason.

There are plenty of other roadblocks to productivity.

In the name of the environment, the consumer and the worker, government has swiftly added a heavy new layer to the already staggering regulatory burden borne by the private sector.

Federal regulations tend to decrease productivity in two ways. First, they often require heavy capital investment that does not improve productivity and is, of necessity, subtracted from the capital that would have been available for that purpose. Second, they occupy staff time filling out forms and applications.

As an illustration of the first point, the U.S. Department of Commerce calculates that nonfarm business spent $4.9 billion on pollution control efforts last year and will spend about $6.5 billion this year.

According to McGraw-Hill, industry spent $2.6 billion last year to comply with the regulations of the Occupational Safety and Health Administration, and will spend another $3 billion this year. And that's just the tip of the iceberg. OSHA itself estimates that its proposed noise control standards would cost business from $13 billion to $31 billion, depending on their stringency.

These are just some of the costs posed by the new social demands or requirements.

Senator McIntyre of New Hampshire calculated a few years ago that processing regulatory paper work alone costs business $18 billion a year and government another $18 billion. Thirty six billion dollars is a significant sum even in our trillion dollar economy.

The rules of many of the so-called regulatory agencies actually have the effect of decreasing productivity and raising costs to the consumer.

The excesses and waste of this proliferation of red tape can best be grasped in application to specific examples:

> To build the Alaska pipeline, 1,100 permits were needed from the state and federal governments.

> To renew his license, the owner of a small radio station and one of his employees had to spend four months filling out an application weighing 45 pounds.

> To gain approval of a new drug, a pharmaceutical company had to submit an application consisting of 64 volumes of data, making a stack over 10 feet high.

And then there's the delay:

> It takes the National Labor Relations Board an average of 11.5 months to rule on a routine unfair labor practice charge.

> The Interstate Commerce Commission needs an average of 18 months to rule on a transportation rate case.

> The average time for processing a new drug application at the Food and Drug Administration was 106 days in 1958 . . .
> . . . 327 days in 1963 . . .
> . . . and over 600 days in 1968.

> The Federal Power Commission took 11 years to decide how to fix natural gas prices all the way back to the wellhead.

And so it goes. Beyond the expense and the delay are the contradictions. You'll appreciate the case of the Holston Defense Corp.

Holston operates an Army ammunition plant, under contract.

According to OSHA rules, the fireplugs at Holston's plant must be painted red. OSHA rules apply to Holston, since it is a private company.

However, according to Army regulations, fireplugs must be painted yellow; with a green, orange or red cap, depending on the water pressure. The Army rules also apply to Holston, since it operates on an Army installation.

Sometimes, gentlemen, it's a dog's life.

On top of the expense, and the delay, and the contradictions, there are the counterproductive efforts.

In a burst of concern for the environment, Congress passed legislation calling for an end to all industrial discharge into the nation's waterways by 1985.

A scientist from the 3M Company pointed out that "zero discharge" would be a technically unattainable state of perfection—the water going *into* a plant already contains impurities.

But this scientist did calculate the requirements for bringing the discharge of one 3M plant up to the U.S. Public Health standards for drinking water. His figures are interesting.

To remove 4,000 tons of pollutants per year from the plant's discharge would require the following resources:

> Nineteen thousand tons of coal to produce steam, 9,000 tons of chemicals, and 1,500 kilowatt hours of electricity.
>
> In the course of the "purification" operation, the 3M plant would produce:
>
> Nine thousand tons of chemical sludge . . .
>
> Twelve hundred tons of fly ash . . .
>
> One thousand tons of sulfur dioxide . . .
>
> And 200 tons of nitrogen oxide.

That's just at the plant. To that total must be added the environmental costs of producing the 9,000 tons of chemicals, the 1,500 kilowatt hours of electricity and the steel, concrete and other resources used in the pollution control facilities.

What's the grand total? Altogether, to remove those 4,000 tons of pollutants would take 40,000 tons of natural resources per year and produce 19,000 tons of solid and gaseous waste material, for a net deficit to the environment of 15,000 tons of pollutants per year.

Believe it or not, we are very nearly in the same position with respect to air pollution. The Supreme Court came within a hair's breadth of interpreting Congressional legislation to mean that no degradation of air quality is permissible anywhere. Fortunately, it did not go that far. But the compromise position is not much better. It is still going to be very, very difficult to relocate industry to low-population areas because of these nondegradation rules.

This brief discussion is by no means a complete survey of the federal regulatory trouble spots for business. There are literally dozens of other agencies, bureaus and departments I haven't even mentioned. Nor are all the problems at the federal level. State regulators, too, seem to be becoming more political and less rational in discharging their responsibilities. Nowhere is this more apparent than in the electric power utilities.

Listen to Paul McCracken, a former chairman of the Council of Economic Advisors:

"Our whole electric utility industry is financially almost a basket case. There has been some inexcusable demagoguery about this. The obvious answer is to get rates up enough so that they reflect the higher costs of fuel being converted into electricity."

Mr. McCracken also has some observations about federal economic policy that are very much in line with what I have been saying here today:

"It would certainly be helpful," he says, "if government would attack some of its own price-raising 'sacred cows'—the disgraceful ICC regulation of transportation that has bankrupted railroads and imposed higher costs on consumers, the postal monopoly, the Jones Act that forces higher coastal-shipping costs on people. Or the so-called Energy Transportation Security Act of 1974, by which the maritime unions will add another billion dollars to consumers' gasoline bills—a mislabeling of this magnitude in the private sector would land some in jail."

How true, Mr. McCracken, how true.

Perhaps the most pernicious effect of this growing tangle of red tape and political economics is the damage it does to our small businessmen. And these are the people our government regulators and their backers always claim they are trying to help.

A small businessman cannot afford a staff of sophisticated lawyers, accountants and technicians to interpret and fill out forms. Nor can he always arrange to finance the heavy capital expenditures new regulations often require.

Consequently, we are hearing from small businessmen who are simply ignoring the rules and waiting for the ax to fall; we are hearing from small businessmen who are going out of business rather than try to cope; and we are hearing from small businessmen who are laying off employees to get their labor force below the level that would bring them under the sway of one set of regulations or another.

The result of these multiple follies is what you would expect: Our capital formation lags sadly behind the competition. For the years 1970 through 1972, U. S. gross fixed capital formation averaged 14.2 percent of gross domestic product.

Let's compare that 14 percent rate with the figures for some of the other major industrial nations over the same period: Japan, 34.5 percent; France, 26 percent; West Germany, 26 percent; Canada, 21.3 percent; Italy, 19.4 percent; and Britain, 19.3 percent.

Capital formation, as I have said, is related to productivity gains. So it is hardly surprising to find that our record in this respect is also lagging behind. Productivity gains in the U.S., 1960–1971, were less than half the average in 10 major industrial nations; 2.9 percent here compared to their average of 6.1 percent.

We have gotten ourselves into this mess by focussing on the desirability of goals while ignoring the availability of means. We have been so busy bickering about the distribution of the golden eggs that no one has given much thought to the nutritional needs of the goose. The consequences of such policies ought to be obvious, but evidently such is not the case.

The very people who create the conditions under which business productivity suffers use the lower productivity as an argument to justify still more government intervention.

Up to now, I have been assuming general agreement that the best way to end inflation and provide the resources to meet our national goals is to increase production while making the productive machinery more efficient.

There is another argument that deserves some comment, especially in the context of global politics. This is the argument that growth and pollution are inextricably and destructively linked, that resources are finite and exhaustable, and that if we continue on the path of growth, we will either starve to death or poison ourselves in the not-too-distant future.

The best exposition of this school of thought is the book, *The Limits to Growth,* produced by an organization of wealthy Western industrialists and intellectuals known as The Club of Rome.

What these anti-growth environmentalists are proposing—stripped of delicate euphemisms—is the deliberate and calculated pursuit of stagnation. Such a policy would inevitably lead them into an impossible quandary.

Even if they could get Americans to abandon forever the quest for material improvement that has been one of the constants of our history, there would remain the rest of the world. How do you convince millions of people who are just beginning to dream of a better standard of living that it's "in their best interest" to accept perpetual poverty as the price of a more serene environment? Particularly when this revelation emanates from a group of wealthy Western intellectuals.

If ever there were an issue custom-made for the alert demagogue, this is it. Any shrewd politician anywhere in the world could and would destroy all the elegant arguments with a gut-level appeal to racial and cultural prejudice, coupled with the dangling carrot of material wealth.

When moral suasion fails, the only thing left is force. America—or the entire West—would have to impose economic stagnation on an unwilling world. But, without a population advantage, the only way to muster sufficient force to do that (assuming this madness went so far) is through the technology that has given us our edge over the rest of the world. Technology again. That brings us back to the starting point.

Of course, there is another alternative—one much more palatable to the extremist environmentalists, I suspect. The West simply halts its growth and allows others to "catch up." Then we expect them to do the "reasonable thing" and halt *their* growth. And what if they don't?

At that point in the scenario, we—the West—would be effete and decadent. The other cultures, perhaps younger, certainly more dynamic, would just be hitting their stride, feeling their oats. They would have every reason to feel confidence in themselves, based on their highly visible accomplishments, and every reason to feel contempt for a Western world which, by that time, would appear to be in decline and decay.

In short, the world is going to be run in the style chosen by the power or powers possessing the physical ability to dominate it. That does not necessarily imply political conquest—although it certainly doesn't exclude it, either. Western culture and technology predominate today much more by example—economically and culturally—than by force.

The real problem is not with economic or technological growth, per se. It is that we have lost (or are being importuned to lose) our faith in technology. Technological progress has always created new problems as it solved old ones. It *will* always create new problems as it solves old ones. But for some reason, some of us have focused on the problems of the moment and concluded that they are permanent, eternal and immutable. Nonsense!

Zero economic growth as now understood would be a disaster. What we want is to produce a given quantity of goods and services with less waste and pollution. For the vast majority of people in the world, more goods and services is the same thing as increasing the quality of life. In advanced societies, the poor share this view; and it is the poor, here and elsewhere, who would bear the major burden of a no-growth policy.

The evidence of history is overwhelming that increases in real income for the poor have come mainly from growth in the economy as a whole. Even though tax policy for years has tried to redistribute income by taking from the rich and giving to the poor, the distribution of income has not changed much if any. Nor could further attempts at redistribution add much to the welfare of the poor. But the heavy tax burden on upper-income individuals and businesses has increased the relative costs of saving. In other words, the tax burden has reduced the amount of saving and capital formation from what it would otherwise have been. And thus economic growth—the prime factor in improving the status of the poor—has been undercut.

In summary, you can see that in the name of a multitude of worthy goals, we have been progressively destroying the ability of our economy to provide the resources to attain these goals.

Yet, the cause of our present problems is seldom recognized. Quite the reverse: The symptoms of damage in the economy which result from inept government intervention are actually used as evidence of the need for still more government intervention.

We are but a short step to the suggestion that since private enterprise cannot raise sufficient capital for its needs, the capital should come from government. That, of course, is virtually identical to the suggestion that government should own the means of production.

It has now been over 126 years since Karl Marx issued his "Communist Manifesto" in which he called out in a voice that has ricocheted around the world for the abolition of the private ownership of the means of production. In the intervening years, his views have been adopted in varying degrees in many parts of the world, ranging from the confiscation of virtually all private property as in the Soviet Union, to lesser levels of government ownership, such as the nationalization of natural resources and public utilities in some developing countries or the nationalization of some basic industries such as in the United Kingdom or merely to the creation of some government owned facilities that compete with private facilities, such as the Tennessee Valley Authority in the United States.

A thoughtful and careful appraisal of the results of government ownership of the means of production will demonstrate that in no case does such a system provide the general public with as many advantages as does the system of private ownership as practiced in the United States.

Despite this demonstrated superiority of the free market system, there are many distinguished leaders from both government and business who warn that future generations of Americans—perhaps even the next generation—will witness the elimination of free enterprise in America—the elimination of capitalism, and the substitution of state ownership of the means of production and a centrally planned economy.

Senator Barry Goldwater recently stated:

"The competitive enterprise system is now under attack by demagogues who would like to nationalize all basic enterprise in this country, and there is a greater chance of their success than at anytime in our history."

C. Jackson Grayson, chairman of the Price Commission during our recent unfortunate experience with economic controls has said in his new book "Confessions of a Price Controller";

"I am personally convinced that our economic system is steadily shifting away from private enterprise and a free market, and toward central direction and control. At some point, possibly in fifteen or twenty years at the present rate, the essential characteristics of a competitive, private enterprise system (nonregulated prices, profit motive, risk taking, collective bargaining) will no longer be characteristic of the American economy. Call it what you will—managed capitalism, socialism, a planned economy, a post industrial state—in the end, it will mean the virtual elimination of the free market system as we know it."

And if you read the entire book, or if you know Jack Grayson, you will understand that he views these developments, these predictions, with considerable alarm and concern.

Paul McCracken, whom I quoted earlier, is equally grim:

"The more detailed and severe the controls over economic life," he says, "the more difficult it is for an economy to generate progress, and for democracy to function in a normal way. We could move toward a police state, toward government ownership of industry, and toward controls that breed economic arthritis—and, not so incidentally, growing corruption. That has been international experience."

Arthur Burns, the chairman of the Federal Reserve Board, concurs:

"I do not believe I exaggerate," he says, "in saying that the ultimate consequence of inflation could well be a significant decline of economic and political freedom for the American people."

If our free market economic system outperforms every variation of government owned and government planned economies, we must ask ourselves why it is that so many knowledgeable people are freely predicting the early demise of the free market system in America. Those of us who realize that all of our freedoms—freedom of the press, freedom to work at a job of our own choosing, freedom to bargain collectively—yes, even political and religious freedom are based on the freedom of the market place and the private enterprise system; those of us who realize this must quickly find the reasons for the threat to our free market economy and rally to its defense. If Grayson, and Goldwater, McCracken and Burns are correct, we don't have much time left in which to reverse the direction in which our economy is drifting.

And when I use the word "drifting," let me suggest the analogy of a Sunday sailor drifting lazily down the Upper Niagara River. It's a warm sunny afternoon, and the current is not yet so rapid that the amateur skipper is alarmed about the rapids ahead that lead to complete destruction at the Falls. There is still time and opportunity to change course and work our way back upstream; or at the very least, work our way over to the shoreline where we can tie our craft to a sturdy tree to prevent being caught in a current that will sweep us over the Falls. The thunder of impending doom is still only a faint rumble in the far distance.

But the longer we procrastinate in changing course, the more dangerous becomes our position. It is high time that we begin to identify and seek to avoid currents that can carry us downstream at an ever accelerating pace until we reach a channel from which there is no possibility to return.

2

MYTHS ABOUT BUSINESS
THAT THREATEN YOUR FUTURE

RAYMOND J. MARKMAN

There is, I think, a tide tugging at the underpinnings of our American economic system. It is a threat to our society as real as any outside peril ever has been because it masks behind the face of life as normal.

That threat is what I call "the Great Rip-off that nobody talks about."

Not quite nobody, of course. In boardrooms it is touched upon. In retail managers' offices it is an everpresent fact of life.

I'm not talking about the kind of rip-offs that news media, the politicians and the federal regulators have been having great fun with lately.

No, I'm talking about the far more pervasive rip-off of business itself.

The widespread, near incalculable and, worst of all, seemingly acceptable rip-offs of business by the consumer-rip-offs that threaten not only our profit margins, our jobs, our companies, our industries, but also our very economic system itself.

For example, how about the phony long-distance collect calls people make to themselves to let someone know they've arrived? Where they slip in an extra message at the same time. "No, operator, don't bother leaving word. I'll see him when I come home Tuesday anyway."

It may or may not be a prime example of consumer rip-offs of business, but its symptomatic of a widespread—and growing—attitude of acceptance.

After all, business is so rich and impersonal, isn't it? I'm not really hurting an *individual*—am I? AT&T is a billionaire!

So what if I return something to Fields for a refund a year later . . . Or not pay the final bill to a utility company . . . Or pick up ashtrays or beer mugs from a few restaurants . . . So what if I ask the attendant to "fill 'er up," then claim I asked for only $5 worth of gas . . . Or don't tell the clerk when I pay with a $5 bill and get change for a ten . . . Or take the introductory selection of books or records with no intention of *ever* buying a thing, no matter what the coupon says . . . Or contribute to the $50 billion pilferage of retail merchandise that occurs every year.

So what about the consumer rip-offs of insurance companies . . . the cents-off coupon misredemptions that run into hundreds of millions of dollars? Misredemption that almost closed the doors for good for Pam Industries in Chicago. A full 90 percent

14

SOURCE: Reprinted from the October 1977 issue of *Success Unlimited* Magazine. Copyright © 1977 by Success Unlimited, Inc. 6335 Broadway, Chicago, Ill. 60660.

of the coupons retailers redeemed for Pam Dry Fry were honored *despite* the shoppers'
failure to buy the product.

Are we such economic illiterates that we can't see the boomerang effect of the rip-offs in terms of higher prices, lost jobs, or reduced dividends to the 50 million of us who are stockholders in corporations or members of pension funds? Can't we see that we're all consumers—and when we step on business' lifeline, we're ultimately cutting our own?

Am I overstating society's view of business today? Not according to Lou Harris, who finds that Americans' confidence in the leadership of business has slipped from 55 percent in 1966 to 18 percent in 1975. And not according to the massive research project just completed by the Ad Council—the National Survey on the American Economic System. It shows quite clearly that most American people are indeed illiterate for practical purposes about the unique system under which they work and live. Just how serious is that misunderstanding? Here is what Max Wrays wrote in *Fortune* magazine:

"Current antibusiness sentiment is no summer squall—no election year flap, no recession-born disenchantment, no transient hostility stirred up by a few malcontents. It would be unwise . . . to assume that Ralph Nader created the wave of consumer resistance. He vocalized feelings already present in the public.

"The declining reputation of business could, unless it is reversed, weaken the internal morale of corporations and so poison the relation between business and the rest of society that the quality of American life would deteriorate."

Early this year, a survey by Standard and Poor's revealed that the average profit U.S. industry makes on the sales dollar after taxes comes to about 5 cents. But do you have any idea of how much the public *thinks* we make: 28 cents to 33 cents after taxes and going up! Almost six times reality. What makes it worse is that the public feels a *fair* profit for business would be a dime out of every dollar—twice as much as we're actually achieving.

Unfortunately, the consumer's view of American business—his knowledge as well as his psychological underpinnings—is being supported by important and respectable segments of our society: the school system, the politicians, the media, and the regulators.

Begin with the schools. According to one survey only 7 percent of American educators have had *any* economic training. In the 12 years that youngsters are in the school system, do you suppose they are gaining an objective understanding of American business, economics and the free enterprise system? Or at the college level, where young people, quite properly, are questioning existing values? Is the businessman's point of view represented adequately? Are teachers, who themselves have selected nonbusiness careers, best qualified to present our story? Couldn't we do it better—and shouldn't we?

Irving Kristol, Henry Luce professor of urban values at New York University and co-editor of the quarterly *The Public Interest,* reports, "College seniors are much more antibusiness than college freshmen, so it is clear that something is going on in those classrooms over that four-year period to achieve this effect."

Consider American politics—and what the politican regards as his first obligation: to get elected. Think of the out-of-context quotes you've seen in election years—the headline grabbers that appeal for votes using the consumerism movement as their vehicle, as they place American business on trial. With either a lack of economic understanding—or for political gain—they blame business alone for inflation, recession and virtually every other ailment of our time. Yet, many so-called economic problems are political.

Consider the media: Ask yourself if you feel the business point of view is represented adequately. In our own direct marketing industry, when headlines speak of junk mail, are they reflecting *your* business objectively and honestly? Or is your industry being ripped off by emotionally directed reporting that distorts truth? How often have you seen a story attacking business on page 1—an inflammatory "exposé?" And how often have you seen the subsequent retraction buried ever-so-quietly somewhere near the obit page? There's no question that the media control information—and that information is power. But how is that power used by the media? Without debating the rights or wrongs of oil company prices, consider the current conflict between WNBC and Mobil Oil Company. WNBC presented a highly promoted five-part series on the price of gasoline. Mobil called the presentation "inaccurate, unfair, and a disservice to the people."

When Mobil offered to buy and pay for 30 minutes of air time to tell its side of the story, WNBC refused to sell the time for policy reasons. Mobil, in its effort to participate in the marketplace of ideas, was forced to run print advertising under the headline, "What ever happened to fair play?" Could Mobil reach the same audience in print?

Do television reporters and commentators have the depth of economic understanding today to do justice to a business story? Or are they "representatives of station managers with their happy hour news anchored by show business hams?" If that last phrase sounds like I'm being less than objective myself, let me point out that it's a direct quote from no one less than Walter Cronkite.

Consider the regulators. According to the *Chicago Daily News,* the regulators, these "federal officials who haven't been elected now seem to be making rules that affect people more directly than the doings of Congress." A Library of Congress study found that in 1974 Congress passed 404 laws while the federal bureaucracy churned out 7,496 new or amended regulations. That's 18 regulations for every law.

Is all this regulation working?

There has been a litany of gripes. Here are just a few from *U.S. News and World Report:*

- Agents of the Occupational Safety and Health Administration ordered that trucks on a construction site install alarms that sound when vehicles are backing up. Then it ordered workers to wear earplugs to protect themselves from excessive noise.
- A Philadelphia electric utility preparing to build a plant needed 24 different kinds of approval from five federal agencies, five state agencies, two townships and a regional commission.

These are gripes from fairly big businesses—but what about the little guy?

Here's what Irving Kristol says: "One may properly wonder why no greater efforts are made to protect smaller business from the horrendous burden which the newer regulatory agencies impose on them. Big business finds it difficult enough to cope with all the expensive changes required to meet new rules. But in the end, big business has the resources to survive this experience, harrowing as it is. Small business will not survive it and is not. All over the nation, smaller firms are being pushed into liquidation or mergers by their inability to cope with these new burdens."

There's another important and respectable sector of society that has fostered the "Era of the Great Rip-off"—business itself through its silence and inaction has created a vacuum in which the antibusiness sentiment has grown and matured.

Aside from the abuses of parts of the business community, which deserve to be singled out and corrected, the *entire* business community has been guilty of allowing misinformation to grow and lack of education to continue—and when business has spoken, we've spoken inarticulately and with poorly prepared spokesmen. Yet it is business, in its own self-interest, that must show consumers that their interests are not at odds with business, but directly and immediately tied to the success of business.

Consumers must be made to realize that new products, lower prices, rising employment, higher wages, dividend checks, stock appreciation—yes, even government funded programs—are *all* made possible by the continuing success of business to achieve fair profits. Consumers must be reminded that in rip-offs of business, the consumer is the ultimate loser through higher prices and a higher cost of living. And we must do the reminding.

What I am proposing is a national coalition of *all* business groups, crossing industry lines. Imagine a well-conceived, well-executed national program designed to educate and "sell" our system—and its unparalleled benefits—to the rest of society.

The communication tools are available to us—and we know how to use them intelligently: paid and public service advertising; public relations that meets the all-important tests of objectivity and credibility; speakers' bureaus; and political action on a grass roots, one-on-one level, to name a few.

Just in the very broadest of strokes, here are some possibilities of positive equal time action programs using these tools:

To reach the school system, for example, we might establish a council for economic education using the Purdue University program as a model. Through such a council, we would initiate a dialogue with educators—with an eye toward making economics courses a required part of the teaching curriculum—and the development of a resource center for curriculum materials. Purdue has actually instituted such an economic education program throughout the state of Indiana, which is working to give citizens a clearer understanding of basic economics through enriching curriculum and teacher education programs and through workshops.

Now for the media part of the program. We could reach the media in several ways:

Attempting to influence the media by educating the consumer with a broadly based advertising campaign similar to that proposed by the Advertising Council—and also using paid advertising to fight inaccurate or unfair reporting *wherever* it occurs. For example: to force a retraction of a story in as much space and as prominent a position as the original accusation.

We could influence the media by educating ourselves about how to deal with media. We have to learn to present our point of view as dramatically and believably as we sell our products: how to hold a press conference; when to go "off the record"; how and when to prepare for appearances on public issues programs.

We can work *with* the media through the creation of equal time workshops and seminars for media representatives.

We can talk with politicians too, through a political action committee and a precisely defined "fair play doctrine" designed, simply, to convince politicians that it is no longer wise to use business as a whipping boy in the race for votes.

We can develop resource materials for business people to use in one-on-one presentations with their elected representatives—educate business people on how to talk with politicians—and encourage business people to expand their communications with politicians. And as we continue the advertising and public relations programs designed to educate consumers, there is hope that their feelings would be communicated to politicians at all levels of government.

Now these are just a few possible steps. There are many more. So much can be accomplished. We can create an atmosphere in which "consumerism" would be genuinely served, in which regulatory bodies would enforce genuinely constructive guidelines, working *within* the system for the consumer's ultimate benefit, not loss.

Former Treasury Secretary William Simon has said that the misunderstanding and misdirection of the American economy has become "*the* central underlying problem of our times". We can, and must, put an end to that "misunderstanding and misdirection."

Jacob Brownowski's superb book, *The Ascent of Man,* says something very important about this. "We are all afraid—for our confidence, for the future, for the world. That is the nature of the human imagination. Yet every man, every civilization, has gone forward because of its engagement with what it has set itself to do. The personal commitment and the emotional commitment working together as one, has made the Ascent of Man."

Let's continue to make more of a good thing through equal time for business.

Let's start now.

3

WHAT IS THE FUTURE OF
THE CORPORATION?

REGINALD H. JONES

Like most businessmen, I have been addressing most of my public comments to the immediate problems of our economy—inflation, recession, and capital formation. But today, with your indulgence, I would like to step back a bit and take a longer, more philosophical look at a deeper question: the future of the corporation itself.

It would be hard to imagine a more directly concerned audience than this. Last August, *Fortune* magazine listed, for the first time, the top fifty industrial corporations of the world. Twenty-four of them are based in the United States. Ten of the top twelve are American. In fact, three of the top five are headquartered right here in Detroit—General Motors, Ford, and Chrysler. General Electric was number six, so I feel a rather direct interest myself.

THE ISSUE IS SURVIVAL

It seems to me that we have reason to be concerned whether the corporation as we know it—the characteristic institution of our American enterprise system—will survive into the next century. Great social and institutional changes are taking place that will necessarily affect the corporation, and especially the larger firms that are the core of our nation's industrial system.

We in management are no strangers to change. The corporation has survived and prospered precisely because it *is* highly adaptable to changing circumstances. In fact, corporations are perhaps the principal agents of change in the United States, with a highly successful record as engines of human progress. It is not by coincidence that the United States created the first and only trillion-dollar economy in the world. That is the result of our traditions of political and economic democracy, in which the profit-and-loss disciplined private corporation, rather than the government, is the primary economic instrument.

SOURCE: Address to Detroit Economic Club, November 25, 1974. Reprinted by permission.

One would think that an institution which has been so spectacularly successful would have an assured future—at least for another century or so. But curiously, it is almost impossible to find any prophet who sees much of a future for the investor-owned corporation.

WHAT THE PROPHETS SAY

Even the most friendly futurists, such as Daniel Bell, Herman Kahn, and Peter Drucker, forecast trouble. As the economy shifts from goods to services, in terms of occupation and output, we become a "post-industrial society." And the question they ask—and we in management must answer—is whether the post-industrial society will also be a *post-business* society.

Other prophets are less generous. More than a century ago Karl Marx predicted that capitalism would collapse of its own inner contradictions, to be superseded by socialism or communism. Many people around the world still accept this as a historical necessity, and are working to move history along by one means or another.

The gloomy historical philosopher Oswald Spengler, writing of the "Decline of the West" at the beginning of this century, prophesied that our civilization is doomed to end with a great final struggle between Money and Power—business and government. And the inevitable outcome, he said, will be the triumph of Caesarism, raw power triumphant over economic and political democracy.

More recently, the prophets have taken a different tack. John Kenneth Galbraith and Richard Goodwin believe that the bureaucratic necessities of operating an industrial system —the disciplines it imposes on all concerned—will inevitably cause the major corporations to be absorbed by the state, the central planning and controlling bureaucracy.

Then there is the consummate pessimism of Robert Heilbroner. He predicts that the pressures of human population on the earth's resources will inevitably bring us into a system of worldwide rationing and control, wherein such bizarre oddities as private enterprise and private decision-making—at least with respect to industrial resources—simply could not be allowed. Thus the challenge extends to *all* industrial democracies, to their economic *and* political structures.

Now these are the observations of intelligent and serious men, and they are not to be ignored. It's my impression that they tend to overstate the weaknesses of the private enterprise system, and underestimate its creative power and adaptability. Nevertheless there *are* bureaucratic tendencies; there *are* worldwide trends to planned economies; there *are* crises that make the public yearn for strong, authoritarian controls.

EXAMINING THE VULNERABILITIES

My purpose today is not to predict the end of the corporation—far from it—but to surface some of its vulnerabilities, a subject that I think is especially important for those of us with managerial responsibilities. Absorbed as we are with the day-to-day tasks of running successful businesses, we cannot ignore the dangers to the survival of the system itself. Preserving and strengthening the best economic system ever developed is one of our basic responsibilities to future generations.

With this responsibility in mind, let's examine some of the vulnerabilities.

A SHIFT IN VALUES

The deepest challenge comes from a basic shift in the values and beliefs that undergird our society. The counterculture is not a passing phenomenon. The values that have supported and vitalized our business system—the belief in rationality, objectivity, efficiency, self-discipline, thrift, hard work—these values seem to be losing their power. Science and technology, once universally admired, are becoming objects of suspicion.

The shift in values is not confined to the young. As C. Jackson Grayson pointed out in the *Harvard Business Review*,[1] both labor and business nowadays often seek to reduce competition, not encourage it. Increasingly, Americans distrust the market system and demand that government step in to assure them of economic benefits. Much of the public has come to feel that controls—in other words, central planning—are not only desirable, but superior. Grayson concludes, "We are very near the point where further centralization will change our present system into one that can no longer perform its function efficiently."

And at that point, the sustaining rationale for the private corporation disappears.

FINANCIAL STARVATION

Another serious vulnerability is the possibility of financial starvation. Corporations cannot survive without a steady infusion of capital investment in new plants and equipment and new technology. Without this, the system runs down, loses its competitive capability in the world, and fails to satisfy the economic needs of society.

American business today is suffering from several decades of underinvestment. Ever since the depression, public policy has systematically favored the stimulation of demand, the redistribution of wealth, and the growth of government services—and given the needs of producers much lower priority. Now we pay the piper.

Between now and 1985, it is estimated that the capital investment needs of the private sector will be on the order of $4.5 trillion. That compares with $1.5 trillion invested in the past dozen years. Where will that enormous amount of private capital come from?

With real profits declining, investors leaving the stock market, and business going deeper and deeper into debt, the possibility of a capital shortage is not academic.

Major corporations with serious financial problems—Pan Am, Penn Central, Lockheed, Con Edison, Grumman, and others—have been reluctantly turning to the government as financier of last resort. Perhaps that seems a long step from regarding government as the financier of first resort. But if consumption-oriented tax policies continue over time to dry up the sources of voluntary savings and investment, then the United States will turn increasingly to government financing, and the power to tax could ultimately become our primary source of capital. And that, of course, would be the end of capitalism and private enterprise.

UNCONTROLLED INFLATION

Another and related vulnerability that must be faced is the possibility that today's double-digit inflation, if it is not brought under control, could lead to political and economic chaos. Dr. Kissinger has solemnly reminded us of the disruptive social and political effects of inflation, and the vulnerability of the Western democracies.

[1]Harvard Business Review, Nov.–Dec. 1973.

On the other hand, excessively stringent measures to stop inflation lead to a down-spiralling recession. Thus we walk an economic tightrope between inflation and recession.

Either of these problems, getting out of hand, could conceivably lead to demands for major changes in our economic system, with some form of socialism brought into being under the guise of emergency reform measures. The top 100 corporations—the most visible targets of control—would be the most vulnerable in such a situation. That's one reason why we cannot regard a harsh recession as an acceptable solution for our problem of inflation.

PLANNED ECONOMIES

Yet another area of vulnerability is the fact that American corporations are increasingly obliged to compete on the international scene with state enterprises and state-controlled economies. How can individual companies hope to compete effectively against the power of national treasuries, and their power to tax the people to cover their inefficiencies or advance political objectives?

As more and more of the world turns toward planned economies, using the whole resource base of a nation like one single economic enterprise—we in the United States might, in self-defense, find ourselves drifting in the same direction. The temptation to join the march toward government planning and control may be stronger than we think. Well-meaning proposals for federal planning commissions to prevent shortages and anticipate problems have in them the seeds of a planned economy.

Another variation of this theme is the trend toward socialism in Europe.

Unlike the United States, the labor movement in Europe has a Marxist tradition and is trying in several countries to gain control of private industry through the use of political power. This would be a very remote possibility in the United States, with the present leadership of our labor unions, but it is a live issue in West Germany, for example, where private industry is threatened by two major propositions.

One is a bill for what is called increased "co-determination." That is, the managing Board of Directors would be made up of 50% representatives of the employees and 50% representatives of the shareholders, with provisos that make it easy for the employee bloc to exert substantial control.

The other is a so-called profit-sharing proposal under which a certain percentage of industry's profits are distributed annually to employee trusts in the form of stock. Because of co-determination in the banks which manage the trusts, employees and their unions could gain effective control over these shares, which in a few years would amount to a controlling interest in the whole economy. The step from there to a labor government and full socialism could be very short indeed.

In an excellent book entitled *British Nationalization 1945–73,* R. Kelf-Cohen points out that the nationalization of Britain's basic industries was not brought about by a great national desire for socialism, but by pressure from the trade unions—the dominant elements of the Labour Party—in order to attain better control over the management of these industries.

Now the labor movement in the United States, unlike its European counterpart, has not formed a political party. It has been content to work—very successfully—within the traditional two-party system. Furthermore, American unions are for the most part strong supporters of the private enterprise system. Nevertheless, if the European trade unions, with their strong Marxist orientation, were to push Europe still further into socialism, this could not fail to affect the United States in the long run.

REGULATION TO EXTINCTION

But the most insidious vulnerability, and the one most likely to change the major corporations into mere arms of the government, is the slow, evermore entangling web of regulations by which the power of decision is being transferred from the Board Room to federal agencies in Washington. I need not recite here the long litany of statutes and regulations by which the federal government tells business what it may and may not do. The threat of federal charters and the licensing of corporations would be the last straw. Everyone of these regulations is introduced as a protection for the public, and every one is said to be adopted for our own good. The cumulative effect is what we must be concerned about.

Public policy has for decades favored growth of the public sector over the private sector. Expenditures by all governments in the U.S.—federal, state, and local—amounted to 10% of the gross national product in 1929. They have increased every decade and now stand at 32% of the economy. (Including off-budget items, Milton Friedman says it's now 40%!) If the long trend continues, they will be about 50% by the end of the century. The question is—when government is such a pervasive element, at what point do we cease to have a market-oriented, private-enterprise economy?

We have, of course, a highly mixed economy at the present time, and the distinction between public and private enterprise is being blurred. As Professor Galbraith put it in *Atlantic* magazine in 1967, "It requires no great exercise of the imagination to suppose that the mature corporation, as it develops, will eventually become a part of the larger administrative complex associated with the state. In time the line between the two will largely disappear. Men will marvel at the thin line that once caused people to refer to General Electric, Westinghouse, and Boeing as *private* business."

IS IT WORTH SAVING?

What are we to make of all this? If it is all so inevitable, should we plan accordingly? If the major corporations—the core of our private enterprise economy—are ultimately to be controlled or absorbed by the federal government, should we cynically start positioning our companies for power roles in the bureaucracy to come? Or do we have, in our private enterprise systems, some freedoms and values that must be preserved for future generations?

I'm sure I know your answer. Historians tell us that situations of freedom are rare and not very long-lasting in the five-thousand-year history of civilization. What we have developed here in the United States, political and economic democracy, has never been developed elsewhere on such a scale. It would be to our eternal dishonor if we were to let it be destroyed.

There's more at stake than the private enterprise system. If too many of our economic liberties are lost, our political and civil liberties will follow. A government that controls our economic life will soon control the rest of life. Freedom is indivisible.

This is, of course, an old-fashioned message. But then, so is socialism. The struggle between liberty and tyranny, people and governments, is a very ancient struggle, and every generation must work out its own accommodation.

BEWARE THE ELEPHANT

None of us, I'm sure, expects a return to the *laissez-faire* doctrine in which government plays no significant role in the economy. That day is gone.

Nor can we afford the kind of divisive adversary relationship between government and business that so frequently has us working at cross-purposes.

Rather, we need a relationship built on mutual respect and mutual support for common objectives. On some technical projects where the risks and costs are too large for individual corporations, business and government will have to work together if the job is to be done. We will need more governmental support for economic objectives overseas—a really effective foreign *economic* policy. But as one of my associates says, "Beware of getting into bed with an elephant. If he ever rolls over, you've had it."

We'll need to have a proper understanding about who does what, with government determining national objectives and policies, and private enterprise getting the economic work done. Though both business and government serve the public, we must insist on maintaining the essentially private, market-oriented character of the corporation, and try to reverse the long, uninterrupted trend of expanding the government sector at the expense of the private sector of the economy.

How can this be done? My purpose today has been to examine the vulnerabilities, not to present a Grand Plan for Salvation. But certain principles would seem to be basic.

DEVELOP A CONSTITUENCY

First, business must develop a constituency of hard-core supporters. As Irving Kristol has pointed out, "No institution in our society can endure without a constituency—a substantial number of people who are loyal to the institution and who will quickly rally to its defense when it is in trouble. Yet the modern corporation is just about the only major institution of our society which does not have such a constituency."

As Kristol explains, "Constituencies are not born but created—and once created, they need constant cultivation. Politicians understand this, but corporate managers do not."

Kristol stresses the share owner constituency, but I think it's larger than that. Our natural constituency is the middle class that not only invests in, but works in, and buys from the corporation. These are the people with a direct economic and political stake in the corporation's success. We in management need to cultivate their loyalty; engage in serious two-way communications; and specifically ask for their help when we need it.

All of us are aware that this is more easily said than done, or we would have done it long ago. So-called economic education programs for the public have failed miserably, and programs to sell the free enterprise system like you'd sell soap are an insult to the people. In my view, we'll have to win our constituency issue-by-issue, like any successful politician, demonstrating how specific proposals will affect the lives and pocketbooks of the people whose support we need. People don't want lectures. They want answers to problems, and assurance that we really care about the things that concern them.

Another basic principle is to resist unnecessary governmental interference with business decision-making. This is one principle that every businessman seems instinctively to understand, but unfortunately we have too often been purely reactive, forever in a defensive posture. The best defense is a good offense. We must anticipate public criticism and take the necessary action to make regulation unnecessary.

In retrospect, it appears that industry did not anticipate the strength of public feeling that could be aroused on the subjects of safety and environmental pollution. The auto industry particularly has been hurt by the legislative over-reaction.

Energy conservation and consumer information are areas where the danger of excessive regulation runs high today. An ounce of prevention here will be worth a *ton* of cure. Industry must take the initiative in developing *voluntary* standards such as the energy-efficiency ratings of the air-conditioning industry, and move out front with effective programs of consumer education.

Or if legislation is needed or inevitable, as in the case of pension reform, then industry can help to assure a sensible outcome by coming up—on its own—with legislative proposals that are responsive to the real problems.

It's the excesses, the needless and heedless use of governmental power, that must be avoided—primarily through voluntary action that anticipates public concern.

CONSCIOUS EVOLUTION

But more important than resistance to excessive regulation is the positive performance that wins and holds the support of our constituencies. As Irving Shapiro said here a few weeks ago, the American public, the sum total of all our constituencies, is highly pragmatic. It supports institutions that deliver the goods.

Thus the basic strategy for corporate survival is to anticipate the changing expectations of society, and serve them more effectively than competing institutions.

This means that the corporation itself must change, consciously evolving into an institution adapted to the new environment.

PLURALISTIC SOCIETY

Consider the changes. It's quite clear that the United States can no longer be called simply "a business society," as we were from about the Civil War to the end of World War II. Today, we are a pluralistic society, in which many competing groups and institutions strive for power and influence. Thus more decisions will be made, and more resources will be allocated, by political processes rather than the market economy. We must adapt to that.

Moreover, as I mentioned before, the U.S. economy is primarily engaged in the production of services, not goods. Though the production of food, materials, and manufactured products is still this country's basic strength on the world scene, six out of ten of our people are engaged in the services sector, and that will increase to seven out of ten in the 1980's. Higher priority is being given to such things as health care, education, municipal services, travel, and recreation. Does this mean that the post-industrial society will also be the post-business society? Not at all. For one thing, industry has a big challenge to provide the equipment that will make the inflationary services sector more productive. And with some imagination, corporations can provide—as businesses—many of the services now provided by governments and other institutions. This too means adapting to a more political climate.

THE WORLDWIDE OPPORTUNITY

Looking further ahead, we see that the easily available sources of energy, food, and materials on this planet are being used up. Unless the world wants to settle for a regimen of shared poverty, we will have to tackle the economic and technological task of developing the more difficult secondary sources. Nuclear power, for example, as well as oil; intensive farming of submarginal land; farming and mining of the sea; and development of substitutes for scarce metals. These are tasks of economic development for which the private corporation has shown itself to be eminently suited, though it will require adaptation to a new relationship with governments in all nations.

And while the United States may be entering its "post-industrial" phase, most of the nations of the world are striving to reach the industrial level. Who is best qualified to provide the know-how, the technology, and the organizational skill required in the developing nations? The initiative has already been taken by the corporations, many of which are now operating on a world scale.

There are many critics of the so-called multinational corporations, but as Peter Drucker points out, "Business is the only institution capable of being multinational . . . The nation is too small a unit to make rational economic decisions." If the gap between the rich and the poor nations is to be narrowed, the business corporation has the best chance of succeeding because it is the only effective international institution we've got.

NEW DIRECTIONS

These, then, are some of the directions in which the corporation should be evolving:

> toward a new and more productive relationship with government;
>
> toward competing more effectively for influence and resources in a pluralistic society;
>
> toward business ventures in the fast-growing services sector;
>
> toward the development of new technologies, new sources of food, fuel, and raw materials;
>
> and toward economic development on a world scale, to help narrow the gap between the rich and the poor nations.

These are noble and self-justifying purposes, but they do not assure the successful future of the corporation. For we have many points of vulnerability, as I have tried to show today.

The sportswriter Damon Runyon once wrote, "As regards the human race, it's 9-to-5 against." At this juncture most of the prophets seem to give the same odds against the long-term survival of the corporation.

But we have all seen the underdog emerge as the winner because he had the will and the energy to prevail.

That's the challenge: in the words of William Faulkner, "not merely to endure, *but to prevail.*"

THE DETERIORATING IMAGE OF BUSINESS

JOHN L. CURRY

There has been a drastic deterioration in public attitudes toward business and businessmen in recent years, particularly since the first Watergate revelations. Telephone companies have not been exempt.

That is the clear implication of a number of public opinion research findings recently compiled by Louis Harris, Roper Reports, Opinion Research Corporation (ORC) and AT&T's Public Overview.

Telephone companies come off slightly better than most major corporations in the public mind. However, this does not diminish the significance of our own declining image, particularly at a time when regulatory pressures are severe and rate increases essential to maintain satisfactory service standards.

In 1966, 1973, and again in April of 1974, people were asked whether they had a great deal of confidence in the leaders of various American institutions. There are no real winners, as Figure 4–1, compiled by Lou Harris, clearly indicates.

Only the people running television news have improved their image since 1966, but an interesting fact shows up here. In 1973, before the first of the Watergate-related disclosures and televised hearings, fewer people had confidence in television news than in the seven-year-earlier survey. A similar surge of confidence is seen in the Press category between 1973 and 1974.

Other data concern reasons why 72 per cent of the people surveyed by Harris expressed "only some" or "hardly any" confidence in the people running companies. Although many factors are involved, some relating to social changes and scandals of the past decade, the chief complaint of 30 per cent is based on profit making. This is especially significant in light of the ORC data on the "bigness dilemma."

Over the years between 1959 and 1973, more and more people came to believe that major companies have grown too powerful (53 per cent to 75 per cent) and that many should be dismantled (38 per cent to 53 per cent). At the same time, however, the data show that the same people continue to believe that large companies are essential for growth and expansion of the economy (82 per cent in 1959 to 81 per cent in 1973).

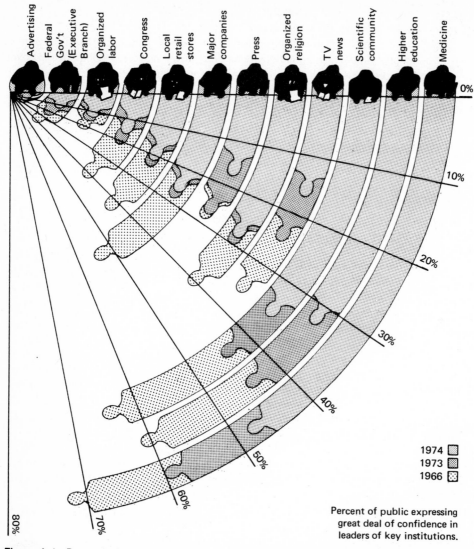

Percent of public expressing
great deal of confidence in
leaders of key institutions.

Figure 4–1   Percent of public expressing great deal of confidence in leaders of key institutions

The public's concern that companies have grown too large and powerful is further re-vealed by other data from the Harris 1974 survey. Over half of the people wanted more federal regulation of the oil industry, clearly because of the energy crisis. These results also show that while about the same percentage of the public feels business in general should be more regulated, certain industries are viewed with more apprehension than others. Drug companies were close behind oil companies, for example, with 48 per cent saying there should be more federal regulation of this industry. More people said utilities, the auto industry, and insurance companies should be more fully regulated than said the same of telephone companies (28 per cent).

A major factor contributing to the public's declining esteem for American business is clearly a wide-spread misunderstanding of the nature of profits and what they are used for. A recent Harris survey shows just how uninformed the average person can be about profits. Fully 77 per cent of Americans are either unsure or believe the average company nets over 30 per cent on sales after taxes. Only 10 per cent of the public realize that the average is actually under 10 per cent—this is an unfortunate commentary on our ability to communicate the facts of business life.

MISTAKEN VIEW OF PROFITS

Table 4–1 demonstrates that the public widely uninformed about the profits of particular industries. Congressional leaders were somewhat more realistic.

More importantly, ORC data from 1959 to 1973 reveal that the public's faith in profits as a "good thing" has diminished steadily. Asked whether the profits of large companies help make things better for all, only 46 per cent responded affirmatively in 1973—compared to 60 per cent in 1959.

Another aspect of the public's view of profits emerges from a Harris question on business and social problems.

People were asked what would happen to profits if business did more to eliminate social ills, and 51 per cent responded that profits would increase.

The reasons given for this rather startling economic viewpoint ranged from a majority opinion that the "goodwill" engendered would cause people to buy more products, to statements of faith that a "better world" would increase profits.

Another increasingly misunderstood aspect of profits is revealed in data from ORC

Table 4–1 THINK PROFITS ABOVE U.S. INDUSTRY AVERAGE

	General Public	Congress. Leaders
Oil industry	81%	80%
Food products	68	50
Drug industry	64	67
Banking	62	70
Electric & gas companies	62	27
Steel	55	44
Telephone company	53	23
Auto industry	51	20
Computer industry	47	57
Insurance industry	46	47
Retail stores	42	17
Stockbrokers	29	3
Airlines	28	3

SOURCE: Louis Harris (1974)

studies between 1953 and 1973. In the former year, 55 per cent of those surveyed believed that most companies in the U.S. could afford to raise wages without raising prices. By 1973, the percentage agreeing with this fallacy had climbed to 67 per cent.

These surveys clearly demonstrate that the American public has not been adequately informed about the true nature of profits in business. Most people who have any opinion at all on the size of corporate profits have a grossly inflated idea of their magnitude. And the purposes of profits are not only misunderstood, but are misunderstood by a growing percentage of the public from year to year.

MORE CONCERN ABOUT QUALITY

The reasons for this growing misapprehension, the increasing suspicion of "bigness" in companies and the perceived need for more government regulation are almost certainly tied to the overall decline in public confidence in all of our major institutions.

The recent Harris Perspective studies have documented the idea that Americans are growing more concerned about their quality of life in general, and the quality of products and services provided them.

By a three to two margin, respondents felt that the quality of life today was worse than ten years ago. In replying to the question of why it is worse, economic, political and social reasons were cited. Inflation was mentioned by 24 per cent, for example; scandals and government corruption were named by another 14 per cent; and 11 per cent felt crime was cause of the decline.

One aspect of this pessimism is the growing belief on the part of consumers that the quality of goods and services is not what it was in earlier years. Table 4–2 shows the increase in this sentiment for specific types of products and services over the last three years. Only automobile tires have held their own, no doubt because of the introduction of

Table 4-2 THINK QUALITY IMPROVED IN PAST TEN YEARS

	April 1971	June 1974
Television sets	67%	58%
Drugs & medicine	66	51
Automobile tires	50	50
Packaged foods	55	39
Major household appliances	54	36
Small appliances	45	30
Automobiles	39	30
Clothing	39	25
Fresh meats & vegetables	38	23
Service from airlines	xx	22
Telephone company service	xx	22
New home construction	22	16

SOURCE: Louis Harris

radial tires in this country. (No Harris data are available on attitudes about our service in 1971.)

To gain further insight into why people feel the quality of life has deteriorated, Harris put agree-disagree statements to respondents. One, to which 87 per cent agreed, was that "Too many businessmen are more interested in how they can make profits than in serving the public's needs."

Another was, "There is nothing wrong with the government leadership in this country; it is simply a matter of people getting erroneous information from the news media." Only 25 per cent of the respondents agreed with that statement in the 1974 study, reflecting the effects of Watergate.

This general tone of public pessimism is further reflected in a recent Roper Reports study, in which respondents were asked to look ahead.and say which of a list of possibilities were "likely to happen in future years." A dismaying 56 per cent said that "people not caring about anyone but themselves" was likely. Another 59 per cent said "rapid depletion of our natural resources" was likely to happen.

At the same time, Roper asked which of the possibilities posed a "serious threat to our life and society." Some of these findings reflect basic misunderstandings. For example, 53 per cent saw, "overcrowding in the cities" likely, but only 20 per cent considered it a threat. The possibility of "increasing difference between the 'haves' and 'have nots' " was considered likely by 36 per cent, while just 14 per cent said it was a serious threat.

EFFECT OF SOCIAL CHANGES

Other causes for the declining public confidence in institutions in general and business in particular can be inferred from demographic and social changes. The population "center" has shifted to a younger group, as has been widely reported and documented. People are better educated and, despite inflation, more affluent.

The long and unpopular Vietnam War has left many scars on the national consciousness, as have political disasters beginning with the assassination of President Kennedy and continuing into Watergate.

Equal rights movements have created dissension in some sectors of society, as long-overdue changes occur too slowly for some and too quickly for others.

AFFLUENT ARE MORE LIBERAL

Another Harris study, completed last year, reveals an interesting fact about how people are reacting to some of these changes. Table 4–3 shows that the affluent, who are also generally better educated, are clearly more liberal on most issues than the unaffluent.

Surveys showing a deterioration of public confidence in the overall business community have produced evidence of a decline in people's attitudes toward telephone companies and service as well. Although most of the available data suggest that we are more highly regarded than most other businesses, the fact remains that the image of the Bell System is worsening in the public mind.

Our own measurements of public and customer opinion are more specific. Two years can be compared in this respect—1966 and 1974.

For 1966, our data are based on the last of the Customer Attitude Surveys (CATS). The

Table 4-3 FAVORABLE TOWARD THESE POLICIES

	Unaffluent	Affluent
Raising taxes to curb pollution	42%	71%
Legalized abortions	27	62
Public financing of federal elections	43	58
Tax reforms with rich paying more	76	73
Comprehensive federal health insurance	50	58

SOURCE: Louis Harris (1974)

Table 4-4 TELEPHONE COMPANY IMAGE

Service Items:	1966	1974	Change
Service good or excellent	93%	83%	−10
Something unsatisfactory	14	30	+16
Usually or always treated in way liked	85	88	+ 3
Cost Items:			
Usually or always get money's worth	87	72	−15
Telephone is quite or very good value	80	68	−12
Company Image Items:			
Run very or quite well	91	62	−29
Not sure	xx	15	
Good or excellent place to work	52	55	+ 3
Not sure	41	28	−13
Good or excellent reputation in community	91	73	−18

SOURCE: CATS 1966 Public Overview 1974

current figures are from the Public Overview, its successor. Table 4–4 demonstrates the general decline in telephone company image over the eight-year period, although there is a slight improvement in the way customers feel they are treated.

The fact that our cost of service image is down considerably should not be especially surprising, considering recent rate increases. Yet rate increases will continue to be necessary to finance the service necessary to satisfy customers, so the question arises of how much of this sort of decline we can afford.

The comparison of company image items for the two years shows a significant decline in the public's view of how well we are run and of our community reputation. The public idea of us as an employer has improved, although 28 per cent have no sure opinion on this.

In summary, it is clear that there is a real and worsening image problem for business today, and that it is likely to continue unless the business community does a better job of telling its story to the public.

Social, economic and political changes in the past decade have contributed to the problem of general pessimism toward the major institutions in our society—including business—although much of the disillusionment with some products and services may be justified.

The Bell System's image with its customers has also declined in the past decade, and this is a problem to which we must address ourselves in a time of increased regulatory pressures and growing capital needs.

Managers of business in general, including those in the Bell System, have for some time been uncomfortably aware of the growing public mistrust and apparent misunderstanding of the purposes and methods of business enterprise. Having such fears corroborated, as indeed they are by the most reliable public opinion research available, is no particular comfort to any executive of a major company. The deteriorating image problem will be with business for some time to come, and will apply to different industries and companies in obverse proportion to their ability to communicate to the public the real nature of their business methods and objectives.

Meanwhile, for Bell System managers, the need to communicate more effectively to the public in areas such as the consumer benefits of the Bell System's structure, the interrelationship of earnings and service, the objectives of our construction budget, and the comparatively low increase of telephone costs to customers in recent years is clearly of the highest priority.

But even effective communications can do no more than complement the manner in which the Bell System fulfills its basic public obligations, especially the obligation to provide good service. The quality of our service has never been better than it is today—and continuing to do the best possible service job is imperative if we are to reverse the public's declining regard for business.

PART ONE
DISCUSSION QUESTIONS

1. Do you agree with Charles Smith's assessment of private ownership's future?

2. Who pays for business rip-offs? What specific steps can be taken to educate us to "sell" our system to the rest of society?

3. Describe the major points made in Reginald Jones's article "What Is the Future of the Corporation?"

4. What is the public's image of business?

PART

MANAGEMENT OF THE
ENTERPRISE

What is effective management? According to Boone and Kurtz, management is the achievement of objectives through people and other resources. Management may be you, perhaps a natural-born leader, who will develop in your position in the enterprise you join upon graduation. Management is the chief executive officer, whether Lee Hess at Dana Corporation in Toledo, or Boyd Schenk at Pet, Inc. You will not start at that level, but perhaps in the sales department, showing that you have the ability to handle materials and money. Perhaps you will start in a line position in a manufacturing concern, learning to manage manpower and machinery. When you have demonstrated such capabilities, you will have your opportunity to move into a management job.

Management styles vary greatly from person to person and from organization to organization. Two outstanding performing persons are described in Readings 5 and 6, Boyd Schenk at Pet, Inc., and Lee Hess at Dana. *Forbes, Fortune, Business Week,* the *Wall Street Journal, Nation's Business,* and the business sections of such news weeklies as *Time, Newsweek,* and *U.S. News & World Report* regularly profile leaders in business and industry. People are moving from one type of organization to another these days since management is essential to any enterprise. Therefore, you should also be aware of leadership styles in government, hospitals, and other enterprises.

What kind of an organization has evolved during these past decades as a result of people involved, both as leaders and as participants? Reading 7, reprinted from the Centennial Issue of *Fortune,* addresses the concerns of the corporation today, "The Intricate 'Politics' of the Corporation." No longer limited to making a profit, today's corporation must meet goals deemed necessary by employees, shareholders, suppliers, consumers, and the public at large. You who enter our corporations can no longer be content with making a profit but must have multiple goals if you are to be successful.

One definite change to anticipate, and prepare for, is that modern organizations are going to demand professional people, not the organization man characterized by a book in the fifties. You who are planning to grow into managers from your entry-level first job will need to develop a professional role, especially women and minorities new to the management arena. Some guidelines directed toward this goal are discussed in Reading 8, "Exit the Organization Man, Enter the Professional Person."   **37**

Your activities in any organization will involve you in individual tasks, but many will demand your interrelationship with other people. The committee meeting is perhaps the most time-consuming, despised, but essential activity in any organization. Improving this type of activity, pointing out opportunities and demands, and considering proposals for streamlining the committee system are stressed in Reading 9, "The Committee in Business: Asset or Liability?"

Motivation is a topic frequently discussed in journals and magazines. Beginning with the Hawthorne experiments in the 1920s, the study of motivation continues today on an international scale. Reading 10, "The Japanese Are Coming—With Their Own Style of Management," talks about motivation and discusses the unique approach taken by Japanese businessmen. Utilizing a different approach to motivation, the Japanese are the only nonwestern developed country and are opening plants throughout the United States. Few managers in the West understand Japanese management and organization and the very different ways in which they tackle a common task such as the determination of profitability, the organization of work and workers, or the making of decisions.

5

THE ROUTE TO PERSONAL SUCCESS IN BUSINESS

Boyd F. Schenk, president and chief executive officer of Pet, Inc., is a friendly, articulate businessman whose company's sales have doubled since he took over eight years ago. Its earnings have tripled.

At 55, Mr. Schenk is comparatively young for a man in the top position at a billion-dollar, multinational firm. He was 47 when he took the helm of Pet.

In the previous year, 1968, the company's sales were $537 million and its earnings, $1.43 a share. In 1977 sales were $1.1 billion and earnings, $4 a share.

Once a company with just one product, evaporated milk, the 92-year-old firm is now in nearly all areas of the food business. Many of its brand names—Downyflake waffles, Whitman's chocolates, Old El Paso Mexican foods, Musselman's applesauce—are household words.

"The company's success," Boyd Schenk says, "is due to the people who work there.

"I sit in this office. I can't manufacture the product. I can't sell it or distribute it. There are 17,000 people out there doing those jobs."

His office is on the top floor of Pet Plaza, the company's international headquarters. Mr. Schenk has a glistening view of downtown St. Louis, the mighty Mississippi River as it flows by the city, and the wide, rich farmlands of Illinois that stretch eastward from the river to the horizon.

Actually, Mr. Schenk doesn't sit in the office very much.

He spends a great deal of time in the field with Pet managers, reviewing their performance. The managers run the company's profit center—from divisions down to a single warehouse.

Mr. Schenk and the company's three executive vice presidents, who comprise the office of the chief executive, make about 50 such visits a year.

"Our role," he says, "is to provide help and counsel."

Mr. Schenk is intent on creating the kind of environment in which Pet people feel free to use their initiative, skills, and common sense to improve company performance.

SOURCE: Reprinted by permission from *Nation's Business*, November 1977. Copyright 1977 by *Nation's Business*, Chamber of Commerce of the United States. **39**

"People tend to live and work somewhat below their true level of capacity," he says. "If we can find out what it is that will make each individual in this company contribute to the best of his abilities, we can achieve a kind of turned-on company that is hard to beat."

In this interview with a *Nation's Business* editor, Boyd Schenk talks about himself and his executive philosophy.

You grew up in the West, didn't you?

Yes. I was born in Providence, Utah, July 23, 1922. I was reared in Missoula, a little town in western Montana. My family lived there until I was 13.

Generally, people think of Montana as being flat, like the Dakotas. Probably two thirds of the state is that way—really high mountain plains. Then, when you get further west, toward the Rockies, the country really gets rough.

Missoula is down in a valley, right in the heart of the mountains.

What did your father do?

He worked for Amalgamated Sugar Co. at a plant in Missoula. A lot of beet sugar is grown in that area.

Did your dad like that kind of country?

Yes, he loved the outdoors. He was a great hunter and fisherman. He used to take me and my brother and my mother, the whole family, camping out near a good fishing stream, Rock Creek. It was about 35-50 miles from town, and that was wild country.

At night, sitting around the campfire in front of our tent, we could hear the coyotes howling in the dark.

As a kid, I used to sit on the banks of the stream where we fished and watch an old mother bear come down to the water and flip the fish out for her cubs.

Where did you go to high school?

In Twin Falls, Idaho, for two years. Then I finished in Rupert, Idaho, where my father was superintendent of an Amalgamated Sugar plant.

Weren't you voted the boy most likely to succeed and elected president of the senior class?

Yes, but it was a small class.

Did you have a business career in mind when you went to college?

No. In 1940 I went to the University of Idaho as a pre-med student. I had always wanted to be a great surgeon. But then World War II came along. I started out as a machine gunner, but wound up as a surgical technician in the 87th Infantry Division, part of the Third Army.

Wasn't the Third Army Gen. George Patton's command?

Yes. The 87th Infantry Division and the Fourth Armored Division, Patton's favorite outfit, used to work together as a combat team.

After the invasion of Europe, we went straight down the autobahn and ended up at the tip of Czechoslovakia.

Did you see the movie, "Patton"? Remember that scene where Patton was on this muddy, snow-covered road directing traffic? I was there that day.

You didn't go back to medical school after the war?

No. I was accepted at Duke University, but I couldn't see how to finance that long medical training. Besides, I had been in service for three years. Another four years at medical school seemed like an eternity.

What did you do?

I went to work for my father. In 1943 he resigned from Amalgamated Sugar Co. and bought a small wholesale and retail ice-cream business at Buhl, Idaho. He had this dream of having his sons, my brother and me, in business with him.

But it didn't work out too well. My dad was very authoritarian. He wanted to emphasize the retail business, and I wanted to emphasize the wholesale.

The manager of Sego Milk Co.'s plant at Buhl asked me to work for him as a lab technician. Sego was a Western subsidiary of Pet. I had some college training in bacteriology and chemistry. So I took the job. That was in 1947.

And that put you on the path to the presidency of Pet, Inc., 22 years later?

Well, at the Buhl plant I did get visible within the company.

In what way?

We were making evaporated milk there. Basically, we received raw milk, heated it under a vacuum to remove water, and then canned and sterilized it.

The evaporated milk had to have a butterfat content of 7.90—a federal regulation. If the butterfat went below 7.90, you might have to throw away the whole batch, maybe 100,000 gallons of milk.

To play safe, Sego told lab guys like me to standardize the content at 7.96 percent. In other words, Sego was leaving a safety margin for error.

After about the first week, I thought: Now if we could come closer to 7.90, we'd get more cans of evaporated milk from the same amount of raw milk. We could make every gallon of milk go further.

I felt that by making one extra test, to be sure my percentage figure was right, I could get closer to the federal standard without going below it.

How long did the extra test take?

About an hour for each batch, and I processed three a day. So I would have to work three hours longer to get my day's work done.

What happened?

I began hitting 7.91 or 7.92 percent every time.

Now samples of every batch of milk processed at all Sego plants were sent to Greenville, Ill., where Sego had its central control laboratory. Normally, if the sample came in under 7.96 percent, Greenville sent you a warning telegram, figuring you had made a mistake.

So the telegrams started to fly to Buhl.
In Salt Lake City, Sego's headquarters, they were beginning to bite their nails, too. They rushed the production manager down to Buhl to find out what was going on.

I explained what I was doing, and I pointed out that my method had already saved Sego about $80,000 on milk costs.

What did Sego do?

I was made a production supervisor and later an assistant plant manager.

Where did you go from there?

To Orland, Calif., in 1952. The Sego Milk plant there had the highest operating costs of any. I was sent there to cut costs.

The man I succeeded said: "I don't think much can be done with this bunch of guys. They're pretty independent."

And they were. Each worker had a little farm, or orange grove, or a few acres of almond trees. They weren't totally dependent on the plant for their livelihood.

Did you get costs down?

Yes, for 16 straight quarters, even though the unions were getting the men regular increases.

There are lots of ways to cut costs in a plant like that.

You motivate people to be cost-conscious. You get them to use a lift fork properly instead of jabbing it through a case of expensive cartons. You get more production on the line and more cars loaded with the same number of people. You make sure your equipment is running smoothly; your maintenance men have a lot to do with that.

But basically, I think people who feel good about their work are more productive. If you feel useful and needed, and if you believe that what you are doing is important, you'll be more productive.

It is management's job to create that kind of atmosphere.

Sounds like you learned a lot there.

Most of the lessons I have learned about people I probably learned from those guys at the Orland plant. In a sense, a small plant is a whole corporation in microcosm. At both places, 99 percent of your problems are people problems.

How did you make the jump from a little Pet subsidiary to corporate headquarters in St. Louis?

In 1955 Pet started on the acquisition route. It bought a company called Pet-Ritz Foods and went into a new venture, the frozen food business.

Pet also took over an old, bankrupt bakery in Fresno, Calif., and wanted it turned into a frozen pie plant. In early 1956 I was picked for the job of plant manager.

What did you know about frozen foods?

Nothing. I had never even been inside a frozen pie plant. Pet sent me to one in Michigan for a week's training; then I headed back to the coast.

What was your biggest problem in starting this project from scratch?

Getting rid of the old equipment. I sold off so much old equipment that I got the reputation of being a junk dealer. In fact, I almost recovered the cost of the plant from the stuff I sold.

And then?

Then I went out and recruited people to work in the plant.

We hired a young crew—the average age was 22. I didn't want people who were already trained in other, old-fashioned ways of doing things. We were doing something new and different. It's easier to teach someone from scratch than have him unlearn first.

As a result, that plant did extremely well. We set all kinds of production records.

That also drew the attention of Ted Gamble, who was president of Pet. He was very interested in this new venture; it was his baby. In 1958, after I spent two years at Fresno, Ted Gamble brought me to St. Louis to be assistant to the general manager of the Pet-Ritz operation.

So in 11 years you went from a job as a lab technician in Buhl, Idaho, to a position in a corporate executive suite in St. Louis. What was the main reason?

Visibility. In all three jobs I held, in Buhl, Orland, and Fresno, the results were visible in St. Louis. That's what every young man needs who wants a career: visibility.

Reaching the chief executive's office is largely a question of getting better-than-expected results from each assignment. That gets the attention of someone at the top.

What was the next step for you?

In 1955 the company reorganized and made Pet-Ritz frozen foods part of the food products division. I was made production manager of Pet-Ritz.

I told Ted Gamble I didn't think the structure was right. I thought that putting frozen foods in with other food products was a mistake.

Why?

In the first place, sales. We had evaporated-milk salesmen trying to sell frozen foods. It's a different ball game. It's a much faster track, and you have different kinds of customers.

Also, we had problems coordinating between marketing, sales, and production. We had what we called a coordinating committee. What we needed was all elements of the operation reporting to one guy.

Isn't that what you wound up with?

Yes. In 1961 Ted Gamble told me: "You may be right on this structure. Set up a frozen foods division as a separate operation. You're general manager, and you've got a year to straighten it out."

At the time we were losing about $1 million a year on frozen foods. Under the new setup we made $30,000 the first year. It began to grow, and in 1963 I was made president of the division.

When Ted Gamble died unexpectedly at 44, where were you in Pet?

I was executive vice president-operations and part of the office of the president, which had consisted of Ted Gamble and four vice presidents.

What did you do?

All four vice presidents got together and then went to a committee of outside board members who had been appointed by Pet's board to pick Ted's successor. We told the committee that, if they chose one of us, we had all pledged to support whichever one was selected. But, we said, if someone outside management were named, we would have to decide individually what course we should take.

Why did the committee pick you?

Perhaps because I was the youngest of the four.

What major changes have you made since becoming president?

We have concentrated more on growth from within, but not because I don't approve of acquisitions. The need to diversify was pretty much accomplished by Ted Gamble.

How do you make big decisions?

I talk to as many people as I can who might shed some useful light on the subject.

Then I like to let that information jell. I guess I'm sort of a believer in psycho-cybernetics. I think you have input all the time into the cerebral computer that we call the brain. So if you can use all the time possible for input, waiting until about the last moment, you can push a mental button and the mechanism will spit out an answer.

I have been accused of being a procrastinator. When I learned about psycho-cybernetics, I discovered I wasn't a procrastinator at all. I was just using the maximum amount of time for input.

How is Pet's management organization structured?

Around the individual—his capabilities, background, and expertise. We tailor our organization to fit the talents our people have. As those talents change, the structure will, too. It's an evolving structure.

Do you have a formal long-range planning program?

Yes. We brought in a man several years ago to set one up. Since then our own people, who trained under him, have been carrying it out.

What kind of goals do you set?

Things like market share. We have a lot of profit centers in the company, too. Each has its own separate objectives and long-range plan. Then we control the operation through the review process.

Could you explain that?

We sit down with managers of a profit center, go over recent performance, and let them talk about their strategies and what they intend to do to reach the goals they have set for themselves.

Who sits in on these sessions?

Any one or more members of the office of the chief executive. That includes me and three executive vice presidents.

How many of these sessions do you sit in on in a year's time?

Close to 50.

How far down does this review process go?

Every department, division, and group must hold at least a monthly performance review. We get a schedule of these meetings, and any one of us, or all four, may just show up and sit in on it.

Many companies pay lip service to the idea of encouraging initiative and giving individuals lots of elbow room. Is that the attitude for real at Pet?

Yes, because I believe down to the soles of my feet that that's the best way to get performance out of anyone. Let me cite an example from my own experience.

When I was in high school in Rupert, Idaho, I was in a geology class that was taught pretty much from the textbook. I read ahead and finished the book in pretty short order. From that time on I was bored, and I believe I became sort of a nuisance in that class.

The principal taught the class. He was a savvy guy, and he sensed this restlessness on my part.

So he said: "Look, is there something else you'd like to study in addition to this?"

I said: "Sure, there are quite a few other things."

He said: "You pick out the subjects, and you can study them in the library instead of coming to class."

So I went to the library, and I suppose I studied three or four other subjects—toxicology, embryology, and one or two others. Then the principal gave me a test in geology, and I passed that and got credit for the course.

What's the moral of the story?

Give people a challenge, an opportunity to take it up, and authority to do it their way—and you get results.

What if you take the opposite approach?

Then it's like being in the army. Everything is done by the numbers. You stifle initiative, increase costs, and cut down on productivity.

How do you get people more involved in the job?

By participative management.

And that means?

Letting them in on what's going on.

Years ago, when I was plant supervisor, no one told us much about results. We didn't even know if the plant was making a profit or not. When I became general manager of the frozen foods division, I changed that. The division was losing money then. I went around to all the plants and told the employees that. The employees were surprised. I pointed out that, if a plant keeps losing money, it isn't going to be open very long.

I said that everyone probably knew more efficient ways of doing his own job. I challenged them to do their jobs better.

Then we began to give them progress reports, to which they could personally relate, as to the profitability of their own plant. In a short time profit improved greatly.

Any advice to a young man who wants to get ahead?

As I said, get visible—stand out by tackling every assignment, whether it's getting a single truck loaded with a product or moving a $200 million profit center ahead, as though it is the most important one in the entire corporation. It is, for you. You must build your career on a base of solid, superior accomplishment.

Also, don't be too impatient. I'm afraid too many young people are much too concerned about a quote, career path, end of quote. Instead of concentrating all their ability and efforts on the present job, they worry too much about that next promotion, which, as a result, may never come.

I have often pointed out to our people that they probably do not have large financial resources to invest—if they did, they wouldn't be seeking a career at Pet. But they are investing what they do have—the sum total of what they have to offer as an individual, the strength of their minds and bodies, their energies and know-how, and that most precious element of all, their time.

It behooves them to get the best possible return on their investment from the full utilization of those personal assets, not so the company flag can fly more brilliantly, but in their own self-interest.

A lot of our people are doing just that. And Pet therefore will continue to move ahead solidly and aggressively, by any measurement. In the final analysis, Pet is people.

6

PROFILE OF A MANAGER

PROLOGUE

Lee Hess walked into an empty, 220,000 square-foot building at Edgerton, Wisconsin, in late May of last year and after a quick glance around, said to himself . . . "My God, what have I gotten into?"

It was a good question. At that moment, all Dana Corporation had at Edgerton was Hess and a building. Nothing else. No machinery, no equipment, no employees, no production. Nothing.

Yet, 105 days later, the Edgerton plant turned out its first Spicer axle. By January of this year—seven months later—Edgerton was building 18,500 axles per month! And today, production exceeds 20,000 per month.

That's quite an accomplishment.

As plant manager, Hess will be quick to tell you . . . "the guys who really did the work are the department heads. I'm just here to listen and help solve problems."

Those are nice-sounding words.

They are also true.

Lee Hess (as you are about to discover on the following pages) doesn't say something if he doesn't mean it, and believe it. And do it.

This isn't an article about Edgerton. And it's not really about Lee Hess, plant manager, either.

It's about a philosophy of management. A philosophy that develops people like Lee Hess and gives them the opportunity to ask themselves . . . "what have I gotten into?" . . . and then do something about it.

It's difficult to pinpoint exactly where or when Lee Hess began to formulate his ideas of management . . . of what a manager should be. You don't acquire the beliefs and convictions that eventually become your philosophy of management at any one stage of your career. They come to you bit by bit as you go along.

SOURCE: Courtesy of Dana Digest, Dana Corporation, Toledo, Ohio.

Someone—or some thing—makes a marked impression on you . . . good or bad . . . and that impression becomes part of your belief . . . for or against . . . and it's a continuing sort of thing.

And after a while, you take all those beliefs you have and mold them together into a philosophy of management . . . your credo of what it is.

For two days, recently, we talked to Hess about his views on being a manager. And they are his views. No one has censored his comments to avoid possible controversy. Nor has anyone "reviewed" what he says here to make sure it follows company policy . . . because Dana's policy is to let Hess—and others like him— pursue their personal management beliefs as freely as possible within broad guidelines . . . and with an absolute minimum of control or direction from higher echelons.

The first thing that impressed me when I began working at the Auburn (Ind.) plant of the Atwood Vacuum Company in 1941 was seeing "the boss," Carl Thelander, come through the plant every day just to talk to the guys. He would stop and chat a while . . . some days with one group, another day with others . . . and as an 18-year-old, just getting started, I appreciated the attention and the interest he showed in me and my fellow employees. I decided that if I ever got into management, I would try to do the same thing. So, at an early stage in my working career, this thing of communication and interest in people was impressed on me.

When the war came, I did a hitch in the army, came back to Auburn in 1946, and worked in the plant until 1947. If a fellow had initiative, they gave you an opportunity to learn. They put me on a trainee program and I spent a lot of time finding out about different pieces of equipment and operating various machines. This gave me a chance to spend time in different departments . . . tool room . . . machine repair . . . inspection . . . and so on, and the opportunity for training was a great thing for me.

But I wanted to go to college, so I took a leave of absence in 1947 for that purpose. They were hoping I would take engineering and come back to work after I graduated; but instead, I got a degree in education and taught for a year. The pay was so low, I couldn't make it, so I decided to go back into industry.

Dana Corporation had purchased the Auburn plant while I was away at school, and it was being operated as a division. I didn't know who Dana was . . . what kind of a company . . . or anything else about them. But I needed a job, and heard that Dana's Aircraft Gear plant was in operation at Fort Wayne, so I got a job there in 1953 as a time study man.

Fourteen months later, the operation was shut down and I went to General Electric for two years. Then one day I got a call to come to Toledo as a procedure analyst on J. R. "Rudy" Miller's staff. Rudy was then director of manufacturing (later, president) of Dana Corporation.

My job was about 50% working on office procedure and 50% investigating incentive systems and working with the various Dana plants. I took a course in MTA (motion time analysis) and went around the company teaching MTA in the plants.

Along with that, Bob Hoyt and I worked together and wrote the "corporate procedures manual" . . . a big, thick thing . . . and we had a heck of a time putting it together. It was later outdated, scrapped, and replaced by our present one-page "Policy Statement." And thank God for that!

At that time, Dana still had a lot of the old-school, hard-nosed type of managers, and the approach to "people" was nothing like it is today. Spread your arms out and look at your right hand. That was management, out there . . . and your left hand was the union . . . 'way out there. That's how far apart they were. And in my opinion, Dana brought that sort of thing on themselves. Now remember, I'm talking about twenty years ago. Because Dana didn't communicate with the plant managers in those days . . . and the plant managers didn't communicate with their people, either. It just wasn't done!

A plant manager, back then, didn't even know what his profits were! The plant controller knew . . . but he reported directly to Toledo, and all the plant manager knew was what his works expense sheet showed. So if the company didn't communicate with the plant manager, how could it expect him to communicate with his people?

There wasn't the openness about things that we have today. People didn't trust each other like they do now . . . and I'm talking about *within* the company.

I worked for Corporate . . . and when I went into one of the plants to investigate something, the plant manager might be nice and polite about letting me into his plant, but in many cases he was really careful about what I learned while I was there. I can remember going into one plant to study the incentive system for three or four weeks, and I got real good cooperation until the plant manager found out what I was learning. After that, it took me another four or five weeks to prove that what I'd originally found out was true!

And I used to think about how crazy the whole thing was. Toledo didn't tell the plants anything and the plants didn't tell Toledo any more than they had to . . . and I don't think Dana was any different than a lot of other companys in that respect. It was just the way things were done. Everything was centralized. Engineering, sales and the money end of it were run by Toledo . . . and the plant manager was nothing more than an operating manager . . . a manufacturing manager. He didn't control his accounting, his sales, or his engineering. He just had manufacturing. And I used to wonder how the plant manager could be expected to improve his operation or be really concerned with things like profits or costs or return on investment when he didn't even know what they were.

In 1958, while still on the Corporate manufacturing staff, I was temporarily assigned to the Fort Wayne plant to help establish a new time study program I had recommended. A year and a half later, the company moved me to Fort Wayne as supervisor over the time study system I had helped put in there. And I liked it, because it gave me a chance to prove that some of the things I had suggested would work. I think it's important to let people prove that some of their ideas are workable . . . and it's equally important to let them make their own mistakes.

Along with time study at Fort Wayne, I was made cost control supervisor . . . which included the responsibility for estimating, budgeting, and cost control. So I was getting experience in a number of areas that would help me a great deal later on, although I didn't think much about that part of it at the time.

After serving as Fort Wayne's assistant plant manager for a brief period, I was transferred to Chelsea (Mich.) as plant manager . . . and it was a whole new ball game!

Chelsea manufactured power take-offs and had never had a plant manager, as such, since Dana had acquired the company in 1958. I don't know what caused the problem at Chelsea, but at first, the union-management situation was bad . . . and management's credibility was practically non-existent . . . so we had a rough situation at the beginning. I had union committeemen tell me that anything we (management) tried to do there was to the detriment of the employees. Automatically! They just felt that every time we did something it was against their best interest. Well, that wasn't true . . . but it takes a long time to turn people back on once they have been turned off . . . and those people were turned off!

So we worked—real hard—at building up an honest approach with the union committee. Doing the things we said we would do . . . and not doing the things we said we wouldn't do. In other words, being honest with them. But I don't think things really started to turn around until we began having monthly meetings with the whole group. Before that, we had meetings from time to time . . . usually when something went wrong. Putting out fires, so to speak.

And we found out, the hard way, that you can't build credibility with your people by going to them just when there's a problem! You have to have regular, face-to-face contact . . . communication . . . with them. So we started having monthly meetings out in the plant, and you'd be surprised at some of the "wisecracks" we got from the back of the room at first . . . and we knew they weren't listening to what we were saying . . . we weren't getting across to them.

But we believed that if we continued meeting with them, eventually they would start listening . . . and they did. And once we got communication going both ways, things began to change.

Right here, I want to say that no one person . . . no plant manager . . . can do what we were doing at Chelsea by himself. He's got to have people all through the organization working hard at a program of communication, involvement, or whatever it is. And believing in it . . . or it just won't succeed.

I think one of the reasons we got things together at Chelsea was that there was a big change taking place in the whole corporation at that time. A lot of things were happening, and some of them went back to Mr. Dana and Mr. Martin and things they had started years before. Those two gentlemen had seen a growing need in the Corporation for training people to fill future management needs as the company grew. They believed that a "promote from within" policy was the best way to attract good people and keep them with the company. And they had started informal "discussion groups" made up of young people . . . beginning their careers, so to speak . . . who met with various members of top management and exchanged ideas about all sorts of things pertaining to the company and its operation.

A little bit prior to the time I went to Chelsea, some of these fellows (including me) were getting out into the organization in management positions. And they had some new ideas . . . different approaches . . . about "management" as a result of those discussion groups.

Today, we have Dana "U" and educational programs like that going on all over the company. A lot of them are direct continuations of those early, informal groups started years ago by Mr. Dana and Mr. Martin.

So what I'm saying is that I think education and training was one of the things that helped turn Chelsea around. I think that a manager . . . any kind of a manager . . . has to be willing to look at, and accept, new ideas. They have to be sound ideas, but I don't think they necessarily have to be proven. A manager, at any level, has to allow the people that work for him the opportunity to implement some of their ideas. Because you can stifle a person's initiative and enthusiasm if he doesn't have a chance to express himself, interject his ideas, and feel he is a part of whatever it might be.

At Chelsea, we wanted to try some new ideas, and we had to have a receptive attitude not only among the union people, but among our management as well . . . all through the plant. We also had to have a receptive attitude on the part of top management . . . the people we reported to . . . if we were to succeed in selling our ideas to Toledo. And thanks to this new attitude that was beginning to flow throughout the whole corporation, we were successful in getting Toledo's blessing. They said "let's give it a try" . . . and I have to say here that if it hadn't been for people like Bill Herring who was general manager over the Chelsea operation, we wouldn't have made it. Bill was a tremendous help in allowing us, at Chelsea, the opportunity to express ourselves and "sell" a new idea.

The first direct approach we made to the people in the Chelsea plant was the "Quality Control Circle." It's been written about before (see Dana Digest, February, 1971) so I won't go into details. But it was a joint union-management approach to solving a big problem we had . . . and it gave the people out in the shop an opportunity to sit down and work with quality problems . . . work directly with management . . . make suggestions to management on how we could make improvements. And they could see their efforts bearing fruit. This was a real good foundation for building credibility with the union and I think we built up a relationship there that made the program succeed. They didn't mistrust us any more and that made it easier for the union committee, as well as management, to operate and to get things across to the entire body.

So there was a great attitude change taking place not only at Chelsea but all through the Corporation. Management's ideas of how to manage were changing. Things like the Area Manager Concept . . . putting responsibility for operating a plant at the lowest possible level of management . . . giving people an opportunity to express themselves instead of merely implementing instructions from above . . . letting them utilize their own initiative. All of this helped make it possible for us to put the Scanlon Plan into the Chelsea plant in May of 1972. (Editor's note: See pages 10–13 for more on the Scanlon Plan). When I look back at it, an idea like the Scanlon Plan was a real "shocker" even for me! Here I was, a plant manager with a substantial background in time study programs and production procedures and used to measuring "productivity" down to hundredths of a minute and things like that . . . and now we were talking about a new idea based on everybody at Chelsea working together instead of competing against a stopwatch! While I believe in trying new ideas and not stifling new approaches, it took me a little time to understand that maybe this "Scanlon Plan" was a better way of doing things.

When we presented the Scanlon Plan to the people at Chelsea, I think we were all surprised when 90% of them turned out to vote on whether or not they wanted to try it. And 93% of those who voted were for the Plan! So we had succeeded in turning that plant around from a really "anti-everything" attitude to one where they were willing to try an entirely new venture that neither the union—or management—knew very much about! We felt real good about it. It was a willingness to cooperate . . . something both groups had worked to achieve . . . that made it possible.

When Bud Giauque (then president of Spicer Axle Division . . . now, group vice pres., Drive Train) asked me to come here to Edgerton in May of last year and get this plant started, I knew the Axle Division was running full blast and had been for some time. We had an empty building here . . . nothing more . . . and time was very critical because of customer requirements. The first thing I had to do was put together an organizational staff . . . production, quality control, personnel, controller, area managers, and so on . . . to get things going.

That's the hardest part of the job . . . getting the best people available.

What do you look for in people? Well, you look for the usual things, of course, education, work experience, stable personality and life style . . . and see how they fit into the job you have to do. In the case of a new plant like this, you concentrate more on getting specialists . . . somebody that is particularly knowledgeable at that job.

And I look for one more thing. Enthusiasm!

That ranks very high with me. I don't care how much experience a person has, or how much education, if he doesn't have the drive and enthusiasm, then he's going to do a mediocre job.

I think what has happened here at Edgerton is a testimonial to enthusiasm. The people we brought here to put this thing together have done a beautiful job, and I can't say enough about them. None of them got cold feet. They rolled up their sleeves and went to work. And the guys who really did the work were the department heads.

Fort Wayne (Axle Division headquarters) gave us a lot of help and cooperation of course, but they gave us a free hand in putting this organization together. The first line management people I selected had to be approved by Fort Wayne, but that's true throughout the company. I was free to go to Fort Wayne and discuss problems and try to get answers, but they didn't sit on my shoulder, and if mistakes were made, I made them myself. I told them what I wanted to do and if it wasn't too far out and was in line with corporate guidelines, there wasn't any problem.

I sat down and made our forecast for this plant . . . told them what we were going to do . . . and from then on, it was pretty much a case of letting us do it ourselves.

And right here, I've got to say something about Dana Corporation and our sister divisions around the company, that is absolutely tremendous when a situation like Edgerton comes along.

Here I was, trying to build an organization to run this plant. I needed people . . . good people . . . to make it go. We have excellent relationships with the other divisions of Dana . . . and when I approached those divisions and asked for some of their people they said "yes . . . go and talk to them if you want to." And I know it hurt some of those plants when I took these people. But it was a matter of plant management being willing to give up some of their top people and letting them have the opportunity to grow. And that's something that has been built up at Dana over the years . . . promote from within . . . and its a tremendous thing.

I believe you should never hold anybody back to protect yourself or your job. It's wrong! And I'll tell you why. Sooner or later, those people will find out that you are holding them back, and if they have any initiative at all, they are going to leave you.

But if the people in your department, or plant, or company know that you are promoting them . . . trying to push them along . . . even though they are your best people . . . they will respect you and work for you.

I don't know of any case where I pushed a person along or moved them up that hurt me. In fact, I think it always helped. And I convey this approach to my own people. I let them know if we are looking at them, at the job they are doing, and they know that if I get an opportunity to move them up I will. I think that's how to get a real aggressive management group . . . and if they believe in this same philosophy and apply it to their people you have an unbeatable organization!

WHAT LEE HESS, MGR., THINKS . . .

. . . About Unions

When the union insists on having a say in everything you try to do in a plant, I think it's because mistrust exists. You eliminate mistrust by being honest . . . consistently honest.

That's what turned things around at Chelsea. The people there who told us that everything we did was "anti union" were the same people who voted for the Scanlon Plan a short time later. I think that happened because we proved to them that we meant what we said . . . and did what we said.

. . . About the Generation Gap

One of the things I insisted on when we started operating here was that we hire a cross-section of age groups . . . 20–30, 30–40, 40–50, and 50–60. A lot of people might say "nobody hires people over 40." Well, we did! And they are doing a great job. They add stability to the organization. Those young people look up to them and have some respect for them . . . and for their experience and know-how. I think we got this plant into operation a lot better and a lot more smoothly by getting a good "mix" of age groups.

. . . About Motivation

Education and training . . . selling an idea . . . or a method or an approach to a problem . . . is the best motivation I know of. Sometimes you get a hard-nosed sort of guy who fights everything you're trying to do. And in that case, you have to say "O.K., this is the way I want it done" . . . but in any case, you tell him WHY. Maybe it doesn't get through to him, but the time you spend explaining why is important, and maybe he'll become more receptive the next time.

. . . About Respect

Nothing is more gratifying than to have people respect you. It's nice to have people like you, of course, and say you're a "good Joe" and all that . . . but they have to have respect for the position. And that means they have to know you . . . know you're the right kind of guy . . . know you're doing a good job for the plant or division . . . so that next week, and a year from next week, they have a place to work.

. . . About Hiring People

When we came here to start this plant we spread the word that this was going to be the best place around here to work. And I think the word got around, because we haven't had any trouble getting the kinds of people we want.

We can't sell products (axles) with local publicity, but we can sure sell Dana . . . the type of company Dana is . . . that it's a good place to work . . . and that's what we did. Now I'll admit that our motives are selfish . . . we want the best people working here that we can get. We've had more than 5000 applications for about 540 jobs here, so far. By next July, we're going to have 1100 people here.

Our personnel department doesn't hire people. They interview them . . . screen them . . . and then turn them over to the foreman and the foreman does the hiring. If he doesn't think an applicant is going to work out, he doesn't hire him. I think it makes sense doing it that way, because that applicant is going to be working for the foreman . . . not for me . . . not for the personnel manager.

For years, companys told the foremen out in the shop that their job was to get pieces out . . . make production. Quality wasn't his job. The inspection department had that responsibility. So the foreman left it up to inspection to worry about. Here at Edgerton, we've put that inspection responsibility under the foreman. The inspector reports to him. So he's responsible for both production and quality In his particular department. He can't blame the inspection department or the quality control people . . . he's managing that area. Quality control specifications and procedures are the responsibility of the plant quality control manager, but the department quality is the foreman's job.

. . . About Being a Manager

I think a person has to be sold on the organization he's with to be a good manager . . . any kind of a manager. And he has to spend hours preparing himself to do a good job. Personal time is always at a premium, so he needs an understanding family. He has to be willing to listen to the people who work for him . . . be receptive to new ideas. He must be fair . . . and honest. He must give people security and opportunity and responsibility. And he must earn their loyalty and respect.

7

THE INTRICATE "POLITICS" OF THE CORPORATION

CHARLES G. BURCK*

One weekend recently, the chief executive of one of the country's biggest industrial corporations pulled Oswald Spengler's *Decline of the West* from his bookshelves and reread it. Spengler, as the executive knew from reading him years before, predicted that Western civilization would end in a bitter struggle in which raw Caesarean power would triumph over money. The businessman did not and does not share the German philosopher's pessimism, but he wanted to check—just in case he'd overlooked something that first time around.

The environment in which the corporation finds itself these days encourages a certain amount of gloomy speculation. American manufacturers are not earning enough to replace their deteriorating plant and equipment, and their productivity is lagging. With the stock market drying up as a source of equity capital, companies have fallen heavily into debt to the banks. The interest charges on that debt were easy enough to support in an era of rapid growth, but now have become an onerous burden. The explosive leap in energy costs, along with the relentlessly advancing expense of recovering other resources, has raised serious questions as to whether yesterday's glorious growth rates will ever return again.

These problems, while worrisome, are at least conventional and familiar. More difficult may be the newer problems caused by changes in what U.S. society demands from the corporation. Consumers, once docile in the marketplace, have discovered their discontent and are uniting to attack the corporation in adversary proceedings. Environmentalists have called it to account for ravaging the landscape and befouling the air and water. Local communities that provide a home for company plants are loudly asserting their claim that the corporation owes them something. In Detroit a public outcry against the impending loss of jobs forced financially troubled Chrysler to reverse an earlier decision to close down an obsolete plant.

*Research associate: Lorraine Carson.

SOURCE: Reprinted from the April 1975 issue of *Fortune* Magazine by special permission; © 1975 Time Inc.

Management has to concern itself a great deal more with how employees feel about their work. Says Irving Shapiro, chairman of Du Pont: "In the past, people wanted a steady job, and income was all-important. In the future, people will want a sense of participation, satisfaction, contribution." No less difficult to manage than blue-collar workers are executives who no longer tend, with single-minded dedication, to sacrifice everything for their careers. They are increasingly inclined, for example, to turn down promotions that would require them to uproot their families or move to an "undesirable" city.

Corporations, to be sure, have been adjusting to new demands for many years. Classically, these demands have arisen mainly from the marketplace, either in the expressed desires of consumers or in some inchoate yearning for a product or service that was not yet in existence. The most successful corporations have been those whose leaders anticipated these demands and marshaled the capital, technology, and people needed to produce what was wanted. Thus Andrew Carnegie, foreseeing what a large and integrated steel industry could do for the world, brought the Bessemer process together with coke, iron ore, and manpower to build what in 1901 became U.S. Steel.

HOW IT GOT TO BE "HUMANE"

As it evolved, the corporation gradually began to encounter a greater number of demands emanating from outside the classic marketplace. Around the time of the nation's birth, when the small, atomistic firm described by Adam Smith fought it out in a rowdy free market, the sole obligation of the business enterprise was to produce goods and charge what the traffic would bear. Conflicts between this narrow economic interest and broader social expectations began to arise in the late nineteenth century, but did not become pervasive until the 1930's. It was not until 1938, for example, that the first federal child-labor law went into effect.

With some pain, corporations learned to live with the growing power of unionized labor and laws guaranteeing a minimum wage, unemployment compensation, and safer working conditions. Through each round of new requirements, the corporation took on greatly enlarged responsibilities. It also became more "humane."

The process of hanging a greater variety of diverse obligations upon the corporation might be viewed, in one sense, as a radical expansion of its marketplace. Every choice a corporation makes these days—to close a plant, to fill a swamp, to hire a quota of blacks —affects thousands of people who had no voice in the classical marketplace but who are increasingly creating new market conditions through social pressure, moral suasion, and law. Simply trying to gauge the corporation's responsibility to these diverse interests is still a relatively new job for management. It may also be the most complicated.

Though few executives are apt to think of it this way, the corporation has in fact become a "political" institution. Before acting, managers must weigh a multitude of interests, including those of employees, creditors, customers, suppliers, shareholders, and the public at large. All these "constituencies" assert claims that are valid, though often conflicting. In the end, the manager, like the politician, has to resolve the competing claims of his constituents and do something.

In the process, corporations have possibly become the nation's most pragmatic, most adaptable, and most successful instruments of change. Privately owned, individualistically managed, and free to try a wide variety of approaches, they are essential elements of democratic pluralism, critical institutions in the American System.

For all the corporation's past ability to master change, though, there remain real questions about how well it can meet the challenges of today. Its varied constituencies are changing more dramatically than ever—sometimes unpredictably, often with enormous consequences. The Arab oil embargo, for example, represented what might be called the revolt of a constituency of suppliers, but it produced more than a simple extra cost of doing business in classical-market terms. "Everything before it is history," remarks Irving Shapiro. "The future is a whole new game."

BEYOND EFFICIENCY LIES EFFECTIVENESS

Clearly, managements have to rethink their whole function. Peter Drucker, that most prolific of writers on the subject, says, "The assumptions of all the work of management during the past century are being put into doubt by new developments demanding new vision, new work, and new knowledge." Meeting problems is only part of the challenge; seizing opportunities is of equal or greater importance. For every Xerox that grasped the immense opportunities beckoning from an unexploited market, scores of other corporations have bogged down in what Drucker identifies as a preoccupation with efficiency.

To be sure, efficiency—the art of doing the same thing with less effort or fewer resources —is one of the corporation's great and singular contributions to the advancement of mankind. But it is not enough. Management's new goal, says Drucker, must be "effectiveness," which is a shorthand way of describing the *optimum* use of all the resources available to pursue *extraordinary results.* To be "effective," the manager must somehow infuse the whole corporate organization with the intuitive sense that a good entrepreneur has for identifying problems—and opportunities—beyond the horizon.

The notion of seeking extraordinary results is hardly radical, but it can get lost in large organizational superstructures. Does this mean that big corporations are necessarily inflexible and unresponsive? Those who argue in the affirmative rest their case to some degree on circumstantial evidence. Small, innovative companies sometimes seem better adapted to serving markets overlooked by big firms, and have a powerful track record for pioneering new technologies ignored by the giants. Indeed, great numbers of small corporations are flourishing. In addition, some of the suspicion of bigness springs from emotional sources —the traditional American distrust of large agglomerations of power, and the Chaplinesque vision of man crushed in the cogs.

THE FLEXIBLE TITAN

But size need not be an obstacle to flexibility or responsiveness. Where it leads to incapacity, the blame rests with management, rather than the phenomenon of bigness itself. I.B.M., after all, was a well-established maker of business machines, with revenues of $410 million and comfortable profits, when it shifted its entire corporate strategy to make the computers that changed the world.

Sophisticated management will scale down the oversized division or department into a number of profit centers or other sub-enterprises, some of them highly autonomous. The pragmatic manager adapts to whatever works best, a process that extends all the way down to dealing with the consumer. For example, many large retailers have demonstrated their "effectiveness" by restructuring their giant department stores and emporiums into smaller units, such as boutiques, shops, and arcades. This meets the consumer's demand for a more intimate shopping environment, while enabling the store owner to make the most of computer technologies that afford more sensitive and precise inventory control. By fragmenting the mass market into many little individual markets, the companies give the consumer a wider choice and spread their own risks in the fickle world of fashion.

PUTTING OFF THE IMPORTANT JOBS

But to be effective, the manager must also overcome some habits of thinking that have little to do with whether his corporation is large or small. Harold J. Leavitt, professor of organizational behavior and psychology at the Stanford Business School, has identified one of these habits as the tendency of managers to "respond to the programmed tasks facing them before responding to the unprogrammed ones."

The programmed tasks are the routine, familiar jobs. The unprogrammed work is creative: identifying potential problems and seizing opportunities generally apprehended only by the skillful entrepreneur or intuitive executive. One unprogrammed area of inquiry, for example, might be trying to find out how the corporation should structure itself in the future to satisfy the human needs of its employees.

Because unprogrammed work is unusually challenging, managers tend to postpone it while they perform routine tasks instead. Leavitt thinks a kind of Gresham's law applies: programmed tasks chase away unprogrammed tasks like bad money chasing out good. If boredom in the factory appeared to be a major long-range problem, a manager might nevertheless prefer the status quo to restructuring operations, which would involve experimentation and a degree of risk. While some workers might thrive on greater responsibilities, such as they have in Sweden, others might agree with the American auto worker who, upon returning from an experimental stint at Saab, said: "If I've got to bust my ass to be meaningful, forget it. I'd rather be monotonous."

In this case, the plant manager's programmed task is to meet a near-term production schedule, and he is reluctant to sacrifice it to reorganize the work, though that might make for a greater long-run profit. Unfortunately, most of the unprogrammed jobs that are shunted aside this way do affect the corporation's long-run prospects. The long-range planning of corporate strategy is the premier unprogrammed task.

Techniques of planning have been substantially improved in recent years, and a growing number of corporations at least attempt to set goals for five or more years ahead. Multinational oil companies and electric utilities have been among the most assiduous long-run planners; it was easy for them to plan because until recently they enjoyed relatively stable growth rates and predictable markets. But managers are quite naturally chary of getting locked into strategies based on abstractions. They know that the best-laid plans, even when formulated on I.B.M. 360's, gang aft a-gley. The markets of the oil companies and utilities have recently been disrupted by unforeseen events, which caused a dramatic decline in the forecasts for oil consumption and the postponement of power-plant construction that had been on the drawing boards for years.

SOME THINGS WE'D RATHER NOT KNOW

Another impediment to serious long-range planning is the natural human tendency not to think about things that make one uncomfortable. Asbestos manufacturers are about as eager to dwell on the carcinogenic properties of their product as the fat man is to contemplate atherosclerosis. Even the pragmatic businessman tends to find improbably optimistic scenarios less "unthinkable" than more probable pessimistic alternatives. So executives assigned to planning all too often remain sealed off in their departments—consulted occasionally by someone who wants extrapolations of the past rather than troublesome departures from convention.

The result is a dismaying abundance of corporate problems that could have been avoided, and not just in hindsight. For several years, for instance, there have been indications that something of fundamental importance was happening in the oil business. If U.S. automakers had studied the distribution of world petroleum reserves and the course of politics in the Middle East, they might have been better able to anticipate the big price rise. If they had then turned their full resources to designing cars that would run on less gasoline, they would probably be selling more cars today.

The troubles of Reserve Mining Co. provide another case in point. When Reserve's owners, Armco and Republic Steel, chose to fight for the freedom to continue dumping taconite tailings into Lake Superior, they must have been counting, against all probability, on the evaporation of environmentalism. Since 1969, Reserve has earned a reputation for flagrantly opposing the public interest, has spent $6 million in legal battles, and is bound to spend a lot more. It could have filtered the water supplies of affected communities in the first place for an estimated $12 million.

THE MANAGEMENT OF CHANGE

What's needed is not so much new planning techniques as better application of the ones that exist. Peter Gabriel, dean of the Boston University School of Management and a former partner of McKinsey & Co., thinks that "the often spectacular failure in so much of what still parades as—and on occasion even is—highly sophisticated planning largely results from confusion between process and substance." The central need, says Gabriel, is for corporate managers to better understand what it is they need to plan for.

Managers have to stretch their minds to assess the changes taking place in all of the corporation's interrelated constituencies. In doing this, says Gabriel, they must understand that the events of tomorrow may be shaped by "ideological" factors, which have become as important as material considerations in influencing everything from oil supplies to employee relations. They also have to shift their emphasis from "the identification of opportunities specific to the individual company—like new products and new markets within traditional lines of business—to problems related to whole industries, if not the entire economy." In sum, he says, the corporation has to plan "for the management of change, rather than the administration of steady-state operations."

A fine example of long-range planning is the exercise conducted by J. C. Penny last year. Chairman Donald Seibert formed a number of groups of from five to eight middle-management people, each member of a group from a different area of the company. Provided with general guidance on source material, access to libraries and files, and plenty of time to work, the groups independently assessed the company's future. Seibert then commissioned outside consultants to work out future scenarios, and asked the in-house groups to chew over the professionals' work. The exercise, which took four months, contributed an unusually broad range of ideas to what became Penney's own long-range plan.

"A MULTIPLICITY OF IMAGINATIVE VENTURES"

One difficult strategy to plan is how to deal with all those new social forces that have become such a familiar part of the corporation's environment. The concept of corporate "social responsibility" has recently been expanded to include a list of demands as long as the attention spans of business's most vociferous critics. Some of these demands are ridiculous, others seriously important, and still others fall in between. The manager who simply writes off the whole problem of social responsibility does so at his peril. Most often, he has failed to take the time to sort out the issues.

A lot of fruitless verbiage could be stricken from the social-responsibility debate if corporate executives had a clear idea of what their responsibilities really are. Thornton Bradshaw, president of ARCO, puts the case succinctly by defining the corporation's two major obligations as "one, to operate to the full extent within the rules, and two, to create as many experimental situations as possible so that the new approaches can be picked up and become a part of our social pattern."

By creating "experimental situations," Bradshaw means things like trying new approaches to training the "unemployable," providing incentives for employee car pools, and so on. Such experiments, conducted pragmatically and in the corporation's own interest, are among the corporation's contributions to democratic pluralism. As Eli Goldston, the late chairman of Eastern Gas & Fuel Associates in Boston, once put it: "It's probably a good thing in any democratic society to have a multiplicity of decision makers—even if you take a scattering of not-so-bright and awfully conservative and somewhat eccentric executives. There's going to be 5,000 of them, each with a little pot of money to do something with. I'd sooner have them than Congress if what I was looking for was a multiplicity of imaginative ventures. And it is the multiplicity of decision spots that creates a wonderful opportunity for innovation."

Many of the corporation's social experiments are purely discretionary—charitable support for the arts, for example. Others, such as opening up jobs to minorities and women, are mandatory, but the means of implementing them afford the corporation some discretion. And the question of closing down a plant or moving a headquarters is broadly discretionary, though corporate executives must decide whether they need to make some effort to ease the impact of the move on employees, or even, in some cases, forgo it for the sake of the community.

There are no sure formulas for dealing with such issues. The corporation's leaders can only apply their own ethics. Taking refuge in the letter of the law begs the question and is self-destructive. The abdication of ethics will inevitably lead to a situation where every corporate decision will be judged by the applicable legal paragraph, and business will be buried under a mountain of regulations.

Bradshaw's other maxim of corporate behavior—"to operate to the full extent within the rules"—is not quite the obvious advice it appears to be. It is in the nature of the System that the rules are repeatedly being rewritten as people's expectations change. And as new responsibilities are placed on the corporation (say, to stop polluting the air), managers have to add the costs involved (to install and operate antipollution devices) to the price of the goods produced.

The attitude of corporate managers is most critical during the period leading up to the time when the rules are rewritten and set in concrete. During this period of awakening, when people are beginning to discern that some costs of production are being borne by the public, the wise course for the manager may well be to go to the government and say, "We think you should work up some industry regulations on this." It may be that the public will be willing to bear some of the costs.

But whatever the outcome, blindly resisting reform is no answer at all. The automobile industry, for example, fought emission controls at first, and upon losing the battle found itself painted into a corner—having to build all of its cars to standards stricter than are needed by most of the nation, and on a crash schedule too short for the best application of engineering talent.

TESTING A DOOMSDAY PREDICTION

By contrast, Du Pont seems to be handling the fluorocarbon issue with far greater dexterity. Fluorocarbons are a class of chemical products that includes the Freons, the principal gases used as aerosol propellants, as well as in refrigeration and air-conditioning systems. Freons are an invention of Du Pont and have become one of its many profitable businesses. The company estimates that the industries directly dependent on fluorocarbon production contribute $8 billion to the economy and employ 200,000 people.

During the past year, several scientists have, on the basis of computer models, suggested that fluorocarbons rising into the upper atmosphere may damage the ozone layer that shields the earth from excessive ultraviolent radiation. The scientists warn that the consequences would probably be disastrous—including increased incidences of skin cancer and substantial biological and climate changes. Their work is highly speculative at this point, however, as they themselves have acknowledged.

No rational manager would halt production of a major product on mere speculation. Not with the premature and costly elimination of phosphates from most laundry detergents still fresh in his memory. "The fluorocarbon issue troubles me greatly," says Du Pont Chairman Shapiro. "I hear the theory doesn't hold water, but there is great alarm that the atmosphere will be destroyed."

Under these trying circumstances, Du Pont appears to be doing about the best it can. Along with other fluorocarbon manufacturers, it is supporting research sponsored by the National Academy of Sciences and the Manufacturing Chemists Association. The latter group alone has funded, to the tune of $1.5 million, atmospheric measurements to test the hypothesis, and it plans to begin work in the stratosphere this year. Finally, Du Pont has made it unmistakably clear that it will stop production if, as it says, "any creditable scientific data show that any fluorocarbons cannot be used without a threat to health."

Particularly now, when their credibility is so low, corporations need to show convincingly that they can move quickly and conscientiously when such problems of potential public concern arise. Environmentalists tend to set standards of minimum or even zero risk to public health and safety. But decisions about risk are too important to be weighed in an atmosphere that pits environmental crusaders against corporate villains. The crusaders are apt to win most of the battles, and society will pay enormously for unrealistically risk-free production.

THE DICTATORIAL BOSS IS DEAD

Another area where there are few clear-cut rules for achieving effectiveness is in the art of managing the corporation's people. "Job satisfaction" is the catchall label that defines the primary task, and it is increasingly important to workers and managers at all levels of the corporation. Too much can be made—and has been—of the idea that the new attitudes of workers will cause the withering away of traditional economic disciplines and organizational constraints. The Age of Aquarius is *not* dawning, at least within the institutions that will carry society through whatever we will call the age that is coming upon us.

Nevertheless, the corporation cannot hope to escape some of the very real changes in values and work habits that are the inevitable outgrowth of increased affluence and education. "The leading motivators of the new work force are achievement, recognition, and the nature of the work," says Reginald Jones, chairman of General Electric. "The new management has to set reasonable goals, and encourage and challenge the work force."

This is by no means an altruistic exercise. Gone forever are the days when a dictatorial boss could elicit performance by barking at his workers. Corporate organization has become too complex for that, the boss too dependent on the knowledge and skills of his employees, who themselves have become power centers in the operation. If a corporation is to achieve extraordinary results, its employees have to *want* to take the initiative, to be creative.

WORKERS WANT MORE THAN MAYOISM

From the factory floor up through middle management, jobs in American industry still too frequently owe more than a trace of their structure and definition to the prescriptions issued at the turn of the century by Frederick W. Taylor, the original efficiency expert. Taylor viewed the worker as basically a mechanical being, and his system for organizing work was to carefully delineate all duties, breaking jobs down into the minutest motions and steps, in order to extract from each worker the maximum in efficiency.

Lingering Taylorism has not been particularly ameliorated by the efforts of the "human relations" school of management, which dates back to the Twenties and the work of industrial psychologist Elton Mayo. Stroking the workers' egos may have represented an improvement over the reductiveness of Taylorism. But apart from its doubtful ethical underpinnings (the stroking was calculated, not sincere), it was not particularly productive.

The company that can pinpoint and eliminate residual Taylorism generally finds that it creates not only better employee morale but higher productivity. The tendency for jobs in complex organizations to become highly specialized, and therefore fragmented, can rob the worker of the satisfaction that comes from completing an entire task. For more than thirty years at A.T.&T., the service representatives in business departments were limited to processing new phone orders and the like. Any decision to grant a customer extra time to pay a bill or to require a deposit for a new account had to be made by supervisors. In 1966, the company decided to give the more able and motivated service representatives these decision-making powers. Chairman John DeButts says that "we did it with some misgivings, but it worked out very well. We said, in effect, 'We trust you.' They did a better job, were extremely conscientious, and were proud that they could do the *whole* job."

Innovations in the workplace can do a good deal more than simply lift the mind-numbing restrictions from jobs at the lower corporate levels. Managers, no less than workers, can benefit from imaginative departures from convention and return the rewards to the enterprise as a whole. J. C. Penney's long-range planning effort is a case in point. Besides helping to shape the company's thinking about its future, it dealt a large number of line middle managers into the planning process, making concern about the corporation's ultimate destiny a part of their own job experience.

A LESSON FROM THE ORIENT

The old-line manager may doubt that there is any positive correlation between job enrichment and higher productivity, particularly in such areas as middle management, where productivity is hard, if not impossible, to measure accurately. But the examples of success continue to multiply at a rate that makes a causal relationship almost impossible to doubt.

The Japanese offer perhaps the most prominent body of evidence—and they have begun exporting their techniques to the plants they own in the U.S. (See "The Japanese Are Coming—with Their Own Style of Management," FORTUNE, March.) They have run their enterprises with an almost intuitive understanding of the connection between employee satisfaction and enhanced productivity. They shape benefits to the needs of specific groups in the work force, foster team spirit through informal relations between management and employees, and involve all members of a decision or company in detailed planning.

BACK TO A SENSE OF LEGITIMACY

Here in America (and of late even in Japan as well), the corporation has become widely mistrusted. That is unfortunate for a number of reasons. Several other institutions that once served as anchors for the society, including the family and the church, have also undergone long-term erosion, leaving lots of Americans with the feeling that they have been cut adrift from solid values. Many of these people devote a large part of their lives to their work. For that work to be perceived by the public, and by themselves, as something less than a force for good, is psychologically debilitating. Yet the work of the corporation is often so perceived. Norman Podhoretz, editor of the intellectual journal *Commentary,* notes: "A lot of businessmen are full of self-hate and are lacking a sense of legitimacy." Others wonder why they are so little appreciated.

Perhaps thinking clearly about the corporation as a "political" institution can help return some of the sense of legitimacy. Certainly, that view of the corporation today is more realistic than Adam Smith's description (the merchant who promotes society's interests only because he is unwittingly led to do so by the "invisible hand") or John Kenneth Galbraith's model (the oligopolist who controls his markets and assures his own perpetuation).

The goals of the "political" corporation can be defined in many ways: satisfying consumers as well as stockholders, allocating resources, marshaling talents, providing jobs, bearing a fair share of the total costs of production. Broadly, these are society's goals. If the corporation is effective, it will make a profit. That remains the unique yardstick for measuring the corporation's success in meeting its goals at the lowest possible cost, not only to itself but to all of society.

A THING OF MANY FACETS

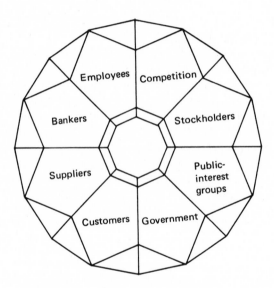

Though it may look like a monolith to some outsiders, the corporation is in fact a multifaceted institution whose managers have to balance the claims of many constituencies. The jewel-like construction above depicts some of those constituencies (such as employees and stockholders) as well as outside forces that bear in on the management (competition). These days the complex and often clashing claims of constituents are harder to assess and resolve than ever. For example, managers intent on serving the corporation's long-term future may feel the need to bend to the desires of public-interest groups concerned about pollution. The stockholders, on the other hand, might worry more about the impact of pollution control on current earnings. To take another case, if a supplier—say, a mineral-resource cartel—raises prices sharply, the corporation's managers may choose to absorb some of the costs rather than drive customers to competing products. But the managers will probably have to defend that action to their bankers when it comes time to negotiate a new loan.

CREEPING GIGANTISM?

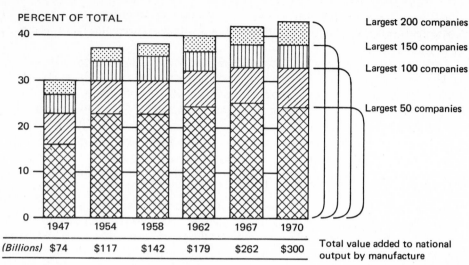

| (Billions) | $74 | $117 | $142 | $179 | $262 | $300 |

Total value added to national output by manufacture

The very large corporation is clearly a dominant force in American business. According to the most recent data from the *Census of Manufacturers,* the top 200 industrial companies produced 43 percent of the value added to manufacturing output in 1970, or about $120 billion. That was a large advance from 1947, when they accounted for 30 percent (or about $22 billion). It is worth noting, however, that since 1954 the 200 have expanded their share fairly slowly, picking up just six percentage points. And between 1967 and 1970, the top fifty companies' share of the total not only stopped growing but shrank.

AN ALTERNATIVE TO SMITH AND GALBRAITH

Characteristic	Classical-market model	Managerial model	Social-environment model
Nature of the economy	Perfectly competitive	Monopolistic-oligopolistic	Effectively competitive
Level of profits	Normal	Supernormal	Normal
Enterprise goal	Short-run profit maximization	Security and growth of business volume	Long-run profit maximization
Locus of decision-making power	Entrepreneaurs	Managers	Stockholders—board of directors
Nature of competition	Price	Price Product variation Selling costs	Multivectored dynamic process
External constraints on enterprise behavior	Markets Markets	Markets	Markets Public opinion Political pressures
Determinants of social activity	None	Social and charitable propensities of managers	Long-run profit maximization

The corporate executive knows that his company behaves according to neither the Adam Smith nor the John Kenneth Galbraith description, but he may be hard put to find a theoretical model that will do justice to reality. Neil H. Jacoby, founding dean of the U.C.L.A. Graduate School of Management, offers one in his book, *Corporate Power and Social Responsibility.*

Of the three models above, the classical-market model sums up the corporation as Smith saw it—the small, owner-managed firm purveying simple products in a perfectly competitive market. The managerial model, developed during the 1940's and 1950's, was, as Jacoby says, "carried to an extreme by Galbraith in *The New Industrial State.*" In it, management is divorced from ownership and the corporation is run not so much to optimize profits for stockholders as to satisfy the managers' own desires for security, power, and prestige. Companies compete by varying their product styles and spending money on advertising and other marketing devices. But since competition is muted by oligopoly, profits are "abnormally" high.

Jacoby's social-environment model reflects the corporation's status as a political institution. Legislation and the prodding of public opinion induce large companies to allocate resources to social purposes they might ignore if they were responding solely to classical-market forces. Because the corporation is financially more secure than Adam Smith's merchant, its managers can afford to look beyond the quick dollar to maximize long-run profits.

Jacoby's formidable phrase to describe competitive forces—the "multivectored dynamic process"—includes four major categories of competition—intraproduct (within the same industry), interproduct (across industry lines), potential (from companies that might enter the business), and international. These categories in turn break down into several subcategories. Interproduct competition, for example, involves not only price, product variation, and selling costs, but also services, credit terms, trade-in allowances, warranties, and competition from secondhand products.

Not everyone will agree with all of Jacoby's conclusions. There is little evidence, for example, that stockholders constitute an effective locus of decision-making power for most corporations. And boards of directors are too often creations of the managements they are supposed to oversee. Jacoby himself recognizes the weaknesses of boards, and proposes they be strengthened. He says the majority of directors should be well-paid outsiders with an independent staff to examine corporate affairs. Since few managers will willingly undertake reforms that would bring them tougher overseers, Jacoby advocates that corporations be chartered nationally, with stringent requirements about their boards' independence written into the charters.

8

EXIT THE ORGANIZATION MAN: ENTER THE PROFESSIONAL PERSON

ROBERT STEPHEN SILVERMAN and D. A. HEMING

During the fabulous fifties, William H. Whyte, Jr. captured the profile of a working person and turned it into a best seller: *The Organization Man.* According to Whyte, a body would leave home—spiritually as well as physically—and sell his mind and soul to the organization. Today, enlightened organizations relegate the Organization Man as an anachronism—a thing of the past. No longer do most working people feel a sense of dedication and belonging to any one organization. Why should they? Exit the Organization Man; enter the Professional Person—the best-prepared man or woman any society ever produced.

The Professional Person has a much higher level of needs, values, awareness, consciousness and sensitivity than the Organization Man. Unlike the Organization man, he belongs chiefly to himself: an individual motivated by competency and personal growth. His loyalty and commitment belong first, to his profession; and second, to the organization for which he may be working, at any particular time. He feels uncommitted to any one organization but willing to deploy his individualism, knowledge and creative abilities to solve problems with resources provided by the organization. Committed to self-actualization, but with the full expectation it will mesh successfully with required organizational roles, The Professional Person appears willing to take risks in asserting his individualism even in large organizations. He looks upon himself as an individual marketing three interrelated products: his knowledge, his skills and his competencies.

Conflict exists in many present organizations between the leadership needs of the Professional Person and the traditional leadership behavior of organizational bureaucrats, who seem to thrive on the decline of innovation and creativity. Traditionally, bureaucratic leaders cannot tolerate risk-taking because their value systems normally revolve around the preservation of the status quo. The traditional principles of management involve organizing, planning and controlling to preserve the status quo. Human relations, to many bureaucrats, have relevance only because they ensure the proliferation of the status quo, at the expense of individuality, if necessary.

SOURCE: *Personnel Journal,* March 1975. Reprinted by permission.   **67**

The Professional Person has a give and take attitude in relation to organizations and, therefore, expects something from it. Once this restructuring of self-consciousness has occurred, a gap opens up between The Professional Person and those who have not changed. When the restructured consciousness of The Professional Person encounters the traditional status quo manager, an Organizational Generation Gap results.

Without recognizing the realities of the organizational problems surrounding them, the older generation manager has had to fumble with solutions based on outdated organizational principles. The older generation manager interprets the behavior of The Professional Person in terms of his own frame of reference. The Professional Person represents the vanguard of the new consciousness in organizations, but he finds himself in social structures unwilling or unable to reshape and renew themselves.

As expectation levels and need patterns change, upper management levels respond accordingly. When upper management fails to respond, organizational rigidity and stagnation, coupled with an increasing level of frustration, isolation, and alienation, sets in. The Professional Person encounters isolation and alienation from administrative and control mechanisms inherent in bureaucracies, such as the federal public service. Within bureaucracies, interrelationships have lost much of their direct, honest and human quality and have instead assumed a rather plastic character saturated by the spirit of indifference. Relationships between men then assume the character of relationships between things. Before upper management levels can respond positively to the concerns and philosophies of The Professional Person, the new need patterns and value systems of these individuals will have to be discerned.

THE EMERGING NEW NEED PATTERNS AND VALUE SYSTEMS

The Professional Person assumes responsibility for making his job a constructive vehicle for innovative and creative self-expression. He fulfills himself, not only by contributing to his particular organization, but also to the larger world around him. Wanting to contribute his skills and talents to society in general, he brings with him the capacity for developing a learning continuum. He sees education as a life-long process. A practitioner and student simultaneously, he realizes that new knowledge constantly makes previous knowledge obsolete.

The Professional Person won't allow the galloping bureaucratic system to change him from a committed, idealistic individual into another member of the apathetic herd. No educational cripple, he won't sink into intellectual apathy due to lack of challenge and incentive. He traces much of the intellectual sterility and apathy that is evident today in organizations to managements handing down objectives and decisions to individuals in lieu of first-hand experience. Meaningful, productive and challenging work, together with recognized achievement, motivates the Professional Person. But to accomplish the output requirements of his position, he requires performance-oriented, dynamic organizations rather than authority-oriented, bureaucratic organizations—organizations with definite centers of accountability, managed by objectives rather than bosses.

The Professional Person needs achievement, recognition and responsibility; a widening range of responsibilities and a broadening control over these responsibilities. He needs to operate in his own way without interference, bringing only exceptional situations to the attention of his superior. In this way, he feels important, needed and trusted to do his best. This style of management permits him to utilize, in a synergistic fashion, his experience and total knowledge.

The Professional Person needs the tangible participation in the organization, achieved by creating decentralized organizational units, in order to manage within the control of the overall organization or by establishing task team, temporary work assignments and other ad hoc groups. Fast-moving, dynamic thinking proves alien to some present day federal public service managers, who find it difficult to share authority, responsibility and accountability. The Professional Person will eventually alter traditional organization structures drastically by the temporary task-team approach which cuts radically across functional, divisional and departmental lines. Most federal public service managers profess an academic understanding of the participation ideology, but mistake human relations for participation. To the Professional Person, good human relations exist when management treats each individual as a unique entity and when the organization does everything possible to create conditions in which each individual can use his capabilities to the fullest.

The supervisor only can give a worker self-respect, and no one else can deprive him of it as easily. Without self-respect, employment in large organizations: i.e., the federal public service, will become an increasingly empty and unrewarding experience, regardless of fringe benefits. And without self-respect, work gradually deteriorates from an opportunity to discover one's own potentialities into a breeding ground for frustration, conflict, grievances and appeals. When management promises more than it can deliver, the conflict in approaches to participation and human relations precipitates an expensive loss of talent. In large organizations—such as the federal public service—the very people able to contribute to the broad social aspects of bureaucracy will leave in quest of self-actualization.

The Professional Person doesn't seek to dictate organizational policy, but merely to contribute to the decision-making and policy formulation processes. He believes that, as a member of the organization, he should have some voice in making decisions that affect him and the results of his labor. He seeks to serve as catalyst, in emphasing that organizations should not wait until problems become major crises before introducing change. Trapped in an ineffectual bureaucracy, the Professional Person views himself an inert component of a group, not a participant in any significant way—simply carried along with the crowd.

The Professional Person believes that all organization members should have the opportunity to participate in the formulation and execution of plans, policies and objectives. He thinks that traditional management should cast aside any preconceptions about employee-employer relations and introduce a viable system of communication and participation that will allow him to contribute his knowledge and expertise to solving organizational problems.

MANAGEMENT BY CREATIVE OBJECTIVES

Traditionally, federal public service management styles have emphasized decision-making at the highest level, and then implemented the decisions by working through other people. The Professional Person needs a new style of management and leadership because he reacts to creative ideas rather than to ideologies, precedents, policies and orders. Some Bureaucrats argue that the Professional Person has little, if any, respect for authority. Quite the contrary, he does respect authority, the type of authority earned through competence, performance and leadership ability, rather than merely position. Competent leadership, stressing performance and creative organizational objective formulation, coincides with the philosophy of The Professional Person. Under effective management, the leader stimulates the group to high levels of performance by instilling a sense of competency motivation. The Professional Person accepts responsibility and the accountability for its risks and results.

The recent trend in the federal public service towards Management of Objectives illustrates the growing pressures from both inside and outside government organizations for more creative management. Unfortunately, too many public service managers attempt to integrate Management by Objectives into management systems presently in use, rather than implement it as a completely new way of managing. Today, no federal public service manager has any real chance of maintaining a level of credibility with his subordinates, peers and perhaps his superiors, unless organizational objectives tune in to the needs, abilities, values and personal aspirations of the achievers of these objectives. By failing to include appropriate objectives within the ambition and capability of a manager's staff, the organization risks losing capable and ambitious people.

By working under a system that forces leaders and followers to work together on the establishment of individual and organization objectives, the intellectual atmosphere needed for situational sensitivity is provided. When intellectual sterility sets in, due to objectives imposed by a rigid bureaucratic approach, the most productive and creative people will leave. If they don't actually leave, one can expect continuous conflict. The Professional Person needs an environment in which he can identify his effectiveness areas and standards. There, he can attain a realistic sense of involvement and participation in the establishment of creative objectives. Management by Creative Objectives requires openness, trust, a sharing of responsibility; it allows the individual to function as a whole person within the organizational context.

INDIVIDUALISM

The Professional Person, by seeking participation and creative objectives, finds personal expression within his organization. He chooses to act as himself, not as the organization would prefer him to act.

Most modern bureaucracies do not foster or reward people for unorthodox or individualistic behavior. The Professional Person, however, demands relevance, responsibility and individualism in his job. The intellectual and awareness gap which exists between younger and older subordinates and managers, will continue as each new generation experiences a technologically, intellectually and emotionally different world. The problem is to find acceptable means of reaching mutually acceptable organizational and individual objectives. The Professional Person will respond positively to managers, who have an informal managerial style and a direct honest approach that recognizes him as an individual and equal —even though less experienced person. Ideally, organizations should create atmospheres in which the experience of the older generation meshes with the knowledge and enthusiastic individualism of the younger generation. When the organization does not run smoothly, the status quo manager traces a failure in communication. In many cases, however, the message has reached the Professional Person clearly, but has been found unacceptable. When an organization becomes too tightly integrated and pre-empts all available resources and methods with policies and procedures, then it fails to provide a margin of spontaneity and individuality that makes growth possible for the Professional Person. Stifling formality drives the Professional Person from the organization due to apathy, lack of incentive and withdrawal of commitment.

Justification for too many organizational formalities is found only in their continued use. Silence and conformity provide the illusion of tranquility. Loss of inner self, on one hand, and outer conformity on the other, create a lulling and discontinuous organizational atmosphere, in which mediocrity flourishes and individual initiative evaporates. The Professional Person has launched a quiet revolution to gradually change the face of organizations. When armed with situational sensitivity, management skills and style flexibility, the Professional Person fulfills the measurable, time-bound output requirement of his position without relinquishing his personality. And that has made all the difference.

9

THE COMMITTEE IN BUSINESS: ASSET OR LIABILITY?

ANGELOS A. TASKLANGANOS

Opinions on the utility of the committee in business range from enthusiastic support to vigorous dismissal. For some committee watchers, the organ has about as much functional value as a vermiform appendix. For others, it is as indispensable to corporate life as the digestive tract.

Advocates and antagonists alike would probably agree with Joseph L. Massie's purposely broad description of what a committee is: "any group interacting with regard to a common explicit purpose with formal authority delegated from an appointed body. . . ."[1] They part company on the issue of what it should do. Initially formed to provide advice to a single executive to help him arrive at decisions—a role it continued to play, of course—the committee of today may also move in other and more powerful directions. It may receive, exchange and test information;[2] it often makes decisions itself; and increasingly, especially in the large corporation, it acts as personnel training ground, of sorts, for junior executives. Some feel that these extensions of function overload the committee's capabilities and that it should be restricted to its original design. Others feel that the "group think" process can be applied even more broadly. There are good reasons behind each viewpoint.

ADVANTAGES OF THE COMMITTEE

The majority of economists favor the use of the committee in the large corporation. One advocate, John Kenneth Galbraith, adopts the notion of a company as a hierarchy of committees. The system, he states, involves coordination, a good in itself. The effective unit, made up of appropriate talent, intervenes on occasion to force a decision, announces a decision or carries it out, or gathers facts to transmit to a higher committee for further action. Galbraith also argues that the working association provides considerable mental

SOURCE: *Personnel Journal,* February 1975. Reprinted by permission.

[1]Joseph L. Massie, *Essentials of Management* (Englewood Cliffs, N.J.: Prentice Hall, 1971), p. 55.

[2]John Kenneth Galbraith, *The New Industrial State* (New York: Signet, 1967), p. 75.

stimulus for members, from the exchanges with their counterparts in the organization.[3]

Other proponents of the committee system also advance the last point, specifying that the suborganization provides a unique marketplace of ideas, enables each member to know the intellectual resources of his colleagues, and stimulates each to keep himself informed on the subject the group is handling. Discussions in meetings allow members to pool information under circumstances that foster immediate probing, as well as to assess the relevance and reliability of the data and opinions offered. The committee thus contributes to a more solidly based decision because it generates a deeper understanding of the problem under consideration. Furthermore, it can deal with certain questions more palatably or more equitably than any single authority. This would be the case, for example, with such delicate issues as the annual bonus and salary of the firm, executive performance review and reappraisal of a high-level policy that is proving risky.

DISADVANTAGES OF THE COMMITTEE

Most critics of the committee assert that it is far too expensive in relation to the service it renders. To begin with, the work hours it requires are massive. It entails not only the (hopefully productive) time of the members in the meetings, but also the time for preparation, travel when they do not work in the same location, and follow-through. Moreover, little or no allowance is ordinarily made for the extra effort that committee service adds to the executive's primary duties, and this in turn may not only heighten the strain of his overall job, but also will certainly affect his committee efforts.

Opponents of the system feel too that the slow committee process bottlenecks the solution of company problems because it is out of synchronization with the fast pace of business life. By the time members have met and deliberated, a decision could have been made long before, and implemented by a single well-informed executive. Positive and creative committee interaction precludes speed, and accelerating the process tends to destroy its raison d'etre—collective thinking. Critics also assert that because the duties and authority of the usual committee are couched in the broadest language possible, theoretically to allow maximum flexibility once discussions get under way, its mandate is frequently unclear and its powers ill-defined. These factors legislate against fruitful deliberations and effective outcomes.

Opponents of the committee contend further that the interchange among the participants does not always stimulate a deeper understanding of the assigned subject and a consequent better decision. Particularly when members are specialists, they can—and often do—cling tenaciously to their respective convictions of rightness, with the result that any decision emanating from the group is often diluted to a meaningless common denominator in the attempt to accommodate all viewpoints.[4] Even when dilution is not drastic, the weakening of a strongly held position can lessen its proponents' sense of responsibility and pride in the results of the group's work, and the compromise produced is, in turn, likely to lower the commitment to carry through recommendations.

[3] *Ibid.*

[4] John Medlin, "Individual Responsibility vs. Group Decisions: An Analysis," *Administrative Management,* Vol. XXVIII, No. 1, January 1967, p. 28.

A final criticism, one often launched, concerns the composition of the committee from the point of view of personality. It is possible for one or more members to suffer from an excessively modest view of their role and remain utterly mute, while others are afflicted with an inflated ego and manifest a severe case of logorrhea. Either malady can cripple the group's effectiveness, making the average member functionally neurotic. When personality differences take a more heated turn, the meetings can become a struggle over who is to emerge strongest; in this case the decision is a single person's, and the whole concept of the committee is more or less negated. Or, if no one will give way, any decision suffers the same dilution as in a group of experts immovably committed to their individual positions.[5] Shepard Mead has commented, "Committees are like tournaments; individuals can win and lose meetings. I've never seen an original idea come out of committees. It's the function of committees to knock corners off ideas and turn them into shapeless blobs."[6]

SOME CORRECTIVES

Most supporters of committeedom admit the accuracy of some attacks on the system, but they have rebuttals. Addressing the complaint—which he agrees with—that meetings often waste time, R. Alex Mackenzie formulates a number of time-saving devices, short of abolishing committees altogether. An amusing but sensible proposal is that members hold stand-up meetings, denying themselves the comfort of chairs and maintaining an inclination toward brevity.[7]

Robert F. Bales, a Harvard sociologist, and his co-authors, Edgar F. Borgatta and Paul A. Hare, have studied the committee from the standpoint of size and structure, troublesome variables that have scuttled many an otherwise well-formed unit. They report that the ideal number of participants appears to range between four and seven, with the optimum being five.[8] Both these commentators and a team of investigators from the University of Michigan's Institute for Social Research present findings that the selection of the committee head is especially critical to the group's functioning. The Michigan team, whose research embraced 23 interdepartmental district committees and 131 middle-management executive committees, concludes that a skillful chairperson can make a 35 per cent difference in the soundness of the group's work.[9]

Some proponents of the committee system go farther and claim that there are criteria which, if met, can make successful functioning almost certain. William H. Newman, for example, feels that the following ensure the effectiveness of any committee:

1. Its duties and authority must be clearly stated.

[5]*Ibid.* pp. 28, 30.

[6]Quoted in "Still Pricking Business Balloons," *Business Week,* March 21, 1964, p. 90.

[7]R. Alec Mackenzie, *The Time Trap* (New York: American Management Associations, 1973).

[8]Robert F. Bales, Edgar R. Borgatta and Paul A. Hare, *Small Groups: Studies in Social Interactions* (New York: Knopf, 1966), pp. 495–596.

[9]Angelos A. Tasklanganos, "Is the Committee a Corporate Albatross," Canadian Business, February 1974, p. 49.

2. Committee members must be selected in view of the duties involved.

3. The committee must be supported by the necessary staff assistance.

4. Procedures must be designed to obtain prompt and effective action.

5. The right chairperson must be chosen.[10]

Others proffer additional rules, but Newman's principles constitute sound generalities that accord with common sense. In their broad span, however, they do not provide the brass tacks—the specific how-to's—for effective utilization of the committee. Nor do they or many other overviews tackle the heart of the matter: the justification for continuing, reducing or even abolishing this long-lived corporate institution.

PROPOSALS FOR STREAMLINING THE COMMITTEE SYSTEM

Is the committee a universal instrument suited to almost every internal business activity? Or is it, as the cynics would have us believe, made up of the unfit appointed by the incompetent to do the unnecessary?

That the committee has important uses cannot really be gainsaid. In its prototypical capacity of providing information to a manager whose time limitations or training prevent him from exploring thoroughly the problems under his review, there is a consensus that it serves a critical need. If given a clear mandate, adequate guidelines and an appropriate membership, it stands a good chance of performing very well.

Many of the criticisms of the committee in fact relate not so much to the institution itself as to its misapplication. It is by nature unfitted, for example, to substitute for a decision-making manager. It obviously should never be used to delay confronting a problem or to "spread the risk" of a sensitive decision. (It is an appropriate instrument, however, for spreading the *base* of a decision, as mentioned earlier.) Nor should it serve, except incidentally, to help young executives learn their trade. Such abuses of the committee's purposes do indeed turn it, as its detractors claim, into a costly and wasteful appendage.

In positive terms, a firm can do much to tap the very real potential of the committee system if it practices the dictum that underlies good management of all human resources —to assign the appropriate task to the proper person at the right time. The following list, incorporating a number of points introduced earlier, spells out this adage in guidelines for strengthening the committee's contribution to company operations as a whole:

1. Avoid erecting a committee unless there is clear evidence that a question cannot be handled effectively by an individual. Use a well-designed communications system (featuring frequent information bulletins, weekly and monthly reports and periodic reviews) to eliminate as many committees as possible.

2. Retain most of the decision-making power in the central administration. This increases individual initiative and innovation.

[10]William H. Newman, *Administrative Action* (Englewood Cliffs, N.J.: Prentice Hall, 1950), p. 249.

3. Define each committee's jurisdiction and duties explicitly and clearly. Only major needs, such as resolving large-scale problems, generating important information, ensuring interdepartmental coordination and planning policy should be assigned to a group, rather than a single executive, for action.

4. Curtail the size of the committee to between three and seven members. Select these carefully, not only for their credentials in relation to the group task, but also for the ability of each to function effectively with the other participants. Group dynamics is as important as group expertise.

5. Appoint a chairperson who has demonstrated competence as a leader, who can tactfully repress the overexpressive and encourage the hesitant, and who can keep the discussion focused on the agenda topics without hampering the flow of the interchange.

6. Allocate to the committee the necessary ancillary factors that will free members for their task of group thinking: appropriate physical meeting place; adequate secretarial assistance; audiovisual, computer-terminal, or other needed equipment, etc.

7. Plan each committee meeting thoroughly. Prepare a detailed agenda and distribute it in advance.

8. Hold the frequency of meetings to a minimum, and restrict the time of each session to one hour.

9. Check the progress of the committee's work periodically, if its assigned deadline is one month or more beyond its first meeting. Be prepared to change its constitution if it is moving too slowly.

10. Discontinue the committee's meetings immediately when its primary task has been accomplished. Utilize the communications system (guideline 1) for as much of the follow-through and review as possible.

The veritable population explosion of committees today derives from a widespread recognition of how useful this business suborganization can be, if it is utilized intelligently. Its thrust as a collective instrument of information and action derives from its economy and efficiency. But these qualities are lost when the group organism multiplies indiscriminately within the parent body, the company. It is obvious that the number, sizes, types and functions of committees should be determined by each firm on the basis of its specific needs; it is equally obvious that the bigger the concern, the more these formal subgroups will be needed. Particularly, therefore, in the large corporation, they must be skillfully shaped —and pruned—to serve the integral business structure effectively.

10

THE JAPANESE ARE COMING—WITH THEIR OWN STYLE OF MANAGEMENT

LOUIS KRAAR

Japan's latest export offensive in the U.S. features, not products, but factories. A number of Japanese companies are opening, or taking over, production facilities here. They're making zippers in Georgia, bearings in Illinois, television sets in California, soy sauce in Wisconsin. Along with capital and technology, the Japanese are bringing their own extraordinary style of management—and it is proving remarkably effective with Americans.

The Oriental manner of motivating people emphasizes a highly personal approach to corporate life and encourages employees to participate in all aspects of company affairs. While there is no single Japanese way of management, most companies rely on similar basic techniques. Their plants typically have an open atmosphere that allows any employee to talk easily with top executives. Rather than issuing direct orders, the men in charge prefer to rule through consultation; supervisors down the line help formulate policy decisions. Above all, the Japanese go to exceptional lengths to keep their employees happy. Layoffs are rare (although not unknown) in Japanese companies, even in hard times.

Like U.S. multinational corporations that build plants overseas, Japanese manufacturers invest abroad in order to gain cost advantages and expand vital markets. Lately the benefits of producing in the U.S. have become clearer than ever, for Japan's inflation rate of 25 percent last year was the highest of any industrial nation. Plant sites are cheaper here than in land-scarce Japan, and labor costs are about the same. Many raw materials are less expensive and more available in this country. Moreover, the Japanese figure that making products in the U.S. will help counteract protectionist pressures, which could sharply curb sales in Japan's largest foreign market.

GOOD FOR THE COMMUNITY

The big march into America began flamboyantly in mid-1971, when Tokyo had an almost embarrassingly large foreign-exchange surplus. All together, more than $2 billion has been committed to investment in the U.S., nearly half of it in the fiscal year that ended last March.

SOURCE: Reprinted from the March 1975 issue of *Fortune* Magazine by special permission; © 1975 Time Inc.

Despite the recession, the Japanese are still coming in a big way, although at a somewhat slackened pace and with greater selectivity.

In the beginning, they rushed in with more money than prudence, buying up Hawaiian beach resorts and California country clubs, and even starting a girlie magazine called *Genesis*. Now the Japanese government insists on investments in enterprises that directly bolster industry at home. Last spring, for instance, Matsushita Electric Industrial paid about $100 million to acquire Motorola's TV production facilities. Matsushita, Japan's largest manufacturer of consumer electronic products, made the acquisition to enlarge its modest share of the U.S. market. Its American operations will eventually use machinery and product components made in Japan.

States and municipalities are competing to attract Japanese investment, and the jobs and tax revenues it will provide. Some localities are luring Japanese companies by offering to finance plants through bond issues that carry relatively low interest rates. In Camden, South Carolina, the trading firm Marubeni has established a textile mill with $4,750,000 in capital raised from county revenue bonds. "Some people still feel that the Japanese couldn't beat us in the last World War, so now they're coming to buy us," says an American manager at the mill. "But most folks think this is good for the community."

As is the case with Americans doing business in Japan, there is no way that the Japanese can leave behind what they have done and known at home. Venturing out of Japan's clubby, insular business community, they bring along a unique management approach rooted in their own traditions. Japanese business is accustomed to workers who are dedicated lifetime employees, identifying closely with the quality of the final product and the welfare of the overall company. A production worker in Japan just naturally corrects mistakes made by anyone preceding him on the assembly line. And managers patiently make decisions by consensus, a custom so ingrained that chief executives usually act mainly as catalysts to encourage proposals from below.

THE YEN FOR HARMONY

In their U.S. operations, Japanese companies put their own nationals in the top managerial positions, and these executives painstakingly adapt their style to the decidedly different conditions they find here. A primary aim of the Japanese managers is to shape and influence workers' attitudes toward their jobs; they consider proper attitudes to be crucial to productivity and quality control. In pursuit of internal harmony, most companies have resisted unionization—in most cases with notable success.

Though specific techniques vary with each company, the Japanese approach requires that executives become personally familiar with what it takes to do every job performed by their subordinates. Their own diligence and long working hours provide an example that they hope American employees will emulate. The Japanese not only know workers by name and encourage suggestions, but often pitch in on the assembly line. Shunji Ishino, president of NTN Bearing, circulates every day among all his employees in Des Plaines, Illinois. He greets them by name, stops to chat and to listen. His rounds make them feel important, and he often comes away with useful suggestions. During semiannual inventories, Ishino works as a manual laborer in the warehouse—partly to show the customary Japanese team spirit, but also to check on the effectiveness of his American supervisors.

Because the Japanese assume that supervisory employees have a long-term commitment, they rarely fire anyone for making an honest mistake. At NTN Bearing, Ishino recently discovered that $300,000 worth of excessive inventory had piled up in the warehouse without anyone realizing it. He brought the matter to the attention of his operations manager, Lauren Sams, who is responsible for controlling inventory. "Anywhere else," says Sams, "that would have brought a serious reprimand or even discharge." But Ishino simply said, "Well, now you see what you have done." The mild remonstrance reflected the Japanese view that employees best serve a company by learning from their errors. Sams was prompt to unload the surplus bearings.

NO POWER STRUGGLES

Most Americans seem to respond well to the Oriental style. After all, almost everybody wants to feel that his or her work is important—and appreciated. Though initially many supervisors are befuddled by the Japanese habit of hashing out virtually everything in long, face-to-face meetings, they usually come to like the sense of participation. As one of the American managers at Sony's TV plant in San Diego observes, "It helps that everyone agrees before things are done. You don't have the power struggles and infighting common in many U.S. companies."

Living and working in the U.S. require the Japanese to make some traumatic adjustments themselves. In Japan, executives rarely reject any proposal flatly and directly; that is considered impolite and a threat to the group harmony. Katsuo Goto, treasurer of Mitsubishi Aircraft's operation in Texas, says, "I've had to learn to say 'no,' instead of 'that's very difficult.'" His Americanization, however, causes conflict with the home office, where Goto's acquired habit of saying "no" shocks associates.

Little in their culture prepares the Japanese for many routine aspects of American life. To win acceptance in small towns, they make a great effort to participate in local civic and social activities. Few Americans realize what an effort it takes for the innately clannish Japanese. "We really don't have community life in Japan," notes one Japanese executive, "because there your company *is* the community."

In New York and other cities, there are enough Japanese businessmen so that many are able to live and work in a Tokyo subculture. They leave home early each morning, speak their own tongue in the office, eat lunch at Japanese restaurants or clubs, and relax at a Japanese bar after working late nearly every night. Few ever plunge fully into an American life-style. "In order to succeed in a Japanese company, you have to stay in Japanese society," explains Tetsuro Iwabe, a vice president of Mitsui & Co., who is based in New York. "That means we have to entertain and take care of people visiting from Tokyo, even on many weekends."

The socializing is generally males only. Quietly and alone, the wives bear the brunt of adjusting to American life. The companies give them surprisingly little preparation for the experience, and their husbands are too busy to help. "Japanese wives here are lonely and isolated," says the exceptionally outspoken wife of a Japanese banker in New York. "Why, I know some women who have stayed here for over two years and never taken a bus or subway. About once a year, a wife will jump off a building or have a nervous breakdown." Recently, Japanese women in the New York area have started organizing orientation courses in such inscrutable Western ways as how to hire baby-sitters and fend off door-to-door salesmen.

The plight of the wives must be counted one great management failure of the Japanese in this country. In most other respects, they have been exceptionally successful at adapting to life here. Visits to a number of Japanese-owned plants scattered throughout the country offer convincing evidence that American workers and Japanese managers usually make a successful combination.

At YKK Zipper's new $15-million factory in Macon, Georgia, Japanese management techniques have been introduced with notable success—but not without difficulty—by YKK's vigorous local president, Yoshinori Kitano, thirty-seven. His working costume is the company uniform, a gray windbreaker with zippers on the sleeves and front. His desk is located in an open area and jammed close to those of his American and Japanese subordinates, so they can overhear all his conversations. "In YKK, no secrets," he says. "Everyone open, everyone same."

Though he speaks in broken English, Kitano has no difficulty communicating with his 100 employees, most of whom are Georgians. For an hour or so daily, the chief executive goes to the production floor and works as a machine operator. This is more than a gesture, for it keeps him in personal touch with production problems. As he likes to put it, "If we forget zippers, our company is finished."

Kitano's stints in the plant also show that the boss is willing to do everything he asks of his workers. His example is emulated by the managers under him, a dozen Japanese who serve in tandem with an equal number of Americans they are training. Though the factory has been in full operation only seven months, productivity is already up to 85 percent of that of YKK plants in Japan. The Macon plant is expected to go into the black this year.

Kitano normally works a twelve-hour day—and then he often takes American managers out for dinner and long philosophical discussions that emphasize the work ethic. At one such session in a local restaurant, he urged them, "Be like Americans 150 years ago— pioneers—for YKK." And one night a month, he gathers together all managers in the plant to discuss specific problems. Kitano purposely never tells them what to do, but asks managers to "aim their thinking" and tell him what should be done.

YKK proudly proclaims itself the world's largest zipper manufacturer, and it has set up assembly operations in thirty countries. The Macon plant is different; it is fully integrated, using highly automatic machines to convert yarn, metal, and plastic into the finished product. Most of the production workers only monitor the equipment that spews out components. But the process demands close attention. The human problem, Kitano says, is that "everyone must be thinking and care about zippers."

THREE MONTHS IN TOYAMA

To instill that sort of devotion across vast language and cultural barriers, Kitano had to figure out a way to make company men out of young Americans. He personally selected half a dozen recent graduates from Georgia engineering and technical schools, then dispatched them for three months—without their families—to YKK headquarters in Toyama, a town 150 miles northwest of Tokyo. The Georgians worked eight hours a day as machine operators, spent evenings studying the new equipment with Japanese engineers, and fell into bed at

YKK dormitories. Before they returned to the U.S., they helped Kitano plan every detail of the Macon plant.

The total immersion thoroughly imbued the young American managers with the YKK spirit. They, of course, wear YKK jackets, too. Ben Shelton, twenty-four, a shaggy-haired production technician, says, "I was sort of converted to the Japanese system. They seem to have a better way of handling people." Like other trainees, Shelton flew back to the U.S. with the Japanese engineer who trained him, and they jointly supervise a production department. The arrangement provides the American with technical expertise and the Japanese with a friendly guide to the mores of Macon.

Under the open-management system, the American supervisors do not hesitate to point out mistakes in YKK's handling of production employees. Many of the problems spring from the company's policy of having everyone do a little menial labor. Women in the plant rebelled against cleaning their own rest rooms; a janitor has since been hired. In another instance, a Japanese supervisor told a new man on the line to begin his first morning by sweeping the floor. After ten minutes the employee walked off the job and never returned. Managers still sweep, but now they ask rather than tell workers to do so.

Perhaps the biggest misunderstanding at YKK has been between zealous Japanese supervisors and sensitive southern women employees. The Japanese are so emotionally dedicated to their product that at first when they observed faulty work, they went into something of a tizzy and excitedly shouted at the women on the line. They had to speak loudly to get heard at all above the noisy machinery, and their rebukes sounded extremely harsh to the women. "So many girls were crying and complaining that we had to do something," recalls an American manager. To stop the tears and yet maintain quality control, YKK appointed a "floor lady," a woman supervisor who gently passes along managerial criticism.

For a while, the plant had a high rate of absenteeism, principally because workers were dissatisfied with the pay scale. In planning the factory, YKK had checked the prevailing local rates, but did not allow for inflation. Recently, production workers got a cost-of-living increase that raised pay by 50 cents to $2.50 an hour, and absenteeism has declined. "The Japanese had a hard time realizing that unskilled Georgia workers were not as dedicated to the company as they are," observes an American executive. "But they do respond to money."

FAMILY ATMOSPHERE AT THE BILLIARD TABLE

NTN Bearing, which has a plant near Chicago's O'Hare International Airport, relies on a special monetary incentive to promote teamwork among employees. Most Japanese find it natural to cooperate for the benefit of the whole company. To inspire Americans to do so, the NTN management sets a monthly production target for the entire Illinois plant. Every employee, from executives to clerks, gets an identical bonus—an extra $10 if the monthly goal is met, $20 if it is exceeded, and $30 if a new factory record is set.

The company adopted the collective bonus because its high-speed, automated operation requires group effort. The Japanese parent sent its latest equipment to the factory, which started up in mid-1971. Just fifty-eight employees, including thirteen Japanese, work there—primarily on the maintenance and constant monitoring of the automated production machinery. The special bonus, which has been earned most months, has helped to promote high productivity. But some important differences between Japanese and Americans persist. Says Hideo Inamuro, who runs the factory: "If a machine breaks down here, a worker will go home anyway at quitting time. But in Japan, never."

The Japanese managers in Illinois strive for what they call "an informal family atmosphere." The company even provides a billiard table in the factory so that Americans and Japanese can relax together during breaks. The accessibility of top executives particularly impresses the Americans. As Roy Griffith, the warehouse manager, puts it: "It makes a lot of difference in our work when you can walk into the president's office any time without going through five secretaries."

On a much larger scale, Matsushita Electric counts on its special management techniques to turn around the three Illinois plants it acquired from Motorola last year. Keiichi Takeoka, a senior managing director from the home office in Osaka, has come to the U.S. as chairman of Matsushita's new subsidiary, Quasar Electronics Corp. ("Quasar" was the Motorola brand name for color television sets.) Takeoka aims to make Motorola's TV production facilities profitable within three years. The way to do it, he says confidently, is by "changing attitudes" of Quasar's 6,000 employees.

The Japanese company, in all earnestness, attributes its growth to the "Matsushita philosophy." And Takeoka is patiently training Motorola's executives—all but two stayed—to accept the Japanese approach. In essence, the Matsushita philosophy hinges on the belief that when the company serves society properly, the profits roll in as a reward. That belief makes Matsushita acutely sensitive to consumer tastes and to the need for high quality.

CANDOR AT THE TOP

To the surprise and dismay of the American executives, the Japanese chairman sometimes bypasses them to keep himself informed. He may go to the design room unannounced to encourage workers, or he may appear on the assembly line to ask a foreman why a chassis is just sitting there. "The area that cannot be understood immediately by Americans," says Takeoka, "is the vitality and excellent communications we have in Japan within the whole company." As a step toward helping them understand, Matsushita is sending groups of the senior and middle managers it inherited from Motorola to Japan for a close look at its domestic operation. The Americans are required to study the company's history and management approach, not just tour its factories.

Takeoka points out Quasar's weaknesses with a candor rarely heard, publicly at least, from any U.S. chief executive speaking of his own company. "The quality of the sets made here is not acceptable," he says flatly. Later on Matsushita will provide high-speed production equipment of its own design. But Takeoka is in no hurry to modernize the Motorola factories. "We're expecting employees to improve the quality, rather than sit and wait for the parent company to bring in the new machines. Eventually they'll come, but first Americans must show what they can do by their own efforts."

There are already signs of an East-West convergence in management methods. Takeoka has adopted the nick-name "Tex" as a concession to Americans who have difficulty pronouncing Keiichi. And he believes U.S. managers are gradually beginning to accept the

Matsushita philosophy. Recently, one group of supervisors returned from Japan and had
the Franklin Park production lines cleaned up and painted. "That was the result of their
visit," says Takeoka. "We're not rushing or forcing them, but step by step they seem to be
getting the idea."

In San Diego, Sony has been making TV sets in its own factory since August, 1972—long
enough to mold employee attitudes to a Sony pattern. The sprawling factory in Rancho
Bernardo Industrial Park makes picture tubes, and assembles over half the color sets Sony
sells in the U.S. To maintain high quality, Sony believes, workers must have an interest that
goes beyond the mechanics of their jobs to embrace the overall company and the final
product as well.

Sony executives will do almost anything to try to inspire a Japanese-like loyalty among
its American employees. The company "cares about people," says Masayoshi Morimoto,
thirty-five, the assistant to the general manager. In effect, he serves as a morale officer.
An alumnus of Columbia University's Graduate School of Business, Morimoto insists that
workers call him Mike—"to get an informal atmosphere." He listens to their gripes and
counsels them on personal problems. "Sometimes I even have to be a marriage counselor,"
says Mike. At the frequent company parties, he sometimes acts as a volunteer bartender
and always makes a point of dancing with dozens of women employees.

Last summer, the Sony manner of handling personnel came under fire when the Communications Workers of America sought to organize the plant. Sony bases promotions largely
on the attitude shown by employees. This is measured by such criteria as whether work
areas are kept clean; the company believes that precision work requires a neat environment. Some union supporters, however, complained that the promotion policy was too
vague.

A CHASTENING ELECTION

Characteristically, the Sony management reacted to the union drive by personally contact-
ing all 434 of the workers eligible for union membership. Production slackened for four
weeks, while Morimoto and Ronald Dishno, a senior American manager, met with small
groups of workers. The two not only pleaded the company's case in these informal sessions, but also urged employees to propose ways of improving working conditions. In
keeping with U.S. labor laws, management promised only to consider the views of employees.

It also started a "Sony action line"—a kind of electronic grievance system. Anyone within
the plant can dial the number 300 on the telephone and anonymously report problems,
make complaints, or offer suggestions. These calls are tape-recorded and in many instances bring immediate action. A request for more pay telephones in the plant, for example, was met within a couple of weeks; complaints about untidy snack bars were soothed
by expanding the janitorial service. "The best thing was that we all got to know each other
better," says Morimoto. In September, employees voted three to one against the union.

Since the election, Sony has been remedying what managers now regard as defects in
its personnel policies. The promotion system has been revised to put more emphasis on
seniority, as many employees suggested. And executives are trying to figure out how to
improve lines of communication within the company, which they fear have been strained
by rapid expansion. The industrial-relations manager, an American, has been relieved of

responsibility for day-to-day personnel problems because, Dishno says, he "lost touch with employees." The fact that there was a union election convinced management of that. Now Dishno and other manufacturing-department managers directly handle any problems involving their own employees.

Sony considers a stable work force essential for maintaining high quality, and makes it a practice to avoid layoffs. This is a neat trick in today's economic climate. But so far, Sony's sales have remained relatively strong. It never builds up large stocks in warehouses, but maintains a fairly steady rate of output that is adjusted every month. When problems with a new model forced the temporary shutdown of one production line, workers were shifted to other jobs in the plant. Says Morimoto, "Layoffs would be harmful to the morale of employees."

The Japanese company has succeeded in teaching its American executives to adopt something of a consensus technique for making decisions. The manager of TV manufacturing, an American, never hires a new supervisor until the candidate has been approved by at least four other managers. "This way takes a little longer," he notes, "but then others have a stake and commitment in my people."

BATTLING THE HOME OFFICE

The blending of Japanese and American business methods sometimes doesn't go smoothly at all. Mitsubishi Heavy Industries assembles its MU-2 executive aircraft in the southwest Texas prairie town of San Angelo. Its dozen Japanese executives fit easily into the life of the community. But the Texas subsidiary, called Mitsubishi Aircraft International, is engaged in a constant battle with the home office in Japan.

Makoto Kuroiwa, now a senior adviser to the company, says he learned to live and work very much like an American during his three and a half years as president of Mitsubishi Aircraft. He belongs to the country club, serves on a local bank's board, and proudly displays a certificate from the state governor proclaiming him "an honorary Texas citizen." All this helped promote sales, and also to cement relations with his 400 employees. "But I could not train my bosses to do business the American way," he says, a bit forlornly. According to Kuroiwa and other company executives in Texas, Mitsubishi in Japan simply doesn't understand the highly competitive market for executive aircraft here.

To be sure, when the MU-2 was first introduced in 1965, the parent corporation recognized its need for marketing expertise. It turned to Mooney Aircraft in San Angelo to handle assembly and sales in the U.S. Though Mitsubishi's turboprop plane won acceptance here, Mooney's other aircraft business failed. In May, 1970, Mitsubishi took over and expanded the plant, where airframes sent from Japan are assembled with U.S.-made engines and electronic systems. Mitsubishi also assembles the MU-2 in Japan, but has sold only thirty there. The Texas company has sold 350 of the planes.

The parent company's response to changes in the U.S. market has proved sluggish, though. "It takes a long time to get what our marketing people regard as bad decisions," asserts one American executive. Although the recession has weakened demand for executive aircraft, the parent company in Japan continues to ship a steady stream of airframes for assembly of five planes a month at the San Angelo plant. The executive adds: "See all those trailers out there. They are unassembled airplanes. We carry them on our books with borrowed capital, and yet can't sell that many now."

Just as frustrating to U.S. marketing managers is the time it takes to add new features to the aircraft. Nearly two years ago, the Texas company decided to install heated windshields on the MU-2. But the consensus network in Japan mulled over the idea so long that major competitors beat Mitsubishi to the change. The MU-2 will not have heated windshields until later this year. Not surprisingly, the U.S. subsidiary has experienced considerable turnover in American marketing directors—four in the past four years.

When Mitsubishi executives in the U.S. objected to a recent price hike ordered from Japan, M.H.I. responded by reporting that its analysis "shows our plane is superior and therefore should sell easily." Except for one year, however, the company has been in the red. Joe Weldon, the sales manager, maintains: "We've never been profit-oriented. The name of the game is image and prestige. The MU-2 is the only successful commercial aircraft the Japanese have produced."

Actually, there's so much confusion about the Texas company's goals that Mitsubishi headquarters has sent in the American management-consulting firm of McKinsey & Co. to help define them—and point the way toward profitability. Like many Japanese companies, M.H.I. has taken a long view of profits by concentrating first on expanding its market share. Meanwhile that strategy has also kept its Japanese plant busy making airframes, in observance of the national tradition of maintaining steady employment.

But now the home office wants profits, too. Says A. Carl Mudd, controller, "If this were an American company, we probably would have closed in 1969." In January, Mitsubishi took the rare step of laying off workers; it cut its Texas work force by 20 percent.

NO LITTLE TOKYO

Unlike Mitsubishi Aircraft, which found a warm welcome in San Angelo, Kikkoman Shoyu Co. had to contend with the one thing that all Japanese businessmen fear most outside their homeland—local hostility. Before it decided in 1971 to build a $9-million soy-sauce plant in rural Wisconsin, the company weighed invitations from five different states. But the initial arrival of the venerable, family-owned Japanese company in the tiny town of Walworth "was controversial as hell," says Thomas G. Godfrey, a Walworth attorney who is Kikkoman's general counsel in the U.S. Many farmers objected to rezoning 200 acres of agricultural land for the soy-sauce factory, which sits amid wheat fields and towering silos. Kikkoman had to start with a crash course in American grass-roots politics.

Executives flew in from Japan and explained how their automated fermentation-processing plant managed to be nonpolluting. They showed films about the purity of products and the company's ancestry, which dates back to the seventeenth century. As one Japanese executive notes, "The Kikkoman brand was around when American Indians were very much in the ruling position here." Perhaps most important to farmers, Kikkoman pointed out that it purchases soybeans grown in the area. In the end, zoning authorities approved the plant.

ON THE CORPORATE WAVELENGTH

But the experience sensitized Kikkoman officials to local feelings. To facilitate community acceptance in Wisconsin, the company insists that its thirteen Japanese employees and their families spread themselves among four neighboring communities. "We didn't want to make a little Tokyo," says Toyoji Murai, Kikkoman's general manager. "It's better for us to mix more with Americans. You know, sometimes many Japanese gather at one restaurant table and speak loudly in Japanese. That's not bad in itself, but the feeling it causes among local people is not so good."

Kikkoman and the Japanese are now accepted with no great ruckus in Walworth. The company employs fifty-five Americans, and has never had to advertise to get job applicants. Once a week, it receives busloads of students and tourists, who are shown how each batch of soy sauce is blended before being fermented for six months. In downtown Walworth, the Century Supermarket has begun to stock canned Japanese foods and, of course, Kikkoman soy sauce. In every Wisconsin community where Kikkoman's Japanese families live, local women have volunteered to teach the wives English and show them around. Murai has joined the Walworth Rotary Club, and his wife demonstrates Japanese flower arranging for women's clubs. "Personally," he says, "I think it would be better for her to show how to cook foods that use soy sauce."

Murai's half-serious comment on his wife's flower demonstrations expresses a kind of devotion to the product that many American companies would very much like to inspire in their employees, but that few corporations have been able to bring forth. Plainly, there is a good deal to be learned from a management system that so often succeeds in tuning both executives and workers to the corporate wavelength.

PART TWO
DISCUSSION QUESTIONS

1. In their management motivation, do the Japanese use Theory X or Theory Y?

2. How would a professional person as described in Reading 8 function in a company managed by the Japanese?

3. What new values and work habits are effecting change in our corporations?

4. Compare and contrast the leadership styles of Lee Hess, Walter Wriston, and Boyd Schenk. How did their particular situations help them discover their own styles?

5. Do you trust corporations?

6. Have you served on or been chairperson of a committee? Respond to the proposals for streamlining the committee system. If you have not served on a committee, what reasons can you give for not having become involved?

MANAGEMENT OF HUMAN RESOURCES AND PRODUCTION

Yes, Virginia, the work ethic is alive, but perhaps not as healthy as human resources managers would like. As a Royal Bank of Canada Newsletter recently stated, "No one has ever repealed the law of work, but it is in the process of amendment." Should work or the worker change? In Reading 11, a group of personnel managers report on recent developments and problems such as affirmative action programs, pregnancy-caused disability benefits, the new retirement law, and staff reductions and their effect on minorities and certain age groups.

A major phenomenon in our society in recent years has been the big increase of women in the work force. Over 41 percent of our workers are now female, concentrated mainly in lower income occupations. Only 2 percent of our managers are women, so two articles (12 and 13) address these issues. Although more women are attending college and entering nontraditional fields, time is needed for people's attitudes and behaviors to change. If change is to occur, women will have to plan ahead, take risks, and accept a higher ulcer rate. Male managers will also need to establish a climate favorable to the changes necessary for women to move into managerial jobs.

Your text asks where new membership in unions will originate. One area is certainly the public sector. Reading 14, "The Advent of Public Sector Multi-employer Bargaining," addresses this type of concern.

Production, that "utility" discussed in Chapter 9 of your text, is examined in Reading 15. Increasing, sometimes unreasonable, demands are being placed upon the producing sectors of our economy by society.

11

PERSONNEL PROBLEM ROUNDTABLE

Seven high-calibre management professionals explore what organizations can do to deal effectively with today's overriding personnel concerns in this roundtable discussion chaired by Paul King, *A/M* contributing editor on personnel. King has gathered authorities on personnel practices from the northeastern U.S. for this *A/M* exclusive feature which has as its theme—personnel management and the law. Panelists are . . . : Charles Thacher, senior vice president, S. M. Hyman Co., consulting actuaries; Howard Ganz Esq., attorney, Poskauer, Rose, Goetz, & Mendelsohn, labor relations consultants; John Graziadei, director of personnel for the New York office of Allied Stores Corp. and for Allied Stores Marketing Corp.; Mrs. Barbara Wald, manager of equal employment opportunity, Hoffman-LaRoche Inc., Donald Guerette, principal, Arthur Young & Co., CPA's; . . . Paul King, *A/M* contributing editor on personnel; [and] Stephen Jordan, personnel director, Burkey Photo Inc. . . .

The panelists address themselves to such vital issues of the day as equal opportunity commitments, pension plan reform, management awareness, new reporting requirements, contradictions in the regulations, and the layoff situation. The discussion begins with an analysis of commitments imposed by Title VII of the Civil Rights Act of 1964.

AFFIRMATIVE ACTION

Many companies have established "Affirmative Action" programs to bring themselves into compliance with provisions of Title VII of the Civil Rights Act of 1964 and other human rights legislation. Even so, legal requirements are not always clearcut. Here, the panelists delve into the ramifications of these laws for management. They also discuss what business is doing to bring itself into compliance with the law.

KING: To open this discussion and to review some basics, what kinds of discrimination are covered by Title VII of the Civil Rights Act of 1964?

SOURCE: Republished with permission from *Administrative Management,* copyright ᶜ 1975 by Geyer-McAllister Publications, Inc., New York.

GRAZIADEI: Creed, race, religion, national origin, sex. Discrimination because of age is covered by the Age Discrimination and Employment Act, which affects people who are 40 to 65 years old.

WALD: Companies can also put themselves in jeopardy if they do not hire a minority or a female person because of a customer's preferences. Perhaps, Howard Ganz can elaborate on these laws.

GANZ: It's the view of human rights agencies that customer preference for employees of a certain sex, race, or national background cannot be taken into account in hiring.

KING: Is it true that only the bigger companies are being looked at by the government?

GANZ: The Equal Employment Opportunity Commission typically confines itself to larger employers because those kinds of proceedings have a larger impact. One technicality. Under Title VII, an employer must have 15 employees or more to be covered.

WALD: That may be changing. With state and local laws, companies with fewer than 15 employees may not be as scott free as they think they are. Nor are government contractors or sub-contractors.

KING: Is the law the only reason why companies ought to change their employment practices?

WALD: Equal opportunity is just a clarification of good management practices. If you exclude females and minority groups, you're working with a small percentage of the population. Therefore, if you choose from a larger number of people, chances of getting the best person for the job are much higher.

GANZ: Here's a twist. Most agencies now seek in conciliation agreements to establish male goals for clerical positions predominantly occupied by women. The theory is that this will not only "desegregate" the work force, but also that bringing males in will upgrade a position in the eyes of upper management and make for greater status and pay.

KING: If a small employer has a union, it can also bring action against an employer.

GANZ: Yes, if you have a union, it could file an unfair labor practice charge under the National Labor Relations Act of Unfair Labor Practices on grounds of discrimination. And yes, most collective bargaining agreements today do contain nondiscrimination clauses.

KING: What protection does management have against harassment? Say an employee without a case files charges just to get "even."

GANZ: There really aren't too many people trying to blackmail large corporations through the judicial process. The few really capricious instances I've seen go to a local agency for a quick bite at the apple. Finding no apple, they go away. But, people who take the trouble to go to a state agency, then to the EEOC, and then to federal court, are in my judgment no longer motivated on a capriciously held belief. They may be wrong—they may perceive discrimination where none exists—but they are sincere.

GUERETTE: How do you educate employment people in the law?

WALD: Various ways. Interviewing seminars, employment booklets. Usually most individual suits aren't the result of people just walking in the door. They generally involve a hiring manager, who is not aware of the issues and the regulations. Special training helps. We've held many sessions in awareness training. It's my impression that you can't change anyone's attitude. But you can attempt to change certain behaviors. How? Well, you can help managers become aware. Most people unconsciously discriminate because they're not aware of past discriminatory practices that have affected females and minorities. We have put managers in group sessions with a consultant for as much as eight hours, to figure out themselves solutions to problems involving awareness of women or minorities. Boyle Kirman Associates, a New York consulting firm, conducted these eight hour awareness sessions for us. Some 900 of our managers have attended. In addition, each of our equal opportunity managers goes over the regulations with managers in sessions too, usually every six months. Also, we send out literature describing new laws, cases, and discussions that might have an impact. Statistics and analyses are issued to individual departments on their status on a quarterly basis.

KING: John, Allied Stores has locations spread all over the United States. How do you see to it that stores two, three, four, and five do not engage in unlawful practices?

GRAZIADEI: One of the functions of the corporate personnel office is to keep all of our store groups informed of situations that could develop, those that have developed, and the way certain situations were addressed.

KEEPING A COUNT

GANZ: A somewhat valuable technique—one which several companies I know of have adopted—is to include in the evaluation of supervisory personnel their progress in the discrimination area. It instills in the supervisor the sense that a company is really serious about these commitments, or at least, that it will cost the company money if the commitments are not met. This evaluation practice also may be a useful piece of evidence for the company should there ever be litigation.

KING: That makes sense. But aren't there contradictions in the regulations?

GUERETTE: Yes, you have to maintain logs of applicants by protected class. Yet, there are certain questions you can't ask when you screen and you can't take a photograph for your records at that point because the fact that you may have secured information at the point when you're screening an applicant could give the appearance of discrimination. It's clear that the log has to be kept separately from the application. Many companies visually scan applicants for log information required by the government at the time of the first interview. A carefully trained receptionist might do it.

KING: It is recommended that companies review their practices before a complaint is lodged against them. But isn't a company's own audit as to discrimination practices in the company a peril to the employer? Some employee might get hold of it and use it against the company.

GUERETTE: Let me go into this a bit. The purpose of an audit is generally to determine if the financial statement of a company fairly represents its actual financial condition. I'm not aware of any case where an equal employment action has had a material effect on a company's financial statement. Even in the AT&T case, where you had damages in excess of $50 million, the money wasn't material and therefore the auditor wasn't required to footnote its financial statement as to damages in that case. In spite of the fact it's not required, several Arthur Young offices have instituted an abbreviated personnel policies review as part of the audit. The auditors use a checklist to determine if an organization is in a posture to comply. The checklist is quite comprehensive. It includes information on filing of all of a company's forms, affirmative action plans, and posting of notices in appropriate places. It also assesses the state of its personnel records. Are they properly maintained? Do they have all relevant information in terms of promotions, transfers, salary actions, and the like? Once the auditor has gathered these facts, he submits them to one of our EEO consultants; if he determines there is a problem, we inform management. Corporate management, especially in large multi-location companies, may not be aware of some of the practices taking place everywhere.

KING: One thing occurs to me. Having received one of your reports, I don't know to what extent a good faith defense would be available to the employer in the event of a discrimination charge since results not intent seem to count with the EEOC people.

GUERETTE: A good point. Good faith is not an effective defense. The EEOC insists on aggressive action to resolve violations. The purpose of the review I described is to help identify problems so that corrective action can be taken.

WALD: I agree, Don. A company should audit itself and take corrective action. Unequal pay for equal work is a discrepancy that can be picked up quickly by looking over payroll runs that have job titles attached to them.

JORDAN: Even though Berkey has long since negotiated the hurdle involved in placing minorities and females at all levels of the organization, it too must continuously audit itself. Keeping records of affirmative action programs at plant locations with a limited clerical staff can be a problem. However, our corporate and local EEO coordinators are working to overcome these problems. The computer has been extremely useful in generating EEO reports.

WALD: At Roche's Nutley facility, we have 7,000 people. If we have to do all reporting manually, it would take quite some time. We have about six or seven very good quarterly computer reports. We keep the company, including the executive committee and the president, up to date on the progress we've made.

KING: As an attorney, Howard, what preventative measures would you suggest to employers to avoid complaints and lawsuits?

GANZ: This is a rather broad question, Paul. Perhaps, I can relate it to the subject we've been discussing, evaluation of your compliance standards. There really ought to be a continuous system devised to inform management, or at least those with responsibility in the equal employment opportunity area, of what's going on. If you develop an elaborate computerized system to keep tabs on the situation, you develop evidence that in many cases will be used against you when the time comes for trial. You'll have to consider how burdensome it will be for you to answer charges predicated on this "evidence." But, you'll end up having to answer them anyway in most cases. The real recordkeeping problem lies not with the employer with few enough employees so the job can be manually done or the employer with thousands of employees who can probably sustain the cost of developing computerized programs, it's the employer somewhere in between.

MATERNITY BENEFITS

Here, the panelists explore the pregnancy-caused disability benefit issue. Although various state laws may apply to such claims, the Supreme Court hasn't ruled on the matter. Even so, companies find that they must take a stand.

KING: Perhaps you can address yourself, Howard, to what you ought to be doing in the area of maternity benefits and maternity leave.

GANZ: Now, as to whether Title VII requires pregnancy to be treated as a disability for benefit purposes, I suppose it's fair to say that the issue is an open one since it has not yet been decided by the Supreme Court. But it's becoming less open every time another

Federal Court of Appeals deals with it. The majority of judicial views indicate that pregnancy, as set forth in the guidelines issued by EEOC, is a disability and should be treated as such under a disability benefit program. Whatever benefits you extend to a man under such a program must be similarly extended to a woman disabled by reason of pregnancy. The period of disability may, of course, vary from woman to woman—and obstetricians and gynecologists take many different sides on this issue.

KING: Well, an insurance company generally handles benefit claims when they say that the expenses must be ordinary, necessary, and so on. Now, say a woman has a baby on May 1, 1975. Are you obliged to keep her job open for one month? Two months? Is there any limitation?

GANZ: Well, I think you've got to keep it open as long as is reasonably necessary for maternity purposes.

KING: A male who recovers from a hernia operation may take as long as two months to convalesce and it's determinable. Doctors would say it's about time you went back to work Jack. You're ready. But when it comes to having a baby, there are other considerations, not merely physical ones. For instance, a woman might feel she must consider when she's going to be able to trust the child to a babysitter? Is that relevant?

WALD: I would say that just as males are treated for hernia operations or heart attacks on an individual basis, so then women who have just given birth have to be treated on the same basis. Generally speaking, there is a time period after birth that a woman can be expected to resume her former responsibilities.

However, there are cases in which there might be complications in birth, such as a cesarean, which require a longer convalescent period. I don't think the fact that a woman might not know when she can trust the child with a babysitter enters the picture. What kind of convalescent period does Allied Stores allow for maternity purposes, John?

GRAZIADEI: Under our policy, which is one of "reasonableness," sometime within three months after delivery, a woman should be able to return to work. On the other hand, if at the end of a three month period, there is some problem for which an additional month or two away would be required to correct, we'd be reasonable as we'd expect an employee to be reasonable.

KING: Are you obligated to hold open the same job for her? Or, as under the Selective Service Act, can you give her a comparable job?

WALD: Yes, a comparable job, comparable salary, and comparable status can be awarded. However, this is easier to do if a woman is in the clerical area. It tends to be a little more difficult when you're talking about professional women. Many times a woman will have a job title, and she'll be the only one in the company with that title and responsibility. Then you might hold the job open for her and fill it temporarily.

GANZ: It's important to distinguish between maternity leaves and pregnancy-caused disabilities. The disability benefit issue is the one that has not been decided finally. At least, it hasn't by the Supreme Court although state laws may apply. Another thing. Hospital and medical coverage are distinguishable both from leaves and disability benefit protection. I assume most employers' insurance policies cover some portion of the costs of childbirth. Typically, hospitalization coverage extends to a week or a similar period. However, if the percentage allowed for doctor bills for childbirth is less than that allowed in other areas, this would likely be unlawful. Thus, the only open question really is whether you have to provide disability benefit income protection during a period when a woman is physically disabled and prevented from working by virtue of pregnancy.

KING: In view of the pressure from members of NOW and other women who are vociferously asking for equality, it's becoming a morale problem. If for no other reason, it seems to me that personnel people would want to be sure that their women employees cannot criticize them on this issue, regardless of what the law says.

WALD: Yes. There are other considerations. You never know when the government is going to come in for a compliance review or because of a complaint.

KING: If you have stockholders and you are socked with a heavy penalty, it may be that you can be liable to them for mismanagement.

NEW RETIREMENT LAW

New pension legislation—the Employment Retirement Security Act of 1974 (ERISA)—imposes new recordkeeping and reporting requirements on management. Also, this law, signed on Labor Day by President Ford, raises a new question. Can a plan administrator be held personally liable for interpretation of a company pension plan to employees?

KING: May we turn to another subject—retirement plans. A new monstrosity, hailed by Mr. Javits and Mr. Ford as being earthshaking, developed in the early part of this year—the Employee Retirement Security Act of 1974 (ERISA). And earthshaking it is. For one thing, it includes a comprehensive definition of a fiduciary, a person required to act in the best interests of plan participants. Is the personnel officer a fiduciary and if so, is he in a perilous position if he misspeaks?

THACHER: The personnel officer may well be a fiduciary—perhaps not eight hours a day though. Most plans have a retirement, pension, or administrative committee, with authority for deciding the amount of benefits, and who is eligible. The board of directors may have the authority for appointing investment counselors or trustees. But if the authority for making decisions regarding an individual's records is delegated to a personnel officer, who determines whether an employee has the right to a pension and how much, in that capacity he is acting as a fiduciary.

KING: Suppose a personnel officer doesn't make a decision but just interprets a provision?

THACHER: Whether or not he is acting as a fiduciary can only be decided by future regulations or the courts.

KING: Under the new law, are companies obligated to tell an employee what his benefits are? What if errors are made?

THACHER: Yes, because of this requirement I'd say companies of virtually any size will start issuing individual benefit statements on an annual basis. They'll communicate to the employee his accrued pension before an employee comes and asks the personnel manager where he stands on the assumption that once one employee asks, everyone will. Because of the complexity of computing benefits for tens of thousands of employees in a company, you're going to make some errors. And, yes. I think a company will be held responsible for them.

KING: Aren't employers who under the law must prepare pension summaries faced with a new difficult situation? Previously, employers inserted a statement in these summaries saying the text is only a colloquial description of the plan. We added that the plan itself, filed with the personnel department and on view there, is what's really binding on the company.

But now, as I understand it, you can be sued upon the document you give to the employee. **97**
So, employers must prepare a colloquially clear draft which also is legally precise. It's a
small eye of a needle to walk through.

THACHER: That will be a difficult thing.

GRAZIADEI: We have lawyers, the personnel staff, and even the president of the company
himself go over the booklet.

KING: Could firms or persons who advise on revising a plan to meet the requirements of
the law . . . including attorneys and personnel managers . . . be acting in a fiduciary relationship? I understand that the law imposes a personal liability on individuals who act as
fiduciaries, a liability that cannot be idemnified by their companies. What ways are there of
guarding against the liability?

THACHER: It won't be clear who the fiduciaries are until court cases settle the matter.
Effective January 1, 1975, a fiduciary must be bonded. Bonding embraces fraud and theft,
but it does not cover errors or omissions. The law provides that a company may purchase
a new kind of liability insurance to protect the individual fiduciary against errors and omissions. This type of coverage is certainly in a formative stage. No one knows what the
ultimate premiums will be. There are about a half dozen companies selling the insurance
now, and there's a lot of discussion about what the policies provide and don't provide.

KING: What about ERISA deadlines for pension and employee benefit plans now in effect?
And the deadline for giving employees plan summaries?

THACHER: The deadline under ERISA for completing two required forms, EBS-1 and the
Summary Plan Description, has been extended to August 31, 1975. EBS-1, a long, comprehensive form outlining company plan provisions has not as yet been issued in final form.
Probably it will in April. For most companies, the Summary Plan Description is represented
by the company employee booklet. The deadline in 1976 for amending most pension plans
will probably not be extended. The law gives employers adequate time to meet the requirements. Some companies are writing new plans today. They may have to be changed
substantially when exact regulations come out. In putting together a booklet on benefits and
compensation, such matters as jury duty, vacation pay, shift differential and any other plan
of compensation must be described to meet the requirements of the new law. However, it
is anticipated that reporting on these compensation plans may be waived by future regulations. But group life insurance, health, and welfare benefits will most likely be included in
the reporting requirements for anybody with 100 or more employees.

GANZ: Take a look at all items that are to be included in the Summary Plan Description:
If you have fine print provisions, you'll have to highlight them. And once you do this, it's more
productive for the company to get rid of them.

THACHER: You'll also have to describe the procedure for an employee making a claim
against the plan, give the identity of the plan administrator, and of the agent for the receiving
process.

KING: When you tell employees about your maternity benefits as required by ERISA, you'd
better be sure you come to grips with the issue.

GRAZIADEI: Yes, under ERISA, we can look forward to more governmental intervention and
more employee involvement. Therefore, companies may have to change certain procedures. For instance, it's going to take a total team effort to put out a benefit summary
booklet. Also, we're coming into an age of specialization. You'll have corporate pension
specialists and others who are more attuned to the insurance side.

KING: You may have to be careful to get a receipt for information booklets handed out to an employee to prove he knew all about it should he make a claim against the company later on. Whenever you give an employee the opportunity of exercising an option, you'll have to clearly state it to him in writing and have him give you a statement that it was made available and was explained to him. All of this must be kept in a voluminous file that will become more voluminous as time passes.

GRAZIADEI: Another thing under the new law. If an employee terminates with a vested right, you must give him a statement as to amount of his benefits and when they are due.

KING: A company may want to mail a summary document to the individual's home and keep a copy in his file so it has some proof the information was given to him. Getting back to my earlier question about personnel people giving plan interpretations, aren't personnel managers wise to say as little as possible and refer the question to the pension committee instead?

THACHER: Yes. A personnel officer may be on the hook because he's performing a function he's not authorized by the plan to perform. He's acting as the retirement committee. Often, retirement committees don't meet regularly, don't keep minutes and don't review all decisions regarding benefits. They merely delegate this authority to the personnel officer. This is especially true for smaller companies and those with fewer than three or four thousand employees. If I were that personnel officer, I'd go to the committee, suggest that the members meet regularly, and that they keep minutes and records of every benefit determination. In other words, they should put in their minutes that employee John Doe was authorized to receive a certain benefit and that the committee is aware of how that benefit is computed. To some extent, this takes the personnel officer off the hook and ensures that the committee is doing its job.

WHEN STAFF IS LIMITED

In a recessionary economy, staff reductions often are called for. But new laws on the books must be taken into account—especially those which affect employees of certain minorities or in certain age brackets.

KING: I am reminded of another problem faced by employment managers today. The lay-off question. What do you do if your hiring rate has diminished substantially making it impossible for you to keep enough minority people and females at the levels needed to meet your commitments under the law? And in view of limited hiring, how can you meet your minority and female employment goals?

GANZ: Any situation like that is going to raise potential age discrimination and reverse discrimination problems.

KING: In a layoff situation, most collective bargaining agreements require that the last hired be the first fired. This will conflict in almost all respects with recently adopted affirmative action programs in which minorities and women were the last hired.

GANZ: Cases put before the Court of Appeals have gone both ways. The question will have to be decided by the Supreme Court. To my knowledge, there's no definitive word from the Supreme Court on the issue of whether you can—or must—follow the seniority provisions.

KING: Howard Ganz mentioned age discrimination. There are risks involved in laying off individuals in the 40 to 65 age group.

This reminds me of the Exxon case. A subsidiary of that operation asked a research chemist, who has since died, to retire early. He refused so they took his marbles away. They wouldn't let him play the research game, and this wore him out. So he agreed to retire—at age 60. The net of it was that the Exxon subsidiary was found guilty by a federal court of discriminating because of age, and it had to pay a healthy sum of money to the widow —some $750,000.

JORDAN: I think that since results are the name of the game, economic realities of the situation would indicate that a personnel manager has to take those actions most beneficial to the company. In most cases, seniority plus qualifications tends to prevail.

We've done one thing. We've accelerated our training efforts. Many companies tend to forget about training during times of difficulty. But Berkey Photo feels if it doesn't have the manpower, it needs people who are cross-trained. We also must assist our people to be better able to move into other jobs that might become available.

WALD: We're also attempting to intensify our training efforts in conjunction with what is essentially a manpower planning program.

KING: Under ERISA, there are complicated provisions regarding rehiring of an employee which may result in considerably additional pension expense. How can these expenses be estimated? Should the personnel officer take this into account before rehiring an employee?

THACHER: Prior to the passage of ERISA, the majority of pension plans said that if a person terminated employment without going on an authorized leave of absence, or military leave, he could lose all of his past pension credit, even if he left only for a day and he was rehired the next day. Of course, if he left but was vested, he would keep any vested right.

Now ERISA has established very specific requirements regarding rehiring of employees. Basically, if you rehire an employee, and he remains in your employ for a year, and works 1,000 hours during that year, if he was vested in a deferred pension based on his prior service, that credit is reestablished. Also if the length of his service prior to his leave exceeds his leave, even if he was not vested you must reestablish his prior service. Not only that. Take an employee whose benefit level was $2 a year when he left. He comes back and it's now increased up to $9 a year. His prior service is rated at the current benefit level of the plan. As much as 20 to 30 percent might have to be added to the employee's salary to reestablish this service.

Your actuary can estimate what the potential cost of rehiring an employee will be. You might have a problem though, if the employee fits into the category of employee you can't discriminate against.

KING: Part-time employees may be excluded from pension and profit-sharing plans without violating IRS regulations. However, ERISA says that employees working 1,000 hours or more must be included in pension or profit-sharing. With pension plans, additional employees—part-timers—will increase plan costs materially. With profit-sharing plans, it may materially dilute the distribution of profit-sharing. Will this result in companies making sure their part-time employees work less than 1,000 hours?

THACHER: These problems always existed. You could always exclude an employee from receiving benefits by taking action when he's just short of meeting requirements. For example, in December, if you've a choice of laying off two employees, one with 900 hours and the other with 500 hours, you could lay off the one with 900 hours and save yourself a pension or profit-sharing contribution. However, I think that employers will not be so callous as to really examine those individual hours records before they determine who's going to work in December . . . but there always has been a potential area of abuse there, which ERISA has enlarged. No question.

GANZ: You're going to have to justify every individual case. You're not going to be able to lay off older workers on the assumption or unproven theory that they're less productive.

THACHER: ERISA does cause some other very real problems. It clearly brings the Department of Labor into the area of pension plan administration. In the past, there were rules on disclosure and the Department of Labor essentially was a filing agency, collecting documents and responding to employees' questions related to them.

KING: The employee also has rights under the law, to bring action on his own. Before, he didn't have any effective way of complaining. However, I think all this recordkeeping is going to be great for *Administrative Management* inasmuch as many of its advertisers sell filing cabinets (LAUGHTER). To record justification for productivity and nonproductivity layoffs, benefit summaries and information handed out and so on, every employee's personnel jacket will be four times its present size.

GUERETTE: We're just going to computerize it.

WALD: Introduce microfilm.

GANZ: I've found it's now customary for EEO agencies, on the national, state, and local levels to insist upon a provision in conciliation agreements which guarantees that any reduction in a company's forces will not have a disproportionately adverse effect upon members of whatever classes—women or minorities—being protected by that agreement.

GRAZIADEI: A great many factors come into play. You have to look at productivity, seniority, and then consider an additional ingredient—company morale. If employees see that senior members of a firm are being terminated without any effort to assist them in improving their performance, the employee who's looking for longer term affiliation may not feel that the company is a good one to be with. As with all other personnel matters, management must not only take care to assess the intent of the law correctly. It also must be attuned to how its practices will affect employee morale—both now and in the future.

12

WOMEN IN MANAGEMENT:
AN ENDANGERED SPECIES?

JOHN F. VEIGA

Doors to the upper levels of the corporate hierarchy recently have begun to open for women, and most of the time, women themselves have opened these doors. But if the typical career strategies of women in management are indicative of how they pursue career advancement, only a few more doors will be opened in the years to come.

Recent studies have suggested that the number of women in upper level management positions is beginning to increase. Currently about 2 percent of all women in business are in management positions.[1] The increase can be attributed in part to affirmative action legislation and to more positive social attitudes towards women pursuing traditionally male careers. However, even with all the pressures for change, the relative impact on the corporate hierarchy will be minimal in the years to come. To increase the impact, women will have to take a closer look at their career strategies and values, and they will have to decide whether or not they are willing to play the corporate success game.

The conclusions of this article, based on a cross-sectional study of more than 500 women who hold positions up to the level of vice-president, could have far-reaching implications for women in, or aspiring to, management. The women studied (coming from 60 firms, including several on the *Fortune* 500 list, and representing 25 industries) attended career development workshops held during the past four years. In the majority of cases, they were nominated by their firms to attend because of their management potential. The participants averaged 35 years of age; half of them were married; almost all had attended college; and they were earning an average income in excess of $16,000. The information received from them was compared to data obtained from men (with similar backgrounds, same average age, and same level of responsibility) who had attended other career development workshops.

In a study of individual career strategies and values, participants were asked to write down their career advice to young persons. Their responses remained anonymous.

SOURCE: Reprinted with permission of the publisher, Division of Research, Graduate School of Business Administration, Michigan State University.

[1]Garda Bowman, N. Beatrice Worthy, and Stephen Greyer, "Are Women Executives People?" **101**
Harvard Business Review 43 (July-August 1965): 14.

Here are some examples:

> Person A: "Don't be a sex symbol or apple polish the boss—do it by merit, being the best worker with the most cooperative attitude."
> Person B: "Don't be afraid to play politics."
> Person C: "Continously develop new skills so as to prepare yourself for advancement."
> Person D: "Be the well wrapped package with the brains as opposed to the brown paper bag with brains—be noticed."
> Person E: "Work hard, aim high, learn something new each day, let the sky be your limit."

Few people have difficulty in attributing the advice given by Persons A and D as coming from women. The sex of the remaining persons is not so obvious: B and C were men, and E was a woman. Generally, only about 10 percent of the advice could be readily identified. However, it was possible, upon closer examination, to distinguish some major differences in career perspectives between men and women.

The purpose of the exercise was to get individuals to recognize the limitations of giving or receiving career advice. When the responses were read aloud, it was easy for the participants to see how varied and naïve such advice would be. For example, one woman wrote: "Work for a male boss first." A newly promoted man wrote: "If you want to become an executive, look like one." When some of the participants volunteered to elaborate further on their advice, it was evident that these were not frivolous responses but seemed to represent an integral part of the individual's career strategy and values.

By categorizing the advice, two distinct perspectives emerged. For the majority of the 500 men, the common theme expressed was a plan-ahead strategy. Often they stressed a need for planning not only career goals but also methods of attainment. It was clear that many of the men felt the need to give opportunity a hand. In contrast, women commonly emphasized the value of proving one's ability by doing a good job. The majority expressed advice reminiscent of Horatio Alger, which can best be summarized as a "work hard and some day you will be rewarded for your effort" strategy.

In a related finding, a researcher of factors contributing to women's success in business found that women are culturally conditioned to feel uncomfortable when making demands in their own interest. Such hesitancy, she theorizes, was probably learned at an early age. For example, at a dance, young girls stand "all dolled up against a wall, waiting to be chosen."[2] Such waiting-to-be-picked behavior appears to have carried over into women's career strategies.

It seems that women are taking a myopic view of their careers, almost a short-run perspective of taking care of today and letting the future take care of itself. One women epitomized this attitude when she said she had no need for specific career plans. "My company knows what is best for me," she said. On the other hand, the men generally were more career wise and questioned the management myth, prevalent until the late 1940s, that good managers, like cream, rise to the top.

---

[2]Margaret Hennig quoted in "Women in Banking: Transition to Management," *Carnegie Quarterly* 24 (Spring 1976): 7.

**"UNLIKE WOMEN, MOST MEN ARE EXPECTED
TO PLAY THE GAME."**

103

PART THREE

MANAGEMENT OF
HUMAN RESOURCES
AND PRODUCTION

Men become more career wise because of their access to what has been described as the "old-boy" network. One executive put this phenomenon simply: "If you are going to play the game, you have to know the rules." Unfortunately, women do not have this access, and there are too few women in management to act as role models and to advise aspiring young women. Myra Strober and Francine Gordon, in *Bringing Woman into Management,* point out that "because most of today's women have been socialized to believe that management, like fatherhood, is for men, women who aspire to managerial careers need frequent reinforcement of their aspirations."[3] Unfortunately, such reinforcement might be long in coming if women in management are unable to break what appears to be a self-perpetuating cycle of passive acceptance in career strategy.

Most women are unwilling to play the game

One remedy for breaking the passive acceptance cycle might be to teach women how to play the game. To some degree assertiveness training has taken this direction. Certainly a nonassertive woman who follows a waiting-to-be-picked strategy will lessen her chance of reaching the top management. However, making a women more assertive and career wise when she is unwilling to play the game is not enough. Basic career motives need to be understood.

Unlike women, most men are expected to play the game. American businessmen often have been characterized as archetypical strivers. In reality, only about one in ten managers can be characterized as possessing the upward or unlimited success orientation.[4] Curt Tausky and Robert Dubin found that many men either are unwilling to play the game necessary to reach the top or do not aspire to top positions. Using the Career Orientations Anchorage Scale (COAS), Tausky and Dubin identified three managerial career orientations: upward, ambivalent, and downward. Male managers with these career orientations were found to possess the following characteristics:

Upward: Value high upward movement; career satisfaction is a function of proximity to the peak.

Ambivalent: Have an uncrystallized career perspective; dissatisfied without advancement but unwilling to actively pursue success.

Downward: Have a limited success perspective; after achieving adequate career rewards, express little interest in further advancement. Career satisfaction is a function of how far they have come in their careers.

Results of several studies which have validated the COAS all have indicated similar career orientation distributions for men in middle management. Male workshop

[3] Francine Gordon and Myra Strober, *Bringing Women into Management* (New York: McGraw-Hill, 1975), p. 79.

[4] Curt Tausky and Robert Dubin, "Career Anchorage: Managerial Mobility Motivation," *American Sociological Review* 30 (October 1965): 725—35.

participants included in this study showed virtually no significant differences from the typical pattern. However, when representative women were administered the COAS, some dramatic differences were found. Results are shown in Table 1.

These findings suggest that even fewer women than men (6 percent versus 10 percent) are strivers. Because the sample was an atypical group of women picked for their management potential, a higher incidence of upward orientation could have been expected. A reduction of more than half in the downward category (20 percent versus 47 percent) resulted in almost a doubling of the number of women (74 percent versus 43 percent) in the ambivalent category. The fact that most of the women were in this category suggests they have uncrystallized career perspectives, which is consistent with their shortsighted career strategies. It also suggests that most women value advancement but are unwilling to play the game necessary to achieve success. However, these results may be overinflated. Women have been subjected to pressures from the women's movement as well as their organizations' affirmative action efforts. Perhaps some career ambivalence is merely a side effect of these awareness-raising efforts?

TABLE 1

Managerial Career Orientation By Sex

Orientation	Women [a] Percentage	Men [b] Percentage
Upward	6	10
Ambivalent	74	43
Downward	20	47

[a] N = 194.
[b] Tausky and Dubin, p. 729 (N = 308).
Note: $X^2 = 47.97$, df = 2, $p < .001$.

As might be expected, most studies show a connection between age and career orientation. By 45 years of age, 73 percent of all males have a downward perspective, in part because these managers have recognized their career limitations and accepted the inescapable fact that only a few will reach the top. In contrast, there is no difference in the career orientation between women over 45 and under 45 years of age. This finding lends credence to the hypothesis that woman are being affected by awareness-raising pressures. While only 18 percent of the males over age 45 are experiencing ambivalence, almost four times as many women (70 percent) at this stage in life continue to experience ambivalence.

In a 1976 study,[5] twice as many younger women were found to be highly disillusioned

[5] John F. Veiga and John N. Yanouzas, "What Women in Management Want: The Ideal vs. the Real," *Academy of Management Journal* 19 (March 1976): 137–43.

with their present management positions (69 percent) as compared to older women (31 percent). Therefore, despite what might be expected, older women are more likely experiencing career ambivalence because of organizational and societal pressures and not because of unhappiness with present positions. However, since a younger person, male or female, often experiences career ambivalence, it is impossible to determine to what extent the higher level of ambivalence found in women over 45 is a result of awareness-raising pressures and how much might be attributed to the acculturation process found in our society today. Yet, it is possible to conclude that woman over 45 are experiencing greater career anxiety than they probably should.

Choice anxiety is a major problem

Consistent with the higher incidence of career ambivalence, woman also have greater difficulty in making career choices. About 79 percent of the women attempting to develop a career plan express difficulty, as compared to 60 percent of the men. In addition, women express different career adaptation problems than men. Milton E. Hahn identifies four adaptation problems normally encountered when making career decisions: choice anxiety, lack of skill, lack of assurance, and lack of information.[6] Workshop participants were asked to identify problems that they anticipated in accomplishing their career plans. The results, shown in Table 2, were categorized by problem type.

"WOMEN MUST BECOME MORE CAREER WISE IF THEY ARE TO SURVIVE IN THE CORPORATE ENVIRONS."

Given the high incidence of ambivalence found in women, it was not too surprising to find almost half with the problem of choice anxiety. Comments such as these were typical: "I have such overriding personal obstacles at the moment that I can't really be as interested as I should be in a career plan," "I'm not sure which way I want to go," and "I just don't know what I really want." Even though their problems varied, many of these women seemed to be expressing anxiety over trying to make decisions they were unaccustomed to making. One women said: "I'm just not accustomed to planning my life the way I want it. I've always accepted things the way they were." Often their expression of choice anxiety sounded like a lack of assurance as well. Hence, even though 20 percent of the problems were classified as a lack of assurance, realistically it was a much greater problem than the table suggests. Surprisingly, lack of skill was rarely mentioned by women even though a great deal of emphasis has been placed on business training for women, primarily because of their lack of business school degrees.

[6]Milton E. Hahn, *Planning Ahead After Forty* (Los Angeles: Western Psychological Services, 1973), pp. 2—3.

TABLE 2

Managerial Career Adaptation Problems
Encountered, By Sex

Problem	Women (N = 400) Percentage	Men (N = 300) Percentage
Choice anxiety	48.5	23.3
Lack of skill	4.0	33.0
Lack of assurance	20.2	12.3
Lack of information	27.3	31.3

Note: The sample size is a result of the number of managers who indicated some problems in achieving their career goals. Out of 506 women, 400 (79 percent) reported problems. Out of 500 men, 300 (60 percent) reported problems.

In contrast, the men expressed lack of information and/or skill as their major problems. Statements such as these were common: "I really don't have the educational background to do what I'd really like to do," "I'm not sure what future opportunities are available to me in my present company." The men tended to obscure any choice anxiety or lack of assurance by rationalizing that lack of skill or information was the major obstacle. Those over age 40 tended to fall into the skill trap. They regarded their careers as continuous investments in skill development and often were unwilling to consider any career options requiring them to start over. On the other hand, women seemed to have the greatest difficulty in deciding where they should invest themselves and whether or not investment was really worth it.

Are women in management an endangered species?

Throughout this article, an attempt was made to avoid any value judgment about which career strategy is best. However, women must become more career wise if they are to survive in the corporate environs. That does not mean that all women should strive for the top. Each one needs to decide where she wants to go, and if the price is worth it.

We all have a choice. We can approach the future as pawns and accept whatever life offers us, or we can recognize our ability to influence our future and take some responsibility for what happens. The outcomes, which vary greatly, often benefit both organization and individual. One woman said: "I've finally discovered that I have wasted a lot of time and energy trying to get a promotion which I thought I wanted. Now that I've decided that goal is not important, to hell with working overtime! I'm going to start taking tennis lessons this weekend." A talented Ph.D. found that by taking an active interest in the direction of her career and by actively pursuing outside opportunities, she won a significant promotion with a major insurance company.

In summary, most of the evidence suggests that it will not be easy for women to assume their rightful place in the corporate hierarchy. While it is clear that, to effect a change, women will have to modify their career strategies, it is unfair to place all the burden for change on them. A great deal still needs to be done to alter the sex-role stereotyping found in business today. Equal pay for equal work has been accepted, but the notion that women and men are interchangeable in management has not.

While there is too much evidence of forward motion to conclude that women in management are an endangered species, it should be recognized that the same pressures that produce change also can be counterproductive. For every woman who achieves a top management position, several others, especially those over age 45, will suffer increased career anxieties and uncertainties. However, along the way women may help modify the corporate environment so that playing the game may become obsolete; or perhaps a new game will emerge.

13

MAKING IT IN A MAN'S WORLD

RACHEL LAVOIE

A women who hits the heights in a male-dominated profession is just as likely to be labeled a token as a trailblazer. For every career success story, there is an equal and opposite tale of woe. When a company with one female and 37 male vice presidents appoints two more women to that post, optimists say that the number of women increased by 200%, pessimists that only 7½% of the vice presidents are women. In short, the situation of women workers today depends a lot on how you look at it: Yes, Virginia, you have made enormous strides—but you've barely gained a toehold at the tip of the working world.

In one sense the statistics are encouraging. In the past 25 years, the number of working women has almost doubled, to over 40% of the U.S. labor force. Women account for almost half of all professional and technical workers and about a fifth of all managers and administrators, the two highest-paid fields. Female enrollment in graduate and professional schools is at record highs.

In another sense the statistics are damning. In 1975, the latest year for which figures are available, the median salary of women who worked full time was $7,504, compared with $12,758 for men; in other words, women earned 59% of what men earned. What's worse is that the gap is widening: in 1971, women earned 59½% of what men earned, in 1965, 60%. Female professional and technical workers earned 66% of males' salaries; female managers and administrators, 57%, female sales workers, 39%.

Since these are broad categories, the differences in income don't necessarily mean that women are paid less for doing the same work as men. What they do indicate is that women aren't where the money is. They are selling clothes instead of cars, managing secretarial pools instead of factories. In the professions, they account for almost 97% of nurses but only 13% of doctors.

A SLEW OF LAWS

108 Some of the earnings gap can be explained by the record number of women pouring into the labor force. The faster they come in, the larger the number of low-paying

SOURCE: Reprinted from the May 1977 issue of *Money* Magazine by special permission; © 1977, Time Inc. All rights reserved.

entry-level jobs. Much of the differential remains unexplained, however, even after adjusting for this and other factors. According to the Bureau of Labor Statistics (BLS), discrimination is the culprit, despite the slew of antidiscrimination laws passed in the 1960's.

The Equal Employment Opportunity Commission has made only "limited progress in eliminating employment discrimination," concluded a 1976 study by the General Accounting Office. In the estimate of Barbara Boyle Sullivan of Boyle/Kirkman Associates, a New York management consulting firm, "Only 20% to 25% of companies are serious about affirmative action, up from about 10% in 1971. Five years ago, there was a lot of activity, a lot of flurry, but significant progress is not being made."

Ms. Sullivan goes on to say, however, that women themselves are "about a quarter of the problem." Her explanation is a familiar one, shared by a good many career counselors. Their assessment of today's working woman runs along these lines: many don't know how to sell themselves, to set a price on themselves, they avoid politics as dirty, not realizing that it is simply a strategy, they don't recognize opportunity when it comes along (see "Keys to the Executive Powder Room," *Money,* August 1976)

TOPPLING MYTHS

Judging how much of the lack of women's progress is the result of outright discrimination and how much is the fault of women themselves is difficult. Recruiters and counselors alike agree that while there is still a great deal of reluctance to promote women in many companies, employers are more and more willing to hire them. Women can take credit for a good part of that change in attitude, since it was they who, in the process of swarming into the labor market, managed to topple at least some of the myths that blocked their way five or ten years ago. Despite employers' qualms that women take an inordinate number of days off to tend to family needs, there is no statistically significant difference between male and female absentee rates. And while it's generally true that women leave jobs more often than men, the BLS says the difference is simply that turnover is higher in low-level jobs. There is still a significant dip in the number of women who remain employed during their so-called child-bearing years, but it looks nothing like the plunge of years past.

One reason so few women have made it to the top is that so few started out with the right educational background 10 or 15 years ago. Educational barriers have all but disappeared these days, though, and industry has responded by opening up many entry-level jobs. "In sales, accounting and finance, and any technical field, entry-level jobs are wide open to any qualified woman who can sell herself," says Ms. Sullivan. Women still meet resistance in middle management, but once they're entrenched at that level, chances of reaching the top should greatly improve.

The best opportunities for women lie in fields in which they've been seriously underrepresented in the past. It's almost a truism that the more technical—and hence the more traditionally "male"—the field, the better the outlook for women. They can, of course, have satisfactory careers in the traditionally female fields, but it's unlikely that they will rise as quickly through the ranks. Following is a sampling of what's going on in the male, female and "neuter" working worlds today.

Since only about 1% of engineers, for example, are women, new ones are valuable to firms worried about lawsuits or bad publicity. Jean Watson (pictured on the cover) graduated from Oregon State University in 1971 with a bachelor's in chemical engineering and landed right in the middle of a switch in employers' attitudes toward women engineers. When she started job hunting, she got a lot of rejections, while her husband was getting an excellent reception even though he still had a year to go before getting his degree in engineering. By the time he graduated in 1972, however, she was getting a good response and he was getting a lousy one. They both took jobs with Standard Oil of California, she at $12,100, he at $11,400. Today their salaries are about equal, with each earning just over $23,000.

TEN FIRM OFFERS

Eva Shaye, 34, had no job problems at all when she emigrated from Sweden to the U.S. nine years ago after solid training in computer technology at the Swedish Institute for Defense Research. She just went through the ads in the *New York Times* for systems analysts, called 10 firms and got 10 job offers. She chose General Electric and worked with its computer time-sharing program until TWA wooed her away a year later. She quit after a few years to have two children, but is currently back part-time, sharing the job with another woman. Plenty of job offers are still coming her way, and she's convinced her field is a good one for women: "With computers, all that matters is what kind of head you have. As long you're good, it doesn't matter if you are a man or a woman."

Besides the scientific and technical fields, women have always been seriously underrepresented in the highest-paying professions—law, medicine and dentistry. One of the most hopeful signs is the rate at which they are enrolling in professional schools. While only about 13% of physicians are women, they currently make up more than 20% of medical students. The number of women receiving law degrees more than quintupled between 1970 and 1975.

It's unlikely, however, that male and female doctors earn comparable amounts of money. When the American Medical Association did a comparative-income survey in 1972, it found that women doctors earned just over half as much as male doctors. The difference is probably about the same today, since women continue to cluster in the lower-paying specialities, such as psychiatry, pediatrics and family practice. Women lawyers are in much the same situation. Although it's becoming easier for women to break into law, there's a persistent shortage of them in high-paying positions.

One woman who made big money in a short time in the legal world, Mary S. Hirschfeld of Beverly Hills, attributes most of her success to her determination. Ms. Hirschfeld, who is 40 and divorced, earned a six-figure income in private practice. Still, she says, "I'm not a wonder woman. I just keep doing things—and I assume I'm going to be successful." She remembers "getting a lot of flak" from her male classmates while she was in law school in the mid-60s, but when she set up her own practice in 1970, she had no trouble getting male clients. "The attitude of most women clients toward me, however, was distrustful," she says. "I even encountered some who wanted to pay me less than they would a man." She's noticed an improvement over the years but still feels that many women are reluctant to put a high enough price tag on other women or on themselves. "Until women start looking at themselves as what is being sold, they are going to remain a bargain," she says.

The percentage of dentists who are women hovers between 1% and 2%, but larger numbers are now graduating from the dental schools. Sheva Rapoport, 40, a practicing periodontist and past president of the Association of American Women Dentists, feels strongly that "it's the individual and not the sex that accounts for any success or failure." She points out that private practice with a home office offers many advantages to women like herself who want to combine a well-paid career ($25,000 to $40,000 a year) with marriage and children.

TRADITIONALLY FEMALE FIELDS

Whatever the drawbacks of the male professions, you can be sure that they're better paying than such traditionally female professions as social work, library science and teaching. These fields all share one characteristic: the work force in each has long been primarily female, but the top jobs have gone mostly to men.

To a limited degree, women themselves are responsible for this state of affairs. In social work, for example, the 1950s and 1960s saw a tremendous increase in efforts to recruit men into the field. The idea was to combat its negative image as a women's field. When the men came in, however, they took over the administrative and organizational jobs, leaving women to be the caseworkers. Though this division has persisted, it may be closing a bit as more men enter the field as caseworkers.

Librarians form the same pyramid as social workers, with women in the majority in every position except director, associate director and assistant director. Even when women reach these positions, their salaries are considerably lower than males'. Male directors, for example, earned an average of $22,242 in 1975-76, their female counterparts $17,062.

Although both these fields have few women at the top, they are not necessarily bad fields for women who want middle-level careers. The salary gap between male and female librarians diminishes rapidly in the middle ranks, with male branch and department heads, for example, averaging only $1,592 more than females.

Women teachers are falling behind in the best-paying area: college and university jobs. From 1974 to 1975 the number of women relative to men declined at the ranks of professor, associate professor and instructor. Average salaries for men continued to exceed those for women at every academic rank.

NEUTER FIELDS

There's a whole other set of fields such as insurance and banking that are not thought of as women's fields but that have a work force that is predominantly female. Women's progress in these areas depends almost entirely on the particular company they work for. In general, the top jobs are still overwhelmingly male; women are moving slowly—but somewhat surely—through the middle ranks, and in many cases they are being actively recruited for good entry-level jobs and training programs.

When 9 to 5, a Boston women's rights group, surveyed that city's insurance industry in 1974, it found that women made up 58.2% of the work force but accounted for only 4.1% of professional positions and ½% of the sales positions. However, Judy McCullough of 9 to 5 says that there's been some improvement since then, especially for women in lower and middle management. A lot of companies are actively recruiting women for their sales forces, she says, and some women are getting good jobs with the insurance companies' computer divisions.

The outlook is more than slightly cheerier across the hall in the banking industry, where women make up over 60% of the work force. When the Council on Economic Priorities, a nonprofit research organization, surveyed 24 major banks in eight cities in 1975, it found that less than 2% of senior executives were women. But 26% of all managers and officials were women, compared with 16% in 1971, and the percentage of female bank officers had doubled during the same time span, from 6.4% to 13%.

Finance-related careers in general look good, especially for women with economics or business degrees. Perry Prestemon, a broker with the Washington, D.C., office of Blyth Eastman Dillon, combined a degree in economics from Randolph-Macon Woman's College with a bit of judicious job hopping through a couple of local brokerage houses to succeed in a field where few women do. The lone woman among the 20-odd brokers in her office, she was No. 1 in sales during 1976, her first full year with the company. She earned herself $46,000 entirely on commission, more than doubling her 1975 income of $22,000. "I don't understand why more women aren't brokers," she says. "It's a neuter occupation."

Another neuter occupation is accounting, which has had a high influx of women in the past four or five years, according to Barbara Rausch, administrative director of the American Woman's Society of Certified Public Accountants. "In my experience, women have a better record than men for staying on the job," she says, "and client acceptance has been good." Though there is parity in pay nowadays for male and female accountants, Mrs. Rausch notes that there are still few women partners in the Big Eight accounting firms. "Accounting firms are slow to promote from within," she says. "Uncertain of their prospects for promotion, many women will leave before putting in the seven or 10 years it takes to become a partner."

The government has always been at least one step ahead of private industry as far as formal equality between men and women are concerned. Just because the pay scales are equal, however, doesn't mean the earnings are.

As in private industry, women make up a huge proportion of the lowest grade categories in the civil service and a minuscule portion of the highest grades. Their position has barely changed from 1970 to 1975, except in the middle grades (GS 7 to 12), where women went from 22.7% to 26.8% of the work force. "Every year we see a good increase from clerical into professional jobs," says Diane C. Herrmann, an assistant director of the Civil Service Commission's Federal Women's Program. "But there's still a reluctance to put women into managerial and supervisory positions."

WACS ON THE MARCH

Somewhat ironically, the armed services have become among the most sex-blind of all employers. "The Army is well ahead of the civilian sector, though of course there's

still more room for improvement," says Colonel Edith Hinton, deputy director of the
Women's Army Corps. In 1972 only 25% of military occupations were open to enlisted
women, compared with 92% in 1976. Only certain combat-related jobs are still closed.

Though ROTC and Officer Candidate Schools have recently been standardized for
men and women, enlistment standards are still slightly tougher for women. WAC
officers are commissioned separately from men, but they increased from 901 in 1972
to 2,036 in 1976. "In the past, women's opportunities for promotion above the grade of
major were extremely limited," says Colonel Hinton, "but now there's no problem at
all—until you get to the colonel level at least."

As the doors swing wider in both government and private employment, one con-
firmation that women are making it in a man's world comes from an unpleasant medical
statistic; the male-female ulcer ratio. Ulcers have long been a male prerogative and,
medical authorities agree, often arise from job-related tension. In 1947 men held a
commanding 20-to-1 lead. Now, after three decades of progress in equal opportunity,
the ratio is 2 to 1.

14

THE ADVENT OF PUBLIC SECTOR MULTIEMPLOYER BARGAINING

ROGER W. MANSFIELD

INTRODUCTION

Many authors have compared the practice of collective bargaining to human systems of behavior such as marriage, business, and politics; the similitude being that each of these follow certain commonly accepted guidelines, although the specific form is determined by many factors that vary from place to place and from time to time. The purpose of this paper is to explore an emerging bargaining form, that of multiemployer bargaining in the public sector. More specifically, the paper attempts to present some of the possible reasons for the use and acceptance of multiemployer bargaining as a public sector labor-management bargaining tool.

Multiemployer bargaining is not a new concept; it has been used in major segments of private industry for some time. As a result, this paper first attempts to present the various bargaining typeologies which commonly fall under the multiemployer heading. Emphasis then shifts to a historical discussion of the evolution of private sector multiemployer bargaining. Drawing on the experiences of the private sector 30 to 35 years ago, similarities are then made with the emerging trends toward the use of multiemployer bargaining in the public sector today. Concluding remarks center around the need for approaches which will help jurisdictions respond more fairly to the demands of public employee unions without compromising the interests of taxpayers and public service recipients.

BACKGROUND

What is multiemployer bargaining? Frank Pierson in his article, "Multi-Employer Bargaining," identifies several of the union-employer relationships which are commonly classified under the multiemployer bargaining heading.

The first of these bargaining relationships is industry-wide bargaining. In its pure form, industry-wide bargaining exists when one or more unions, acting together, bargain with an employer association over wages and working conditions for an entire industry. Industry-

SOURCE: *Personnel Journal*, May 1975. Reprinted by permission.

wide bargaining in this form is rare in the United States. However, in the railroad and bituminous coal industries something close to it exists.[1]

More common than systems of industry-wide bargaining are regional and local systems. In these, employers in a city or wider geographical area join together to bargain for the industry in that area or region with the union or unions representing their employees. Pierson states that what distinguishes between these bargaining types is who is represented by the spokesman for the two parties and what proportion of the industry in the area is covered. Negotiations are on a local area basis when the bargaining representatives speak for a majority of an industry's employers and employees in a given community or locality. Bargaining becomes regional when the coverage goes beyond a local area, but falls short of being industry wide in extent. Several examples of the local arrangements are evident in the brewing, printing and publishing, and retail trade industries. Examples of regional arrangements are industries like the pulp and paper, hosiery, and fishing industries.[2]

The chief purpose of these various multiemployer relationships is to fix uniform scales of wages and uniform working conditions within an entire industry, area, or community. Uniformity may not be achieved; and where it is achieved, it may not last or may be interrupted. But uniformity is still the goal.[3]

The historical development and use of these multiemployer bargaining approaches is traced by Wilson Randle and Max Wortman in their book *Collective Bargaining*. The authors state that most multiemployer associations in this country were founded around 1900. The primary goal of these organizations was to oppose the trend toward unionism evolving at that time. However, by the 1930's, the basic philosophy of these associations changed with the passage of the Wagner Act, which caused them to operate within the new public policy framework favoring collective bargaining.[4]

During the period from 1935 to 1947, trade unionism expanded at unparalleled rates. Throughout this decade unionism radically changed its position in the United States. From a small minority, representing little more than ten per cent of the nonagricultural wage-earning and salaried population, it rose in these years to a minority empowered to speak for forty per cent.[5]

Concurrent with the rapid rise in union membership was a significant shift in the relative and absolute power of the unions. In an article by Leo Wolman entitled, "Industry-Wide Bargaining," he notes that the transformation in the position of organized labor had swift practical consequences. Union policies and practices which previously affected only the fringes of American industry now went to its very heart. Single unions or combinations of them had the power to shut off the flow of goods and services or to determine the conditions under which it was allowed. It was also the first time that organized labor was strong enough to shut down an entire industry or a substantial part of an industry in order to effectuate policy.[6]

[1]Frank Pierson, "Multiemployer Bargaining," in *Unions, Management, and the Public*, pp. 346–347.

[2]*Ibid.*

[3]*Ibid.*

[4]Wilson Randle and Max Wortman, *Collective Bargaining*, p. 109.

[5]Leo Wolman, "Industry-Wide Bargaining," in *Industry-Wide Collective Bargaining*, p. 15.

[6]*Ibid.*

Wolman contends that with the rise and spread of organized labor and the concurrent disappearance of the limited strike, the public increasingly faced the threat of industrial paralysis and crises that endangered their health and safety. Also that it was only natural that such a great shift in the relative and absolute power should place the public's view of the union movement in a new perspective. Therefore, it was to be expected that a public which viewed the behavior of a relatively weak minority with equanimity and indifference began to take seriously the same practice in the hands of a larger and much more powerful union.[7] This increasing apprehension about the growing monopolistic tendencies on the part of organized labor manifested itself in the passage of the Taft-Hartley Act of 1947. The Taft-Hartley Act placed restrictions on organized labor and sought to balance the bargaining rights of management and labor.[8]

Since the passage of the Taft-Hartley Act, the trend from single employer to multiemployer bargaining has continued. Randle and Wortman in their efforts to describe the reasons for this trend have offered the following possibilities. The strength of unionization is cited as the prime factor. From this source have come the continuing bargaining ambitions on the part of unions and the defensive alignment of employers into associations and multiemployer groups. This trend toward larger and more centralized units, in turn contributed to a defensive alignment of the unions into larger bargaining structures. The growth and recognition of collective bargaining, itself, contributed to a standardization of conditions and gave encouragement to collective bargaining. The industry-wide production drives of World War II are also mentioned as contributing toward multiemployer bargaining thinking and action. In addition, the War Labor Board with its Wage Stabilization Program imposed wage ceilings that caused a cluster of rates to accumulate around the ceilings and thus gave added uniformity to wage structures. Finally the development of wage pattern negotiation significantly contributed to multiemployer and association bargaining.[9]

Today's private sector employers associations have developed across industry lines into what are called federated metropolitan employer bargaining associations. These associations attempt to aid their member firms and associations through collective bargaining and the improvement of their employment relations policies. Several examples of this type of association are the Associated Industries of Cleveland, the Employers' Association of Greater Chicago, the Mountain States Employers' Council, and the San Francisco Employers' Council.[10]

Having briefly described the various types of private sector multiemployer bargaining relationships and their historical evolution, discussion will now shift to the emerging use of this approach by public sector employers.

What is the nature of multiemployer bargaining relationships now appearing in the public sector? From the limited literature presently available on public sector multiemployer bargaining, it would appear that most of these evolving relationships fall under Pierson's classification of localized multiemployer bargaining. Under this typeology employers band together on a localized or larger area to bargain with the union or unions representing their employees.

[7] *Ibid.*

[8] Jessie Fredin, *The Taft-Hartley Act and Multiemployer Bargaining,* pp. 1–3.

[9] *Op. Cit.,* Randle and Wortman, p. 104.

[10] *Ibid.* p. 109.

Since the literature on the American experience with this approach is so scarce, the exact extent of usage is unknown. However, the National League of Cities and United States Conference of Mayors have documented the first use of this approach in the Twin Cities area of Minneapolis and St. Paul.[11] The only other governmental agencies known to be using this technique are the cities of Pleasanton, Livermore, and the Valley Community Services District in California.[12]

The limited documented experiences with multiemployer bargaining seem to indicate that there are three primary reasons for its use. These reasons are as follows: The geography causes the parties to draw on the same labor pool; there exists a common union or unions that represent a majority of the employees; and the increasing awareness of municipal and other governmental officials that they are at a distinct disadvantage at the bargaining table when dealing with the full-time professional union negotiators. In addition to these expressed reasons for the advent of multiemployer bargaining, it is felt that in some important respects one can compare multiemployer bargaining in the public sector today, with multiemployer bargaining relationships in the private sector 30 or 35 years ago. Evolving trends of that time are now appearing, as government gains more experience in collective bargaining with public employees.

In examining what has happened in the public sector, one finds some interesting similarities. The first of these similitudes has been the rapid growth in size and power of the public unions. Like the growth period from 1935–1947 in the private sector, the period from 1962 to the present has been a major growth period for public sector unions. From 1962 to the present, public sector unionism has grown from 1.2 million, or seven per cent of the total United States union membership, to nearly 2.5 million, or 11.8 per cent of the union membership, and is still growing.[13]

The prime factors for this growth, according to Harry Cohany and Lucretia Dewey, authors of the article "Union Membership Among Government Employees," are: the passage of Kennedy's Federal Executive Order 10988 in 1962 which sanctioned union organization at the federal level and had wide repercussions for state and local levels as well; the long standing wage differentials between private and public employers; the results achieved by many militant unions; and the need for a mechanism whereby employees, especially professionals, could participate in decision making from which they had previously been excluded. They also note that technology, population, urbanization, and changing concepts of governments role have also had their effects, leading toward greater public sector unionization.[14]

With this growth in size of public sector unions, there has been a concurrent increase in the power of the unions. The power of the public sector unions is evolving much as it did in private industry. At the outset, it was noted that unionization was accepted with equanimity and indifference, but as the power of the unions became increasingly dispropor-

[11]_____, *Cities Join Together for Bargaining: The Experience in Minnesota and British Columbia,* U.S. Conference of Mayors, National League of Cities and National Association of Counties, September 1971, pp. 1–16.

[12]Joint Powers for Labor Relations Consolidated Bargaining, Cities of Livermore, Pleasanton, and the Valley Community Services District, May 1, 1973.

[13]_____, *Statistical Abstract of the United States: 1974,* p. 365.

[14]Harry Cohany and Lucretia Dewey, "Union Membership Among Government Employees," in *Collective Bargaining in Government,* pp. 5–11.

tionate, there came cries that this power be mitigated. This cry was answered with the passage of the Taft-Hartley Act of 1947. In the public sector, the same power syndrome seems to be evolving. During the early 1960's militancy among public employees was met with acquiescence by our society generally. The example of the student war protestors, the civil rights movement and so on, left its mark on the fireman, hospital worker, teachers, and others. Conduct of questionable legality had achieved results where more conventional means had failed.[15] However, this conduct and power is increasingly coming under closer scrutiny as more individual's health and safety are threatened. Or, as George Skelton and William Endicott have pointed out in their recent *Los Angeles Times* article entitled "The Public's Servants—How Big? And How Powerful?" some are now fearing that if this power trend continues the public servant corps may someday overwhelm the electorate it serves. They note that bureaucracy has never shown a willingness to diminish itself, even when the need for which it was created has long since vanished, and they fear that its steady growth in size and power could render the private citizenry powerless to effectively deal with it. Before this happens, it is felt that changes in the structure of bargaining will be necessary. The purpose of such restructuring would be to ensure that a particular interest group, public employee unions, do not gain a substantial competitive advantage over other interest groups in pressing its claims on government.[16]

The second likeness between the public and private sectors has been the trend toward centralized bargaining units. Randle and Wortman note that in the private sector there was a trend towards larger business units with greater centralization of control, which contributed to a defensive alignment of unions into larger bargaining structures.[17] Through centralization, unions are attempting to standardize wages, hours, and working conditions in the labor market, in order to eliminate competition between individual workers or groups of workers. Randle and Wortman also state that centralization occurred because of an expanding technology and improved transportation services which enlarged the area of competition; and local labor markets are becoming increasingly interdependent through wage standardization programs. As a result of this movement toward larger bargaining units, there is a tendency toward increasing multiemployer as well as multiunion collaboration in collective bargaining.[18]

During the late 1960's, the public sector widely used a form of regional centralization such as councils of governments and associations of governments as an approach to planning and problem solving. This was primarily due to the growing number of problems which transcended local jurisdictional boundaries and the areawide planning incentives attached to federal and state grants in aid.[19]

Joseph Zimmerman in his article entitled "Meeting Service Needs Through Intergovernmental Agreements" states that city and county officials have increasingly attempted to meet these joint problems and common needs through the use of formal and informal

---

[15] *Ibid.*

[16] George Skelton and William Endicott, "The Public Servants—How Big? And How Powerful?" *Los Angeles Times*, (September 10, 1974), p. 1.

[17] *Op. cit.,* Randle and Wortman, p. 15.

[18] *Ibid.,* pp. 15–16.

[19] _____, *The Municipal Year Book 1973,* International City Management Association, p. 63.

agreements. The dominant motive for entering into these agreements is to take advantage
of economies of scale. Other reasons cited are the lack of facilities, the lack of qualified
personnel, meeting an urgent problem, citizen demand for service agreements, civil service
avoidance, and keeping the service out of politics. Zimmerman feels that the use of agreements is a limited form of functional consolidation based on a partnership approach,
whereby administration is centralized and policy making is decentralized.[20] Although the
original purposes of many of these regional associations and agreements may not have
been to deal with labor relations and collective bargaining, they do represent the ability and
willingness to establish cooperative approaches to matters of area-wide concern. These
associations have demonstrated that they can deal with activities involving more than one
policy or program area; membership consisting predominantly of elected officials or appointed representatives of constituent local governments; and funded by local cooperation.
As collective bargaining and labor relations become more of a problem for governmental
jurisdictions, it is felt that this demonstrated ability to work together will lend itself to the
creation of multiemployer relationships. A recent example of where this has taken place has
been the creation of the Southwest Labor Relations Council in Southern California. The
Council was set up by the South Bay City Managers Association to handle the growing
problems associated with current day labor relations in the Southern California area.

The third similarity between the private and public sectors has been the increasing
amount of labor relations legislation which is adding uniformity and giving encouragement
to collective bargaining. The Wagner Act, which was passed in 1935, gave collective
bargaining rights to most employees working in the private sector. However, it was not until
1962 that the federal government granted some form of collective bargaining to its employees. Similarly, only the state of Wisconsin had provided bargaining for employees of its
local units of government by 1962. Since 1962, the scene has changed dramatically;
twenty-two states have passed laws granting collective bargaining to state and local employees. Nixon's Executive Order 11491 replaced Kennedy's Executive Order 10988 and
updated and expanded the framework for federal employee bargaining.[21] Also, recent
legislation such as the Fair Labor Standards Act and the Equal Employment Opportunities
Act seem to be directed toward the union goal of uniformity. These statutes seek to protect
and encourage organization among the unorganized and no doubt provide a moral and legal
imperative in that direction. However, comprehensive statutes are generally not enacted
until union organization is substantial. Thus, one might say that organization seems as much
of a cause of legislation as an effect.

The fourth similarity between the two sectors has been with wage and price controls.
During the 1940's the War Labor Board imposed wage ceilings that caused a cluster of rates
to accumulate around the ceilings and gave added uniformity to wage structures.[22] One
must wonder how much of an effect Nixon's 1971–1973 Economic Stabilization Program
has had on added wage uniformity in the public sector. It is doubted that the impact of

[20]Joseph Zimmerman, "Meeting Service Needs Through Intergovernmental Agreements," in *The Municipal Year Book 1973*, pp. 79–88.

[21]Joseph Loewenberg and Michael Moskow, *Collective Bargaining in Government*, p. 1.

[22]*Op. cit.,* Randle and Wortman, p. 102.

Nixon's program on wages would be as far reaching as the War Labor Board's since the program was not in effect as long. However, it is felt that there was a tendency for wages to move toward the imposed wage ceilings.

The fifth likeness between the private and public sectors has been the development of wage pattern negotiations by unions. By wage pattern negotiations it is meant that the employee labor organizations are developing common demands and positions which are presented to a number of jurisdictions. The organization then plays the actions of one of the jurisdictions against the other. In California, the Los Angeles County Division of the League of California Cities has identified this as one of the developing problems in the labor management relations in this area. One means they suggest for combating this situation is the exchange of correct information, including the cities' positions and proposals; and the use of total compensation figures for an accurate accounting of personnel costs to facilitate effective meeting and conferring.[23] The actions suggested and being taken by area wide associations like the Los Angeles County Division of the League of California Cities seem to resemble the actions by private sector multiemployer bargaining associations during the 1930's and 40's.

What have been the advantages and disadvantages of multiemployer bargaining based upon public sector usage? In discussing the alleged advantages and disadvantages of public sector multiemployer bargaining it should be noted at the outset that collective bargaining relationships do not operate exactly the same in any two situations since they are usually the result of different situations and pressures. Consequently, the following advantages and disadvantages are based on generalizations from the limited documented public sector experiences found in the literature.

Proponents of multiemployer bargaining usually aver the following characteristics of the multiemployer relationship:

1. Most multiemployer associations have typically aided in the development of job specs, pay plans, and daily personnel policies.

2. Negotiations and preparations are simplified for the member jurisdictions of the multiemployer association.

3. Since the association does most of the "hard nose bargaining," the CAO and personnel staff are able to work with employee representatives on personnel program activities not directly related to collective bargaining in a more harmonious atmosphere than might be the case.

4. Multiemployer bargaining has brought expertise to the bargaining table.

5. There appears to be an equalization of bargaining between the member jurisdictions and unions which contributes to a better competitive position for each group.

6. Multiemployer bargaining tends to reduce the provincialism on both sides of

[23]_____, *Report of the Task Force on Action Plan Implementation,* Los Angeles County Division of the California League of Cities, August 6, 1974, p. 4.

management and labor by forcing employers and employees to evaluate the area situation as a whole during negotiations and imposes the necessity of compromise as a price of whatever uniformity is achieved.

7. Wages and earning levels do not appear to have risen more rapidly under multiemployer bargaining.

8. Wide salary differentials for similar positions seem to have been eliminated.

9. Unions seem to achieve greater stability in their political structure and greater uniformity of contract interpretation.[24]

Opponents of multiemployer bargaining are also able to present strong arguments against it. These arguments usually center around the following:

1. The jurisdiction may lose direct control over a significant budgetary item-personnel service.

2. There may be inequitable apportionment of costs to maintain the association.

3. More time may be involved in the negotiation of the contract.

4. The entity established to conduct multiemployer bargaining programs may usurp the jurisdictions authority in handling of the personnel function.

5. During the establishment of the multiemployer association, or shortly thereafter, the wages, hours, and terms of employment usually rise to the highest cost firm in the association.

6. There may be possible restrictions on terminating the agreement once it is entered into.

7. It may imply the facilitation of the establishment of make work rules and full crew laws which may impair efficiency.

8. Strikes have not been eliminated and the consequences are more severe when they do occur.

9. Between negotiations the union may obtain concessions through the administrative machinery of the contract by whip-sawing grievances from one firm to another until the most favorable outcome is obtained.[25]

In analyzing the arguments for and against multiemployer bargaining, it is easy to see how heated battles could develop over attempts to outlaw, weaken, or strengthen it through legislated public policy. However, the documented public sector experiences with multiemployer bargaining seem to play down the negative aspects of the approach, relative to its redeeming characteristics.

[24]Based on readings in the bibliography.

[25]Based on the total readings in the bibliography.

CONCLUSION

There is no one "best" system of collective bargaining. What may work well in one place may be entirely inappropriate in another. Consequently, the purpose of this paper was not to present multiemployer bargaining in a context that it might be the public jurisdiction's panacea to its labor management problems. Rather, the purpose of the paper was to explore the use of multiemployer bargaining as a labor management tool which might be used under certain circumstances to counterbalance the growing power of the public sector unions.

In examining multiemployer bargaining systems, it is apparent that there is a need for local and regional efforts to relate to state-wide developments. Labor unions that are dealing with municipalities on a state-wide basis utilize settlements from municipalities in other regions, as evidenced in the recent Southern California Rapid Transit strike where wage comparisons were being made with other major metropolitan cities as New York and San Francisco. Consequently, the entity created to handle the bargaining program should have current and up-to-date information on other municipal developments as suggested by the Los Angeles County Division of the League of California Cities. In addition, it is felt that contract administration and general personnel administration should be vital parts of any total labor management programs established. In this way, it is hoped that governmental jurisdiction may be able to respond more fairly to the demands of public employee unions, without compromising the interests of the taxpayers and recipients of public services.

REFERENCES

Anonymous, *Statistical Abstract of the United States: 1974,* U.S. Bureau of the Census, 95th edition, Washington D.C., 1974.

_____, *The Municipal Year Book 1973,* International City Management Association, Washington D.C., 1973.

_____, *Report of the Task Force on Action Plan Implementation,* Los Angeles County Division of the California League of Cities, August 6, 1974.

_____, *Cities Join Together for Bargaining: The Experience in Minnesota and British Columbia,* U.S. Conference of Mayors, National League of Cities and National Association of Counties, September 1971.

_____, Joint Powers Agreement for Labor Relations Consolidated Bargaining, Cities of Livermore, Pleasanton, and Valley Community Services District, May 1, 1973.

Bakke, W. W., Clark Kerr, and Charles Arnold, *Unions, Management, and the Public,* Harcourt, Brace and Co., New York, 1960.

Cohany, Harry and Lucretia Dewey, "Union Membership Among Government Employees," *Collective Bargaining in Government,* pp. 5–11.

Fredin, Jessie, *The Taft-Hartley Act and Multiemployer Bargaining,* University of Pennsylvania Press, Philadelphia, 1948.

Kaye, S. P., and A. Marsh, *International Manual on Collective Bargaining for Public Employees,* Praeger Publishers, New York, 1973.

Loewenberg, J. J., and M. H. Moskow, *Collective Bargaining in Government,* Prentice-Hall, Inc., Englewood Cliffs, 1972.

Pollak, Otto, *Social Implications of Industry-Wide Bargaining,* University of Pennsylvania Press, Philadelphia, 1948.

Randle, Wilson and Max Wortman, *Collective Bargaining,* Houghton Mifflin Co., Boston, 1966.

Skelton, George and William Endicott, "The Public Servants—How Big? and How Powerful?" *Los Angeles Times.* XCIII, September 10, 1974, pp. 1, 14–15.

Warne, C. E., *Industry-Wide Collective Bargaining,* D. C. Heath and Co., Boston, 1950.

Warner, K. O., *Collective Bargaining in the Public Service: Theory and Practice,* Public Personnel Association, Chicago, 1967.

Wellington, H. H. and R. K. Winter, Jr., *The Unions and the Cities,* The Brookings Institution, Washington D.C., 1971.

Wolman, Leo, "Industry-Wide Bargaining," *Industry-Wide Collective Bargaining,* D. C. Heath and Company, Boston, 1950, pp. 13–22.

Zimmerman, Joseph F., "Meeting Service Needs Through Intergovernmental Agreements," *The Municipal Year Book 1973,* International City Management Association, Washington D.C., 1973, pp. 79–88.

15

U.S. PRODUCTIVITY CALLED KEY ITEM BY LOF HEAD

AL GOLDBERG

The nation is destined for eventual economic collapse unless its priorities are reordered to increase productivity rather than heap additional demands on a shrinking producing segment of the economy, the president of Libbey-Owens-Ford Co. told a group of Ohio journalists meeting in Cleveland Friday.

Robert G. Wingerter's observations came at a conference sponsored by the Business Roundtable of Northern Ohio to examine with journalists what the organization considers the most critical economic issues confronting business and the nation.

The issues—the need for increased profitability, increased productivity, the shortfall in the level of capital investment, and new accounting and financial disclosure requirements—far transcend the current economic downturn, which was touched on only indirectly in the day-long conference.

Mr. Wingerter, who led the discussions on productivity, said that the producing segment of the economy is simply not strong enough to support all of the demands society has been imposing on it.

The Toledo industrialist said, "We have witnessed for many years a declining percentage of our nation's total employed population that is engaged in the production of things holding tangible values, while the percentage engaged in the production of services has grown to over 60 per cent of those employed." He said that those who work in the services and professions, plus the one in six persons employed by national, state, and local governments, can contribute to the nation's economic strength and producing functions only insofar as their efforts increase the productivity of those producing things of tangible value.

In blunt terms, he decried laws and policies by elective representatives that he said have discouraged productivity by "rewarding the nonproducer almost as well as they reward the producer.

"We have permitted restrictive work practices and featherbedding. We have in various ways protected incompetence on the job. We have spent huge sums of money in nonproductive pursuits," he said, conceding later during a question-and-answer session that LOF

 SOURCE: Reprinted by permission of *The Blade*, Toledo, Ohio, May 25, 1975.

had not been a national leader in the area of increasing individual employee productivity on the job.

The Business Roundtable is a New York-based nonprofit organization made up of the chief executive officers of more than 150 large U.S. companies. The Cleveland conference was the first of its kind, a pilot effort designed to help create a better understanding of the economic system for the journalists and a better understanding of the role of the news media for the businessmen.

The group's northern Ohio chapter is made up of 26 chief executives, with Mr. Wingerter and W. W. Boeschenstein, president of Owens-Corning Fiberglas Corp., being two Toledo members.

John Ong, new president of the B. F. Goodrich Co., of Akron, discussed profitability, which he said has replaced sex as the nation's most-tabooed subject for discussion, even among businessmen.

Mr. Ong said there are widespread misconceptions about corporate profits, citing a survey by the Opinion Research Corp. showing that people believe profits to be seven times higher than they actually are. The average guess in 1973 was that the average profit was 28 cents on the dollar when the actual figure that year was 4 cents.

The same question asked about 1974 profits showed people to believe they were 33 cents on the dollar when the average figure was actually 5 cents.

Robert Cogan, secretary-treasurer of Ohio Bell Telephone Co., discussing the shortfall in capital investment, said, "There are sobering thoughts that, unless our capital formation process is improved, our economy will fail to reach goals in the 1980s, which we heretofore had been taking for granted."

Charles Allen, vice president and chief financial officer of TRW, Inc., of Cleveland, called for an accounting system that actually measures performance in the light of comparable past performance. He explained that the objective is to actually report corporate finances in terms of "units of general purchasing power"—adjusted to reflect inflationary forces.

PART THREE

DISCUSSION QUESTIONS

1. From the readings, do you think work or the worker is changing?

2. Which problem in Reading 11 appears to you to be the most difficult to resolve?

3. Can you think of any advice you would give a woman desiring to move into management other than the suggestions given in the article? Name and explain three nontraditional jobs for women and minorities.

4. What do you think will happen to the steelworkers' experimental negotiating agreement when I.W. Abel is replaced as head of the United Steelworkers of America?

5. Should public sector workers be allowed to organize? Should they have the right to strike? Can they strike under your state's laws?

6. Explain your work ethic.

MARKETING MANAGEMENT

Society has seen the goals of marketing change radically since the Industrial Revolution. The Industrial Revolution created vast amounts of goods; with an almost unlimited demand for these goods, there was little need for concern about sales management or consumer issues. After the depression of the 1930s, more concern was given to sales volume and sales management. In the 1950s, many companies gave much more thought to the marketing concept based on a customer orientation. Many of the companies producing consumer products became very good at anticipating consumer needs.

In the 1970s, a series of new frontiers has arisen to confront the modern marketing manager with totally new problems. Consumerism and the resultant legislation have forced companies to change their marketing practices. Social responsibility has even reached the companies that previously had ignored the new marketing concepts. A product today must not only satisfy consumer needs but, in addition, should be ecologically sound, should conform to safety and health rules, and should be a wise user of energy and other resources. To meet all these requirements is difficult, to say the least.

Another element of the marketing scene is the rapid rise of the service industries. Service industries include such areas as finance and banking, recreation, rental agencies, and personal service firms. Because of the rapid growth in the service industries, some have not really begun utilizing some of the better marketing concept techniques. The traditional bank with its 10 a.m. to 3 p.m. hours could not be said to be serving the needs of the customer—compare bank hours with those of the typical supermarket.

There are many companies that have become experts in satisfying customer needs. Reading 16, "P&G's Secret Ingredient," is a good illustration of the methods of a company committed to the marketing concept. Procter & Gamble spends more on advertising than any other company in the world. As you read the article, ask yourself if the huge expenditure is justified in a modern business world.

Regionalized advertising is a new innovation tested successfully by Carter Hawley Hale. Its consumer approach to the middle-income fashion image has lifted its **127** revenues to seventh place in department store retailing.

Limited merchandise has made a multimillionaire of the founder of "The Limited" in thirteen years as it returned 74 percent on equity in 1977.

The eight-billion-dollar cosmetic business is undergoing changes that will help boost sales by ten to fifteen percent per year. Drug and department stores are modifying sales areas to accomodate the increasing demand.

Parking and mass transit proponents are fighting for recognition in their efforts to revitalize downtown shopping areas. The carless poor on the one hand and the affluent suburbanites on the other have marketing managers banging heads. Downtown malls are a part of the commercial revitalization that is exciting merchants.

All of these are examples of the increasing attention of business managers to marketing techniques. Clearly, the consumer has become the focus of attention in marketing management.

16

P&G'S SECRET INGREDIENT

PETER VANDERWICKEN*

Ask almost anybody in the world of business to characterize Procter & Gamble, and chances are you'll get a familiar answer—it's "a marketing company." The cliché implies that only by puffing them up with great gales of advertising can P&G sell its products in such huge quantities. Now, it certainly is true that P&G is very big in marketing—the nation's No. 1 advertiser, in fact. The $200 million that the company spent on TV in its last fiscal year provided one-tenth of the networks' total revenues. And P&G is certainly very *good* at marketing. A company that ranks No. 1 in the U.S. in laundry detergent (Tide), shampoo (Head and Shoulders), toothpaste (Crest), shortening (Crisco), disposable diapers (Pampers), toilet paper (Charmin), and several other consumer products as well has to be doing some very effective marketing. But to repeat that "marketing company" stereotype is to miss the true secret of Procter & Gamble's success.

That secret, in a word, is thoroughness. Procter & Gamble manages every element of its business with a painstaking precision that most organizations fail to approach. Thoroughness extends to the careful and tenacious recruitment of employees, the development of a much-admired executive corps, the design of manufacturing facilities, and the creation and testing of products. By the time a product gets to the marketing stage, the thorough preparation through all the prior stages has already endowed it with an edge on competitors.

Before Chairman Edward Harness will allow a new product to be put on the market, he insists that its superiority (meaning consumer preference for it) be demonstrated by actual tests. "Some people suggest that product differences in our field are minimal or infinitesimal," he says. "I can't agree. When you find a significant body of women who believe the characteristics of what they want are found in a product—this is the essence of consumerism, giving them what they want."

One of the less obvious benefits of the P&G approach is that it helps employee morale. People who work for P&G believe the products they make and market *are* better. As they see it, they're engaged in something fundamentally worthwhile. The high morale accounts in part for the legendary competitive enthusiasm of the company's salesmen. "They eat,

*Research associate: Lenore Schiff.

SOURCE: Reprinted from the July 1974 issue of *Fortune* Magazine by special permission; © 1974 Time Inc.

sleep, and dream P&G," says a vice president of a supermarket chain who sees a lot of them. A campus radical of the Sixties who went to work for P&G and then quit to run an arts foundation says of the company as he recalls it: "Their integrity and fairness permeate every dimension of what they do."

NOW THEY'RE EATING HYPERBOLIC PARABOLOIDS

The top managers of Procter & Gamble are wise enough to know that perservation of this spiritual vitality is more important than any temporary fluctuations in the operating results. Their ability to take this farsighted view, rather than jerking the company from one course to another in response to breezes in the market, derives in part from the leaders' own longevity. The men who reach the top have usually spent most of their careers at the company. Howard Morgens, who stepped aside for Harness in April, was chief executive for seventeen years. Now chairman of the executive committee, Morgens has thought a lot about what has made P&G successful. "We take the long-term view and work for the long-term future," he says. "Anyone can improve his earnings over two or three years."

Procter & Gamble's thoroughness is most apparent in the development of new products, the lifeblood of any consumer-goods company. P&G spends well over $100 million a year on research. Contrary to the general impression that consumer-goods companies belch forth new products in rapid succession, P&G has introduced only two since 1970. One was Sure, an antiperspirant, and the other was Pringle's, a new kind of potato chip. Not infrequently, the company spends a decade or more perfecting a product before bringing it to market. Work on Pringle's began back in the mid-Fifties.

The development of Pringle's is a classic case of recognizing a need in a consumer market and then painstakingly working away to meet it. Americans gobble up roughly $1 billion worth of potato chips a year, but for the manufacturers, potato chips have always had their problems. They are so fragile that they are rarely shipped more than 200 miles, and even at that distance, a quarter of the chips get broken. They also spoil quickly—they can't remain on the shelf for more than two months. These characteristics have kept potato-chip making a fragmented industry, and nobody had applied much technology to the product since it was invented in 1853.

Aware of these problems because they sold edible oils to the potato-chip industry, P&G executives set out to solve them. Rather than slicing potatoes and frying them in the traditional way, engineers developed a process somewhat akin to papermaking. They dehydrated the potatoes, reconstituted them as a mash, then pressed them for frying into a precise shape that a mathematician would call a hyperbolic paraboloid.

That geometrical form looks like a potato chip, is easy to manufacture, and permits the chips to be stacked neatly on top of one another in a hermetically sealed container that resembles a tennis-ball can. Pringle's stay whole and have a shelf life of at least a year. They are selling regionally in the U.S. at a rate that, if they were distributed nationwide, would make them a $200-million-a-year product.

SHAMPOOING HALF A HEAD

After the lab work has been done on a new product, the division that will manufacture it takes over and finances all further development and testing. In some companies, division managers are reluctant to take on new products because the costs of introduction are heavy and hold down short-term profits. P&G avoids this impediment to innovation in several ways. Its executives reiterate in each annual report that they attach no significance to such matters as quarter-to-quarter wobbles in earnings. They also budget by brand, rather than by division, so that a division manager's record is not marred by the cost of a new introduction.

There is, however, a formidable obstacle to the introduction of a new product: the ironclad requirement that any proposed product has to have a demonstrable margin of superiority over its prospective competitors. P&G reaches a verdict on its own innovations by rigorously testing them against the competition. A development team begins refining the product by trying variations of the basic formula, testing its performance under almost any conceivable condition, and altering its appearance. Eventually, the team gets the product into a few alternative versions that differ only slightly—say in odor or color. Then they start testing variants on hundreds of P&G's own employees.

In the company's Hair Care Evaluation Center, women have half their hair washed with a new shampoo, and half with their regular brand as a control. To analyze detergent performance, technicians in a P&G laboratory wash the laundry of five hundred employees every week. Some tests become a little bizarre. Employees sampling a new toothpaste or mouthwash, for example, enter a laboratory where they breathe through a hole in the wall. A researcher on the other side sniffs their breath to judge the product's effectiveness. A new deodorant is tested similarly, by a professional armpit-sniffer.

If the product passes its tests by employees (who tend to be overly critical, the testers say), P&G presents it to panels of consumers picked at random. In all, P&G queries 250,000 consumers a year (church groups are a favorite target), asking whether this or that product fills their needs and whether they would buy it. To be considered for introduction, the product must win the votes of a majority of consumers in tests against each major competing brand.

The required margin of preference varies from one type of product to another. The company has found, for example, that taste preferences vary greatly, so it is difficult to develop a toothpaste or mouthwash that a panel will favor over competitors by a margin of more than 60 to 40. Accordingly, P&G is satisfied if its entrant is chosen by fifty-five out of a hundred consumers tested.

People's sensitivities to differences in paper products are much less acute. Since the capital investment required to produce paper products is much greater than with many other products, the risks in marketing a newcomer are higher. "If the product is perceived to be superior here," Harness says, "it has to be preferred by a huge amount." For a new toilet paper, the required margin is about 80 to 20. It wasn't just marketing, in other words, that made Charmin No. 1.

A CREATIVE TENSION

P&G is no less thorough when it comes to manufacturing. The company's own engineers design or extensively modify most of the production machinery P&G uses. All employees are encouraged to propose ways to reduce costs, but each proposal is carefully tested before it is adopted. The procedure, Harness explains, is that "you get the plan blessed by the engineering division and get an experimental order to jury-rig the machine to see what the new process does. We run EO's all the time on everything."

The critical process in making detergents, for example, is drying and mixing the chemical ingredients to form granules. That takes place in a stacklike "detergent tower." By successively modifying its oldest tower, built in 1946, P&G has been able to increase the output sixfold. If the company had not modified any of the thirteen towers it now has, it would need a total of 108 towers to achieve current production levels. Similar modifications help improve productivity throughout P&G. Its toilet-tissue winders originally turned at 900 feet a minute; now they wind at twice that speed.

Plant managers are judged in part on their ability to devise new ways to cut costs. The resulting not-so-informal competition among plants serves to create both a competitive spirit within the company and an internal tension that keeps operations lean. When the new paper mill at Mehoopany, Pennsylvania, got into full production in 1969, the costs were well below those at the much older mill in Green Bay, Wisconsin. Since then, the Green Bay managers have modified their machines enough to become competitive in cost with Mehoopany. Because methods have been revised in many ways throughout the company, Harness says, "our costs this year are $100 million lower than a year ago."

THE DIFFERENCE 4 CENTS MADE

And then, of course, there's that famous marketing. Here, too, thoroughness reigns. P&G tests its marketing methods as painstakingly as its products. In some cities with cable TV, one sample commercial goes to homes on one side of a block and another to homes across the street. Researchers will then ask residents whether, and how well, they remember what they saw.

Before a new product is introduced nationwide, P&G tests it in one or more cities that are demographically representative of the nation. The company sets up an initial production line, backs the product with a massive barrage of advertising, and puts it on sale in supermarkets. If a product fails this test, it is normally dropped. But occasionally one gets a second chance.

One product that was not discarded after initial failure went on to become a huge success: Pampers, which now rivals Tide as P&G's best-selling brand. On its first market test, Pampers bombed. The product was priced too high—about 10 cents each, which was more than the cost of buying a cloth diaper and washing it. By simplifying the package, speeding up the assembly lines, and using less costly components, the company gradually got the price down to 6 cents.

As the price dropped, each of three subsequent tests over four years indicated a bigger potential market. So management progressively reduced the profit-margin target and raised the volume target. By the fourth test, the price was right and Pampers took off.

Prior research is supposed to prevent P&G from flopping in its test markets. "My boss said years ago," Harness recalls, "that when you go to test market you should be 90 percent sure. That's our approach." According to one survey, 112 of 204 brands put into test markets in the U.S. in 1971 failed to make it to nationwide distribution. P&G's success ratio has been better, but nowhere near 90 percent. Of sixteen brands test marketed in the last decade, seven failed to win general distribution.

THE MISSING MAGIC

The expansion of a new brand nationwide is reminiscent of a military campaign in its complexity and intensity. Generally, distribution is extended outward from the test markets as production capacity becomes available, until, after six months or a year, the brand is sold throughout the country. P&G may spend $25 million or more promoting a brand in its first year on the market, and the company continues to run tests to discover the least expensive combination of ways to reach potential consumers. Surprisingly, giving out samples door-to-door can be the cheapest method of introducing a new brand, especially if it is delivered with samples of another brand that shares the cost.

In the last ten years, P&G failed in an attempt to extend a brand beyond its test market on three occasions. Hidden Magic, a hair spray, turned out to have no magic at all. Stardust, a dry bleach, failed to convert housewives from the customary liquid. Cinch, a spray household cleaner, just never caught on, and the men at Procter & Gamble still haven't figured out why.

On any brand that flies, P&G expects to recover development and marketing costs and begin earning a profit within three years. Getting into the black, though, is only the beginning of an endless process of trying to hold and expand market share. A typical brand budget provides for a promotion of some kind—a "3 cents off" offer, a coupon, or a premium—about every three months.

Contrary to what might be expected, P&G runs its most attractive promotions not to lure customers when a brand's sales are falling off, but when the demand is highest. Cake mixes sell best before Thanksgiving and Christmas, for example, while soaps and detergents move fastest in the late spring and summer. Promotions are aimed at building market share, and it is easier to increase penetration when the total market is growing. If the product can expand its share then, it may be able to hold some or most of the gain as sales fall off seasonally during the rest of the year.

Similarly, P&G and other manufacturers increase advertising expenditures on their fast-selling brands and reduce them on brands that are doing less well. They figure that a dollar spent advertising a high-volume item will return a greater profit than a dollar spent on a brand with lower volume or a smaller market share.

Daytime television is still the most efficient means of selling soap (and Pampers, too), and Procter owns, produces, and sponsors six long-running TV soap operas, which get the attention of housewives as their predecessors on radio did for almost half a century. Products such as deodorants and hair sprays, which also appeal to working women and to men, are more efficiently advertised on evening TV.

Once a brand is established, P&G changes it in some major or minor way twice a year. The company recently changed the formulation of its dishwasher detergent, Cascade, to prevent the granules from caking. It added a new ingredient to Downy fabric softener to help minimize the buildup of lint-catching static on clothes in a dryer.

There is a lot of show biz in the soap biz, to be sure, and a good many of the changes seem trivial. A supermarket executive laments: "One year they'll add blue dots to a detergent and say, 'new blue improved,' and the next year they'll take them out." Ed Harness, though, claims there's a good deal less straining for superficial novelty than there was a couple of decades ago, when the industry was more flamboyant.

UP AGAINST THE LIFE CYCLE

All the attention P&G gives its existing products represents an effort to cope with an inescapable challenge facing consumer-goods manufacturers. Left unchanged, a packaged product will tend to increase its market share for a few years after it is introduced, hit a peak, and then sink into a decline. Though no one knows for sure, many marketing men believe these product life cycles are becoming shorter. A study by the A. C. Nielsen Co. concludes that 85 percent of all new brands can expect less than three years of success before their market shares start declining rapidly. While manufacturers can try to lengthen the life cycle by launching a new advertising campaign or redesigning a package, they don't always succeed. And when they do succeed, the study says, they revive the brand for only an average of fifteen months before it sinks once again.

Procter & Gamble's strategy of frequent, regular improvements, accompanied by an unceasing barrage of advertising, has in most cases virtually overridden the life cycle. Several P&G products introduced long ago are still very much around. Crisco was first sold back in 1912. Ivory soap made its debut in 1879 and is now the most venerable brand sold in American grocery stores. No established P&G product has died in the last ten years.

This stability pays valuable dividends. P&G sells only forty-nine branded consumer products (plus some industrial bulk chemicals and variations of its domestic brands abroad), and that is a rather small number for a $5-billion company. It means that the average P&G brand sold in the U.S. is in itself a sizable business, permitting many economies of scale. And since the company's established products aren't dying off, the sales and profits contributed by newly introduced brands are net gains for the company's growth.

POISED FOR A LEAP FORWARD

For the last 125 years, Procter & Gamble has been growing at an average rate of 8 percent a year, compounded—one of the most splendid long-run performances in the annals of business. For the last two decades, the company has increased sales, profits, *and dividends* every year without a miss.

Its prospects, moreover, seem pretty bright. After a relatively quiet period of introducing few new products, P&G has seven in test markets, including a fabric softener, a paper towel in a counter-top dispenser, a liquid laundry detergent, and a tampon that the company began developing thirteen years ago. Hopes run high in Cincinnati that the tampon, named Rely, will take a major share of the market from Tampax and Kotex. Demonstrating the new product, P&G executives plunk Rely and Tampax into separate beakers of water to demonstrate their own product's superiority. They are confident enough about the outcome to make an explicit claim on the package: "Rely absorbs twice as much as the tampon you're probably using now."

BUT WILL THOROUGHNESS WORK ANYMORE?

To all appearances, the company has great potential for growth abroad. Right now, foreign business accounts for a quarter of its sales and, owing to the recent price controls in the U.S., a somewhat larger portion of earnings. Recently sales have been growing faster abroad than in the U.S.—about 35 percent a year—but the president of the international division, William Gurganus, says that he expects foreign sales "to remain one-quarter of our total business."

This statement suggests that Gurganus, at least, believes domestic business is poised for a leap forward. The burst of new brands could well keep sales rising briskly for several years. P&G took 119 years to reach its first billion dollars in sales, nine years for its second, five years for its third, three years for its fourth, and little more than a year for its fifth. At the recent rate of growth, sales could more than double by 1980. If history is a guide, profits would keep pace.

Some analysts on Wall Street, however, express serious doubts whether Procter & Gamble can sustain its remarkable pace. One big question concerns the time-consuming process of testing that is a crucial element in the P&G system. As the life cycles of packaged goods grow shorter, manufacturers are compressing the time they spend in developing new products. A new shampoo is introduced about every three months now, for instance, and each new one threatens the market shares of all those on the shelves. Under such conditions, can P&G continue to spend years developing and testing its products? Can P&G still count on thoroughness?

Morgens and Harness, at least, seem unworried about predictions that their company will have to change its ways. Morgens, indeed, maintains that some trends at work in the society favor the Procter & Gamble style. "The development cycle may be longer in the future," he says, "because of the consumer and environmental movements and the red tape of government. It can take the FDA a year and a half to clear a product, and this is after it's ready to go to market. All this benefits a company like ours which does its research well."

17

CARTER HAWLEY HALE
ACQUIRES A TOUCH OF CLASS

ELEANORE CARRUTH

Two powerful forces now emerging will dominate the retailing business in the U.S. for many years to come. One is heightened competition among all sellers of general merchandise as an era of easy growth comes to an end. The other is the pervasive influence of fashion in determining what consumers buy and stores sell. Together these forces are challenging the strategies of the big retailers and reshaping their prospects.

Performances have already begun to diverge. In the past year or two, profit margins of several department-store chains have improved markedly over the previous peak of 1972-73, while those of some others have undergone substantial shrinkage. For the entire field of corporate merchandisers, there has been a thinning of overall margin. This lackluster profit performance reflects the restrained pace of the recovery and the cautious mood of consumers, of course, but it also reflects the new intensity of competition.

In the last two decades, retailing corporations flourished by following customers out to the suburbs and positioning themselves in the shopping centers that sprang up there. In this way the big retailers expanded their market share from around one-fourth of total GAF sales (general merchandise, apparel, furniture) to something approaching one-half today. But in recent years suburban growth has slowed down, along with population growth, and so has construction of new shopping centers. In the years ahead, therefore, the big retailers generally will not be able to grow as fast as before, and those that do will have to rack up their sales gains not just at the expense of smaller stores but at the expense of other big stores too. The battlegrounds of the intensifying struggle are the shopping centers, which now account for about half of all retail sales aside from cars and gasoline.

Department stores, in addition to fighting one another, are feeling heat from the major mass-merchandise chains—Sears, Penney, and Montgomery Ward. Over the past decade the success of the discounters—stores offering minimum service, skimpy

136 SOURCE: Reprinted from the December 1976 issue of *Fortune* Magazine by special permission; © 1976 Time Inc.

selection, and slim markups on large-volume standard lines—has forced the mass-merchandise chains in self-defense to stock and sell more fashion goods. As they continue to move in this direction, they will impinge further on lines carried by the traditional department stores.

"Growing the gross margin"

On another front, department stores are running into brisk competition from large and small specialty shops (i.e., shops that specialize in some categories of merchandise also carried by department stores). A great many independent specialty stores are proving nimble at catering to customers' wants in goods and service. They are proving themselves especially adroit at the fashion game, right on the wavelength of fashion-conscious consumers. Their success has led some experts to speculate that the future of retailing may well lie with them. One consultant, indeed, goes so far as to declare that "the time of the department store is past." A shopping center, after all, can be regarded as a single horizontal department store, with a central mall providing access to separately run shops that are in effect "departments."

Under the new stress of competition, the professional managers now coming to the fore in the large department-store chains put heavy emphasis on "fashion," not only in apparel, but also in furniture, bedding, table linens, and housewares. Fashion is the principal weapon now, both for improving or preserving market share and for getting bigger markups on merchandise—"growing the gross margin," as retailers put it. The "fashion explosion" that FORTUNE talked about nearly a decade ago (October 1967) has gathered force over the years. For great numbers of American consumers these days, especially in the rapidly expanding twenty-five-to-thirty-five age group, fashion is no optional frill, but an integral part of life, a necessary form of self-expression. "If we hadn't traded up we would be wallowing in self-pity right now," says Philip Schlein, president of Macy's California. "The customers have become much more fashion-conscious."

No major retailing corporation is more fully committed to a trading-up strategy than Carter Hawley Hale, the nation's seventh-largest department store chain, with sales of some $1.4 billion this year. That strategy represents a continuation of policies set by Edward Carter thirty years ago when he took charge of the Broadway, a group of three price-promotional stores in Los Angeles, with combined sales of only about $30 million. From the first, Carter determined to aim for, as he puts it, "the broad middle—with a little emphasis to the top." There are no bargain basements in The Broadway stores.

He continued to look upward when he moved into the northern California market via merger and acquisition, aligning The Broadway with quality department stores: Hale Bros., Weinstock's, The Emporium, Capwell's. And a decade ago he decided against any move into discounting at a time when most major store groups were taking a stake in it. Instead, Carter went after high-margin businesses. Starting in 1969, he acquired three well-known specialty stores—Neiman-Marcus, Bergdorf Goodman, and the Canadian chain of Holt, Renfrew.

A HIGH CLIMB FROM THE SLUMS OF RETAILING

A competitor once called Edward Carter "the smartest merchant in town." That was thirty years ago, and in retrospect it appears that he may have been right. From a small and very unpromising base—three stores that one industry observer describes as "the slums of Los Angeles retailing"—Carter built up an impressive company, No. 30 on the FORTUNE list of the largest retailing companies in the U.S.

His first critical management judgment when he took over The Broadway at the age of thirty-four was that Los Angeles was going to sprawl. "I was convinced that people were going to move out to the suburbs and I built the best grid of shopping centers out there," he says.

To manage so many stores, Carter thought up the regional-chain concept, with central management and a single set of buyers. "This was a revolutionary idea at the time," he says. "It took me six months to convince the downtown Broadway store that it could buy even for the Hollywood store, and that was only five miles away."

Storing up a state

Carter moved northward in 1950 by merging with Hale Bros. in San Francisco and Weinstock's, the leading department store in Sacramento. In 1956 he began acquiring stock in Emporium-Capwell, strong in the San Francisco Bay area. It took him fourteen years to complete the acquisition. When it was finally completed in 1970, he had the leading department-store business in the state.

Having pretty well "stored up" California, as he puts it, Carter made a rapid-fire series of acquisitions that put the company on the national map. In 1969 he bought Walden Books, now the nation's largest bookstore chain, and Sunset House, a mailorder chain specializing in gifts and novelty goods. That same year he launched his company into high-fashion, luxury retailing by acquiring Neiman-Marcus. He followed in 1972 with Holt, Renfrew, the leading Canadian purveyor of quality apparel, and Bergdorf Goodman, located on perhaps the best site in the world—at the top of Fifth Avenue's shopping district, just off Central Park.

Shortly after that the corporate name was changed from Broadway-Hale to Carter Hawley Hale. The move prompted one competitor, among a number who resent Carter's self-assurance, to dub the company Ego Inc.

Sinking with a country

Carter did make at least one move that in hindsight looks like a mistake. In 1974 he paid $68 million for a 20.5 percent interest in the House of Fraser Ltd., a British company accounting for fully a quarter of all department-store sales in the United Kingdom. Fraser's fortunes have been sinking with those of the British economy. The stock price has fallen by one-third since the purchase, and meanwhile the cost of the money put into Fraser is chipping at Carter Hawley Hale's earnings and stock price.

A long run in the driver's seat

Carter has ensured that the policies he set for the company over his long tenure as chief executive will be maintained, for his protégé Philip Hawley is also his handpicked successor. Hawley, now fifty-one, became president of the company in 1972. Carter, who reached sixty-five last June, has been gradually turning operations over to Hawley for the past four years, and will probably step down as chief executive officer before long.

Having enjoyed a long run at the top, and the advantage of being able to take the long view, Carter wants Hawley to have the same advantage in shaping the corporation's future. "It's a weakness of American business not to give talented prospects a long run," Carter says. "Men in the driver's seat for only a couple of years have a tendency to devote all their efforts to making just those few years look good."

Unlike many men long at the top in the department-store field, men who were primarily good at selling the merchandise rather than at managing a large business, Carter has always been a professional manager. Hawley is from the same mold. Both men have academic credentials from the University of California and the Harvard Business School, and both climbed high in retailing while still young. At thirty-four Carter was already earning more than $60,000 a year as a merchandise manager with The May Co.-California. Hawley had a remarkably swift rise at The Broadway; within two years of his arrival in 1958 as a buyer of misses sportswear, he became, at thirty-five, merchandise manager for all women's apparel.

By common consent, the personable Hawley is a great "people person," but despite his low-key, easygoing manner, one expert observer of the industry describes him as "aggressive as hell" in his approach to retailing. In today's climate he will have to be in order to achieve his stated objective—"to build our sales and margins through a fashion approach."

The difference the mix makes

The use of fashion as a counter in the retailing game starts with creating an "in" fashion image. The object is to lure customers to look and then to sample, for once in the store they will often go on to the more prosaic goods that actually make up the greater part of the merchandise. Some research by J.C. Penney indicates that customers don't really shop around much from store to store—they tend to make most of their purchases at the store they head for first. To become such a "headquarters" store today, the savvy retailer aims to put enough sparklers in the "fashion-merchandise" group—clothing, furniture, and household items—to give the store a fashion aura that carries over to the more basic stock.

The luxury specialty stores fit right in with Carter Hawley Hale's strategy for the department-store side of the business. With their relatively small sales base, the specialty stores will account for only a modest share of the company's overall growth, but they mean a lot in the effort to refashion the image of the department stores. While the company does more department-store volume than any of its competitors in both the San Francisco and the Los Angeles areas, its stores on the whole do not have the trendy fashionable stamp that Hawley wants. The acquisition of Neiman-Marcus,

Bergdorf Goodman, and Holt, Renfrew, Hawley says, "removed any doubt about what kind of company we want to be. They validated the point that as a management we believe in better, more fashion-oriented merchandise." The new cachet markedly improves access to better "resources," suppliers who might otherwise hesitate about selling to Carter Hawley Hale's middle-income stores for fear of downgrading their own fashion image.

The benefits to the bottom line of changing the "merchandise mix" can be, as they say in the trade, fabulous. Joseph Ellis, retail analyst for Goldman, Sachs, has calculated that a well-executed fashion strategy can—on paper, anyway—improve a store's gross margin by as much as four percentage points over a period of time. The difference lies in the mix—two-thirds of sales in the bigger-markup "fashion" fields, with only one-third in the price-sensitive "commodity" groups, instead of the other way around. Gross margins can be increased even more if the departments are selling large amounts of highly fashionable goods with very high markups.

There are great risks in the fashion game, however. Among fashion goods, some will always be more fashionable than others, and if the merchant is either too far ahead of or too far behind his customers' fancy, he will have to do too much marking down. Fashion, moreover, involves a lot of built-in obsolescence. Today's hit often becomes tomorrow's markdown.

The process of upgrading a store to more fashionable levels takes time. "Building the fashion image can't be done on a crash basis," Hawley stresses. "Stores have reputations, like people, and you don't want to go so fast that you leave your customers behind." Upgrading starts with a small fashion "umbrella," a layer of more fashionable merchandise than the store featured before. As sales of the tonier goods catch on, the store builds another layer above them but "chops one off at the lower end," as Hawley puts it. Some customers will be trading one layer for another, and the store will be trading some old customers for new ones.

The upgrading process can eat a lot of profits while it's under way. Inevitably, a store trying to upgrade will have to mark down a lot of fashion merchandise that fails to move. Consider the case of The Emporium, Carter Hawley Hale's major stake in the San Francisco area. The chain has thrived by selling good, solid, unrisky merchandise. Its markdown percentage was one of the lowest in the country, and its return on investment quite high. But The Emporium is now taking a new fashion-merchandising direction, and there have been setbacks in the form of substantial markdowns on new goods introduced to help build a more dashing image. Management is convinced that the strategy is necessary—the chain was obviously headed for competitive trouble. A newly aggressive Macy's California has moved vigorously along the fashion path, spending millions to refurbish old stores and open new ones. Competition is also intensifying in Capwell's territory, San Francisco and its eastern suburbs, where Bullock's, a division of Federated Department Stores, has begun making a determined push.

Trouble right across the way

Competitive pressures are most acute, perhaps, in The Broadway's own home territory. There, the fashion leadership is held by Bullock's and by J.W. Robinson's, the

Associated Dry Goods entry. The May Co.-California, The Broadway's closest
competitor in both sales volume and image, continues to slug it out for market share.
Even with formidable rivals to contend with, The Broadway has slightly increased its
share to the southern California five-county market (to 4.5 percent of general-
merchandise sales in 1975). But the continuing increase in sales has been bought at
some cost to earnings. The Broadway has taken markdowns on fashion goods more
rapidly in the last year or two. The chain has also incurred some additional costs for
new buyers, as well as the staff for four new merchandising divisions to help search
out the right fashion wares.

Some industry observers doubt whether the fashion approach will work for The
Broadway. As one of the puts it, "What kind of luck is The Broadway going to have
upgrading with Saks and I. Magnin right across the way out there in the mall?" The
Broadway has a special upgrading problem, moreover—its very bigness. With sales of
some $500 million, it is one of the largest department-store groups in the world, and
with forty-two stores it surely has by far the greatest number of individual units. "How
do you upgrade so many stores?" asks Maggie Gilliam, retailing analyst of First
Boston Corp. "When you are as big as The Broadway, it's hard."

Lost attunement

Problems of scale will confront quite a few large department-store groups in the
competitive struggles ahead. In some respects, the traditional department store
should be well suited to an age of fashion, being attuned to the preferences of local
customers. It should have an edge over the giant chains such as Sears and Penney,
which are committed to centralized buying and are set up—in the words of Richard
Hauser, president of The Broadway —"to extend last year's successes." But as the
department store itself becomes a chain, with centralized buying, it can lose agility
and attunement to local markets. Says analyst Gilliam, referring to some of the
department-store chains: "Their problems are just beginning."

Carter Hawley Hale is trying in various ways to deal with the local-attunement
problem. The Broadway, for example, is experimenting with ways of testing new
fashions before buying them in volume, and is speeding up computer installations to
get point-of-sale information by location from all the stores. The chain split its
advertising into four separate geographical areas some time ago, for the sake of
closer adaptation to customers, and now plans to increase the number to eight.
Management is also encouraging individual stores to participate more in the buying
process, by signaling headquarters about local customer preferences and, in some
cases, making buying decisions.

Out but not down

As seems reasonable in fashion-minded times, Carter Hawley Hale expects its
specialty-store business to grow faster than the department stores between now and
1980. Neiman-Marcus, though, will account for all of the extra growth, since projections
for Bergdorf Goodman are modest and for Holt, Renfrew about average. Carter sees

no need for any new acquisitions in the luxury field, where the company vies with Saks for the No. 1 ranking. "We already have the best," he says.

Even the best, however, can run into difficulties when they go for growth. The growth on the specialty-store side of the company is expected to come from both broadening of lines and multiplication of units. There are fashion problems along both these courses.

The specialty stores vehemently deny any suggestion that they are "trading down." As one merchandise vice president explains, "No one needs us if we don't stay different." But they are, at the very least, reaching out, carrying a wider range of merchandise than they used to. Says Bergdorf's new president, Ira Neimark: "We are merely adding to the store now the life-style of a group that we didn't have before while keeping what we already have." Still, it will take refined skill to preserve the tone of the luxury specialty store while becoming less special.

Most store names have only local or regional reach and are not candidates for distant colonization. One of the exceptions in the specialty-store field (like Macy's and Bloomingdale's among department stores) is Neiman-Marcus, the Dallas-based company built by the imaginative promotion of merchandising genius Stanley Marcus. Under his direction, the store his parents founded in 1907 acquired national celebrity. He made the arrival of its lavish Christmas catalogue an annually awaited mail event in homes across the country.

From four Texas stores and sales of $70 million in 1968, Neiman's has expanded to eight stores, the new ones all outside Texas, and sales are now up to $185 million. The division expects to double sales in four years, in part by opening at least another half dozen stores.

Scanning the field for stars

But the multiplication of units presents problems. Taste and customs vary from place to place. Cruisewear sells before the Christmas holidays in Chicago, after the holidays in St. Louis. Dresses sell very well in Bergdorf's Fifth Avenue store, not so well in its White Plains outpost. It takes time lo learn the nuances that make a store go in a new location.

It also takes trained people to maintain the service standards and ambience of the original. The luxury store tries to be not only elegant but also pleasant, with high standards of service and, ideally, a personal relationship between salespeople and customers. The service is every bit as important as the merchandise. But there are limits to the number of trained people that Neiman-Marcus, for instance, can send in from other stores. So it will be a difficult trick to maintain the special Neiman-Marcus character with a great proliferation of units. Says Stanley Marcus, who is now an executive vice president of Carter Hawley Hale: "The jury is still out on that. It all comes back to management, whether or not it realizes what you have to do day after day to keep being unique."

The execution of a corporate strategy centered around fashion demands a special competence in the management of store groups, and the premium for star talent today comes high indeed. Heads of major store divisions now commonly command upwards of $200,000, plus plenty of perks, a package that sometimes exceeds the compensation of the company's chief executive officer. (Carter and Hawley, however, draw the top salaries in their corporation—$250,000 and $220,000 respectively.) "The salary numbers are pure economics," says Jerome Buff, retailing analyst for Smith Barney, Harris Upham. "Top management is betting these men can transmit their intuitive merchandising skills through an organization of people, and that is very difficult."

All the big companies are scanning the field for stars. In the past year or so, executives have switched companies in numbers remarkable even for retailing, an industry noted for job jumping. For Carter Hawley Hale the hiring pace has been almost frenetic, because with the great expansion of the company the management ranks had become thin near the top. Besides filling gaps at headquarters—adding high executives for real estate and finance—Hawley has gone outside the company to hire away half a dozen store heads and many more second-layer merchandisers from competitors— Bloomingdale's, Bullock's, The May Co., B. Altman, Saks.

Hawley believes his company will derive a major advantage in the competitive wars ahead from its firm commitment to operating autonomy for store heads. "We give our people a big ball park to play in," he says. "We want every decision in the company to be made as close to the customer as possible." And he appears to mean it. Angelo Arena, who came from Bullock's and is now chief executive of Neiman-Marcus, reports that "I can make any decision I want to make, just as if it were my own business." A new manager recruited from Federated Department Stores observes: "Carter Hawley Hale practices what Federated preaches." This managerial style was established by Edward Carter, and he takes pride in it. "Rarely have I ordered someone to do something," he says. "I would always rather have the heads of divisions wondering what I think than worrying about what I say."

It is a delicate management problem to sustain the entrepreneurial drive so essential in today's fashion-retailing climate and at the same time develop the kind of professional management a growing billion-dollar corporation requires. "There is an intuitive, or green-thumb, element in this business," says Hawley, "and the problem is both how to develop that intuition in people and how to school those who have it without causing them to lose the touch."

Where the art of management comes in

Corporate headquarters, which Carter from the first split away from store management, has two responsibilities. One is to handle long-range financial planning and such nonmerchandising tasks as locating new store sites, financing real estate, and setting up budgeting procedures and controls. The other is to challenge the divisions through the planning and monitoring process, which is steadily becoming more refined. "This is where the art of management comes into play," says Hawley, "knowing when to challenge, and how to do it."

Top management meets with the store groups twice a year to review operating budgets and on a monthly basis to discuss various matters from marketing and personnel development to expense reduction and advertising. Store heads also meet to swap stories and strategies. They come prepared from having studied one another's performance figures, which are kept in the corporation's internal books, red for expense items (e.g., advertising) and black for merchandising data (e.g., sales by segments of the business). "Our job is to make the divisions aware of successes and mistakes," says Hawley.

One of the most important advantages the company obtained with all the new acquisitions is cross-fertilization, as people from different store groups exchange ideas and experiences. Capwell's and Weinstock's swap strategies on hot items (right now, for example, goose-down jackets). Bergdorf Goodman asks Neiman-Marcus for advice on improving its gift department and The Broadway consults with Neiman's on catalogue techniques. Neiman-Marcus in turn has learned something about the foundation business from The Broadway, and all the stores are benefiting from The Broadway's successful way with junior lines.

Carter and Hawley both feel very confident that they have set their strategy on the right track and built the organization to keep moving in the trying period ahead. It will be a period almost made to order for their approach, they believe. They expect sales to reach $2 billion by early 1981, without any acquisitions. Major acquisitions, however, are very much part of the future plan. Hawley is emphatic about that. "It is terribly important to us to acquire, to broaden our geographical base in the department-store field, and we are not going to quit."

He is still unhappy about losing out on a big acquisition last year—a merger with Rich's, an Atlanta-based department-store group with annual sales of some $340 million. The prize went instead to Federated, the nation's largest department-store group. The Federal Trade Commission will ultimately have to pass judgement on the merger, of course.

A lack of chips

The obstacle for Carter Hawley Hale, Carter acknowledges, was the price of his company's stock, then and now selling at only about half its 1972 high. The stock's multiple, once among the highest in the department-store field, is now only middling. Store mergers are generally based on an exchange of stock. "We just didn't have the chips to play with," Carter says. "We would have had to dilute the stock too much."

A source of softness in the stock has been meager growth in earnings per share over the past couple of years, a lot less than that of several competitors. This performance reflects, among other things, the intense competition in California and profit penalties from upgrading.

Both Carter and Hawley, however, take an expansive view of the future. They are counting on the stores to grow at a rate of 11 percent annually between now and 1981, outperforming not only the rest of the retail field but the growth in real personal income as well. Long before that, Hawley predicts, internal sales growth will move the company's ranking up a couple of notches, from seventh to fourth or fifth place among department-store chains. With the profit penalties of the fashion transition behind, margins are expected to increase from the current 3.3 percent of sales to almost 4

percent over the five years. That would open up the possibility of new acquisitions if
opportunity knocks.

In the longer view, too, the expectations run high. Whatever problems the company may have, it certainly does not lack for optimism at the top. "I have told Phil Hawley," Carter says matter-of-factly, "that if he does not build this company into a $5-billion business in his term I'll be very disappointed. I've given him a big canvas to paint on." Hawley does not expressly commit himself to that specific goal, but he apparently expects to meet the challenge. "There are no limits on where this company can go," he said not long ago.

"To the No. 1 spot?" he was asked.

"Why not?"

18

THE UNLIMITED LIMITED

In 1961 Leslie Wexner, then 24, dropped out of law school and went to work for his father's modestly successful women's wear store in Columbus, Ohio. But Harry Wexner and his son soon had a falling-out.

What led to a parting of the ways was young Leslie's insistence that the store ought to drop coats and dresses because it wasn't making money on them. Leslie felt there was no point tying up money in merchandise that couldn't return a profit. Harry countered that you needed a full line in order to attract traffic.

"Dad finally said to me, 'If you've got a better idea, go do it,'" Leslie says. And Leslie did.

In August 1963 he opened a small, 2,000-square-foot store in Columbus' Kingsdale shopping center. It featured young women's sportswear. Wexner describes the stock as "Bass Weejun, pleated skirt stuff"—a kind of female Brooks Brothers. He called the store "The Limited"—limited merchandise, that is.

"I figured that if I grossed $100,000 the first year I could survive," he says. The Limited grossed $162,000. Leslie Wexner began to think big: "I opened a second store and figured that I'd go right on up to building a $1-million-a-year business around Columbus."

Thirteen years later, Leslie Wexner, 40, is worth $50 million.

His first store alone grosses about $1 million a year. The Limited Stores, of which he is chairman, president and chief executive officer, has 188 stores in over 60 metropolitan areas, with more stores planned for this year. Its sales, only $8.7 million in 1972, totaled $117 million in the fiscal year ended last July 31—a 68% compounded growth rate. Profits, $8.3 million last year, have grown even faster than sales in the same period, despite the fact that the chain was opening dozens of new stores and despite the 1974-75 recession.

The company's stock, of which Wexner owns 38%, has soared from a little over $1 in 1975 to $18 today, 18 times earnings.

Petrie Stores (FORBES, *Dec. 1, 1976*), led by 75-year-old retailing genius Milton

Petrie, is the "grandfather" of a group of stores specializing in young women's

SOURCE: Reprinted by permission of *Forbes* Magazine from the November 1977 issue.

clothing. The Limited is a specialty within a specialty. The Limited, like Petrie, sells to the 18-to-35-year-old "junior" woman, but its prices are sharply higher than Petrie's; it is reaching for a more affluent customer. A top or blouse might sell for $8 at a Petrie store, while a more classic version of the same item might go for $18 to $20 at a Limited store. The Limited aims at a relatively small group; its typical customer is a young working woman—an executive secretary, for example. Such clothes-conscious people usually care more about fashion than price.

"The Limited is an excellent example of concentrated marketing using a detailed positioning strategy," says Professor Roger Blackwell, a consumer behavior specialist at Ohio State University business school. "While a lot of women don't go to The Limited, the woman who's 25, making $10,000 to $12,000 a year and 'fashion-oriented' hardly needs to go anyplace else." The Limited capitalizes on this basic fact about consumer behavior: People like to shop where people like themselves—or whom they would like to be like—shop.

The Limited's stores are almost all located in regional shopping malls in large metropolitan areas, and their atmosphere can best be described as tastefully "with-it." The newest stores feature plenty of shiny chrome and mirrors to make the store appear even more chockfull of merchandise than it is. Low volume but definitely upbeat rock music adds an extra dash of excitement. The stylish neon sign in the front costs $3,000. Isn't a Limited store quite expensive overall to put together? "The purpose of a business isn't to minimize expenses; it's to make money," retorts David Kollat, Limited's vice president-marketing, a former Ohio State marketing professor.

The merchandise, which is abundantly displayed throughout the store, is very strongly oriented toward a single "look." For instance, Wexner and his associates decided months ago that the hacking jacket—a tailored, wool riding jacket—would be big this fall with The Limited's sort of customer. Accordingly, the store walls feature dozens of color-coordinated hacking jacket outfits—wool skirts and jackets, with plaid shirts and sweaters underneath. Wexner and Kollat stress that a great deal of thought goes into deciding what "the look" will be. Once they decide, the stores go all the way with it. There is no confusing the customer with a little bit of one look, a little bit of another.

The stores' saleswomen, all of them young and dressed in Limited-style clothes, help reinforce the image. "The Limited expects more of its employees than any of the three other retail chains I've ever worked for," says Laura Cartwright, 22, assistant manager at one of The Limited's Columbus stores (after checking a FORBES reporter's identification to make sure he wasn't there to steal secrets about the store's design and operations). "They expect you to understand fashion, say by reading the big fashion magazines," she says. Employees are motivated by a strong company promote-from-within policy that has turned saleswomen into district managers within three years' time.

Some outsiders are clearly nervous about the company's prospects. Says one analyst who admires the company's management and marketing skills: "I've found that anyone who runs that fast can get hit blind-sided. You try to keep your eyes open, but there are so many vagaries. I've seen too many [examples of this], and they've looked too good."

Sizzling Specialists

The Limited may be a red-hot company, but it's only one of a number of rapidly growing junior women's specialty retailers. The major junior specialty chains (*see table*), many of which had sales of less than $5 million ten years ago, have been growing and earning at rates that put even the best department store chains to shame (although one of the first big chains, Lerner Shops, has slowed down since it became a part of Rapid-American Corp.).

The junior chains follow similar formulas in their operations, although their markets are slightly different. "The customer that we all cater to is the 15-to-35-year-old woman," says Andrew Saul, executive vice president of Brooks Fashions. "She spends a hell of a lot of her money on clothing." Petrie, Miller-Whol and Charming Shoppes serve the lower-income, price-conscious end of the junior market. Casual Corner (a subsidiary of U.S. Shoe), Limited, Winkelman and Paul Harris sell to the more sophisticated, fashion-oriented young woman; Brooks Fashions and Ups'n'Downs are in between.

All of the chains have centralized buying and pricing. Store managers can concentrate on cleanliness, maintenance and personnel in their small (typically 3,000 to 8,000 square feet) stores. As the chains grow, substantial cost efficiencies result from having a few central buyers for large numbers of stores. While a single large department store might have 50 buyers and buyers' assistants for all of its departments, the specialty chains can rely on 15 to 20 or so buyers to select huge quantities of merchandise in the narrow array of items they stock. "Limited or Casual Corner, in the lines they carry, might carry 50 times the merchandise that a Bloomingdale's does," says Noel Davidson, president of Casual Corner.

The narrow selection also makes for high inventory turnover, typically five to ten times per year versus a department store annual turnover rate of four to seven turns.

Not having something for everybody, of course, decreases traffic in the store. But thanks to huge suburban shopping malls, the specialty stores can rely on the promotion-oriented department stores to draw their customers into their vicinity. Since the department stores bring in the traffic, they get lower rentals per square foot than the specialty stores. But the specialty stores have virtually no advertising costs.

But competition is building among the junior specialty chains. "Like any business," warns Casual Corner's Davidson, "we could have our shakeout."

Company	Fiscal 1977 Sales (millions)	Pretax Margins	5-Year Compounded Growth		Earnings Per Share	P/E Ratio	Stock Price Appreciation (1/1/77-10/26/77)
			Return on Equity	Sales			
The Limited	$117.0	13.7%	74%	68%	77%	16	43%
Brooks Fashion	62.5	14.9	46	42	54	8	36
Miller-Wohl	105.3	17.1	50	−3	D−P	11	55
Ups 'n' Downs	45.4	5.9	14	35	18	11	8
Petrie Stores	333.6	21.3	32	20	26	13	−2
Winkelman Stores	76.4	6.3	15	9	29	5	3
Paul Harris	46.2	7.5	27	24	5	7	5
Charming Shoppes	48.2	12.0	28	22	26	9	68

D−P: Deficit to Profit.

Replies Wexner: "We're very sensitive to the velocity that we're traveling. The point is, we review the decision [about how fast to grow]. We're vulnerable, but we're very introspective. The thing I would fear most is the attitude that we're invulnerable."

In order to keep a sharp lookout for trouble spots, the company has instituted a system of financial controls, backed by NCR point-of-sale terminals which permit headquarters in Columbus to monitor inventory levels in every item. Vice President-Finance Robert Morosky calls the system one of "offensive and flexible" controls rather than defensive ones. What are "offensive" controls? Here's the idea: Many department stores plan their markups and markdowns in advance, and stick to their budgets rigidly. By contrast, The Limited aggressively marks down items that aren't selling, even if it is exceeding its initial markdown targets, to move the items out of the store so that fresh—and hopefully hot—merchandise can be moved in. It's hardly a unique strategy, but it's one that helps keep the fashion flops to a minimum, and the stores' "look" exciting and current.

Meanwhile, Wexner has a long-range plan. Once the potential for The Limited's current market appears to be diminishing, Wexner hopes to diversify into related areas of specialty retailing—say, by acquiring or starting a chain of men's stores or stores aimed at the 30-to-50-year-old woman. Although Wexner says he has had "very satisfying" offers from bigger retailers to buy The Limited, he's not interested in selling.

So what happened to Harry Wexner's clothing store, the one Leslie quit? Harry and his wife Bella closed their store in 1965, and joined The Limited, where Harry served as chairman until his death in 1975. Bella is now the corporation's secretary. As for the intrafamily dispute over how to run a clothing store—well, that's all forgiven now. □

19

COSMETICS BUSINESS

Treatment lines, men's toiletries and cosmetics aimed at the black market are changing the complexion of cosmetics areas in leading department and specialty stores across the country.

In fact, the growth of these three areas is expected to help generate a 15 to 25 percent increase in retail cosmetics sales this year.

Top merchants believe the increased emphasis and substantial growth of new products and markets in the cosmetics area will result in additional major dollar and footage allocations by department and specialty stores who are zeroing in on this hot classification.

The most recent statistics show that drug stores now control 35.5 percent of total cosmetics dollars at retail. The fact that many of the more exclusive fragrance, cosmetics and treatment lines are not sold through drug stores appears to represent an opportunity for department and specialty stores to cut into the drug store share of the market, and to bolster their own burgeoning business.

What is happening in New York City is indicative of what is going on around the country. Nearly all the prestigious Fifth Avenue department and specialty stores over the past year have remodeled the main floor of their flagships in order to expand space for cosmetics and to bring the area to up-front locations. In addition, such volume retailers as Macy's and Ohrbach's have also made increased commitments to the cosmetics areas.

Bloomingdale's too is talking about renovating its main floor cosmetics area next year, when more space is sure to be added.

Branch stores, too, are giving increasing attention and space to cosmetics.

Mary Jane Robinson, cosmetics market representative for Associated Dry Goods Co., points out, "Originally management misjudged the square foot requirements of cosmetics areas in the branches. Insufficient space was allocated during the building of many suburban stores, and as a result additional space and fixturing is being allocated this hot category."

150

SOURCE: Reprinted from *Stores* Magazine; ° National Retail Merchants Association, July 1977.

While cosmetics merchandisers have long been advocating adding more footage to their departments to recognize such growth areas as cosmetic/treatment lines, two other expanding areas are causing even tighter restrictions on newly enlarged departments.

These areas are cosmetics for black women and men's toiletries, both of which have shown increases of at least 15 percent over last year's figures. To gain more space on the main floor, some divisionals have set up outposts for men's toiletries within men's wear areas, easing already cramped quarters.

Several leading department stores—such as J.L. Hudson in Detroit and Foley's in Houston—have completely separated men's toiletries from the cosmetics division, thereby creating highly specialized buying and easing the main floor footage crunch, so critical in flagship and urban locations.

Some New York stores are trying to empahsize the treatment lines carried in their long counters by opening mini-salons off the selling floor for skin and/or hair treatments. While this may appear to be a needless and costly expense, the opening of a treatment area requires little more space than a dressing room and one or two treatment chairs.

Macy's Herald Square store, for example, has put in a two-stall, three-chair operation on its main floor, run by Adrien Arpel, to accommodate up to 50 clients on a busy Saturday. With roughly 60 percent of the average $30 bill going for merchandise, mini-salons are definitely business ventures with strong service overtones.

However growing cosmetic/treatment emphasis by the consumer has not adversely affected fragrance business, according to Bloomingdale's fragrance buyer, Pat Ennis, who claims "Our fragrance business has been super." She notes too that Lancome's treatment line is an extremely good-selling product line. Trade sources report Bloomingdale's will be opening a Lancome treatment salon later this year.

Evidently the urban locations provide a different market for cosmetics areas than suburban locations. Ennis identifies city dwellers as more sophisticated and interested in stronger, long lasting versions of fragrances, such as perfumes. Suburbanites are still looking for eau de toilettes and colognes. Recognition of the different tastes has boosted Bloomingdale's fragrance business, which is currently 20 percent ahead of last year's figures.

Treatments offer a new wrinkle to management, pointing up a need for more trained and productive sales people to be on the floor to educate the new customer.

ADG's Robinson notes that getting and keeping high caliber sales help has been a continual struggle in the cosmetics area even though commissions add perks to lackluster retail salaries. "The turnover in sales help is devastating," she adds. "In suburban stores, many store managers are turning to part-time sales help—mothers with children in school, for instance, who can work from 11 to 2—as alternatives to finding competent full-time help."

With more and more treatments being introduced by both cosmetic and fragrance manufacturers, the personnel problem will grow more critical. Clinique, for example, which has one of the most efficient and profitable treatment lines in the country, says its beauty consultants are a key part of the treatment program.

Extensive training programs, ranging from one to three days, are offered to new consultants, and all year-round, Clinique training supervisors travel throughout the country offering established beauty consultants advanced classes.

A Clinique spokeswoman notes "the gal behind the counter is our most important link to the consumer." Not only does the company emphasize the principles of the system, which is based on computer evaluation of the customer's skin type, but the basic philosophy that Clinique representatives don't sell items, they sell a treatment concept.

Computers are being used by another cosmetics firm entering the treatments field. A new one, Helena Rubenstein's Skin Life Beautyscope computer is designed to be handled directly by the consumer, who punches buttons on the 8-foot long counter computer. The system has been tested in Abraham & Straus and in Bloomingdale's. An index number system registers the appropriate products in response to customer's answers. The program will debut in New York this month; in Los Angeles in late

COSMETICS SALES BY OUTLET

General Merchandise group	33.2%
(including Department Stores)	23.4%
Food Stores	23.0%
Apparel & Accessory Stores	2.8%
Drug & Proprietary Stores	35.5%
Mail Order and Direct Sales	2.0%
Other Retail Outlets	3.5%

Source: Fairchild Fact File

COSMETICS AT-A-GLANCE

Net sales change	+14.0%
Cumulative Markon	39.9%
Markdowns	1.5%
Gross Margin	38.6%
Stock Turns	2.8×
% Contribution to Merchandising Division	56.3%
Sales per square foot	$202.50

*1975 MOR figures reported by NRMA member department stores with volume over $1 million.

August or early September. Management expects 1,000 computers to be in department and specialty stores by the end of 1978.

Cosmetics for black women—Fashion Fair, Flori Roberts and Barbara Waldon are the top selling lines—provided many urban store locations with a profitable new cosmetics area. Requiring no special equipment, black cosmetics business offers retailers a market which has been estimated to be between $500 million and $750 million. While Revlon and other major brands have been researching and adding makeup and cosmetic/treatment products for black women, it is the smaller firms, with traditional black lines, that are the fastest growing.

Statistically black women have used far less lipstick and eye makeup than other women. Many cosmetics buyers believe this is because the correct shades were not available and that the introduction of more lines and choices will help.

J.L. Hudson has received good customer response to black cosmetics since the introduction of specialized lines. Still an untapped market, black cosmetics are expected to show strong and steady growth in both school-age and older working women brackets.

The opportunities offered by such new target markets, along with the proliferation of products, are causing market analysts to project strong growth figures over the next three years.

A study by Arthur D. Little, Inc., published earlier this year, estimates retail sales of cosmetics and toiletries will climb from 1976 figures of $7.2 billion to $10.9 billion by 1981.

The fastest rise, 10.6 percent, is projected for cosmetics—which includes skin and eye make-up, women's fragrances, skin treatment products and hand preparations. Presently cosmetics account for more than one-third of total industry sales.

Toiletries, which includes hair preparations, oral products, men's toiletries and fragrances, external personal deodorants, toilet soaps and miscellaneous oil, lotions and powder for the body, are expected to grow at a slower rate of 7.7 percent per year.

"Though mass markets are more profitable," according to Natalia Mitchum, co-director of the Little survey, "most cosmetics companies cannot afford to ignore the fact that department store distribution contributes to an aura of glamour which is essential to a market image of quality."

The survey also reports that fragrances and other cosmetics are being found in apparel department outposts and are not confined to a single store location. Marketing techniques are persuading consumers to match fragrances to specific activities and times of day rather than to the traditional personality approach, and therefore increase their use.

The marketing positioning of fragrances like Charlie (targeted at the career woman) and Aviance (definitely for the housewife, according to TV commercials) is a sign of increasing creativity and sophistication on the part of cosmetics firms, Mitchum claims.

"Fire and Ice," the business biography of Charles Revson, founder of Revlon, points up dramatically the cosmetics business of today—where a former ITT executive, Michel C. Bergerac, a suave, French-born international businessman, now heads the same company—has changed drastically.

And Samuel Kalish, who had been with Revlon for many years and left about a year ago, warns in a *Business Week* article: "Now that the great personalities with their mystique are gone, there is a real danger of the pendulum swinging too far the other way. We're not an insurance company or a bank."

But the trend is that the cosmetics business—like it or not—is being controlled by bottom-line watchers. Revlon and Avon are the leading women's cosmetics producers, with Revlon controlling the biggest segment of the consumer market in foundations, powders and blushers (13.9 percent), lipsticks (16.6 percent) and nail products (33 percent). Avon holds the largest share of market in face treatments (16.3 percent) and fragrances (29.8 percent).

Presently the cosmetics industry is in the midst of a marketing changeover. The biggest challenge is getting distribution. The cosmetics industry, which operates on a 40 percent discount, and provides a whole slew of marketing assists, such as promotional monies for sales staff incentives, co-op advertising, sampling and salaries or contributions toward salaries for demonstrators, is one of the heaviest investors in advertising and promotion. According to IRS data for 1972, the cosmetics and toiletries industry spends approximately 8.79 percent of sales for advertising. The overall ratio for all manufacturing is 1.25 percent of sales invested in advertising. And approximately twice as much is spent on network and spot TV than for print media.

Since increasing numbers of women are entering the work force, media experts note that different marketing strategies have been tried. An example cited by the Arthur D. Little study is that working women tend to buy cosmetics in stores rather than at home—resulting in a decline in door-to-door sales. And cosmetics companies are shifting their advertising expenditures to prime time TV to reach the woman who works during the day.

In-store promotions have been changing as well. Most buyers surveyed say that the gift-with-purchase or purchase-with-purchase, especially when using a product far afield from cosmetics, such as a T-shirt or umbrella, puts cosmetics into the accessories business.

One Midwestern department store buyer suggests another possible promotional approach: samples with purchase. "That's really gift-with-purchase, but it would be a sample of a complementing or new cosmetics product. I feel that would stimulate future business."

Another cosmetics buyer for a leading West Coast chain, suggests there should be more reduced price sales on cosmetics. "Currently, some firms offer half price sales during January on basic products. What would be really important to our department would be special offers on some of the $45 creams and treatment products, annually or semi-annually. It would be fantastic to see really prestige items go on the block. So many women want to try them, but $45 is a lot of money for something that may not be what she really wants."

Retailers are looking forward to lots of changes in the cosmetics business—ones occasioned by a changing manufacturing industry, a changing consumer and a changing product mix. Fortunately most of the changes seem to be ones that will bring higher profits to stores and more glowing faces to customers.

20

CAN DOWNTOWN LIVE WITH MORE PARKING AND EASY TRANSPORTATION?

ROBERT B. MELTON

Trying to revitalize retail business in the central downtown district today without adequate parking plus accessible and reasonable public transportation is like trying to do business from an empty wagon.

The heart of any retail business is drawing customers to the store and without these two essential elements—parking or easy transportation for non car owners—all other revitalization efforts will wither.

In addition, the parking must not be too expensive to draw private vehicle users to the retail business district downtown. Studies show that people are far more likely to change destination than mode of travel when entry to certain areas of cities is restricted or made more expensive.

According to Daniel Brand, an associate professor of City and Regional Planning at Harvard University, 'overconsumption' of the auto has led to high parking fees and traffic congestion in the central business district of most major cities and therefore the CBDs are now an overwhelming market for public transportation.

Unfortunately, Brand notes, most public transportation systems have an under-consumption problem. The result is that the user-fees do not cover the cost of the service even in the well-developed systems.

Development of newer modes of public transportation systems have been under study for a number of years, but most of the developments have not proved to be economical or impovements over previous types, Brand adds. He cites the personal rapid transit experiments in both Morgantown, W. Va. and from the Dallas-Fort Worth airport.

Taking a different view of whether public mass transportation would benefit the revitalization of a central downtown business district is Lawrence A. Alexander, Downtown Research and Development Center, New York City.

Alexander suggests the prime users of any city's public transportation system are people going to and from work in the CBD. "Only about 5 to 10 percent—being generous, 15 percent—of the riders of public transit systems to the downtown area are primarily retail shoppers," Alexander says.

155

SOURCE: Reprinted from *Stores* Magazine; ⓒ National Retail Merchants Association, March 1977.

Alexander also believes that in coming years this percentage of shoppers will decrease. He doubts that more parking will stem the tide of the deterioration of many downtown business districts.

"That's not the number one problem," he suggests, "but only one of many in any revitalization. The merchants also have to realize that they must share the cost burden in some manner, because land costs are rising just like everything else."

Still another factor in downtown parking versus that of parking lots for suburban malls and centers is that the customer in the suburbs will park further away from the store and cheerfully walk to the store, says Norene Martin, executive vice president of the National Parking Association. Thus, the visual psychology is very important when selecting the site for new parking facilities in a downtown revitalization.

Martin states that only about "a half-dozen cities today have any really good public transit systems, so therefore, the automobile and consequently parking is a major factor in any re-developing project." Even in the cities undergoing re-development, she continues, the cost of public transit is so out-of-sight that it is not a viable alternate for drawing more shoppers to the inner city.

Yet, David Stahl, executive vice president of the Urban Land Institute, argues that the initial reaction to the new subway system in Washington, D.C., has been a very positive one on retail business downtown. He agrees, however, that most public transportation systems are not economical and must be supported either via higher taxes by downtown businesses or high fares which work against the principle of drawing more retail customers to the downtown shopping areas.

One solution to downtown parking has been the growth of multilevel garages to make better use of the land area downtown. But this also has its drawbacks, according to the officials of the ULI, because of the "personal safety element in going in and out of the garages."

Although there have been disappointments in some of the previous efforts to establish new public transportation technology and lower costs of moving people to and fro from CBDs, the Urban Mass Transportation Administration of the Federal Government has continued to investigate ways of alleviating the congested traffic situation in downtown areas of some of the nation's cities.

Two of the most recent fundings from the UMTA have dealt with Chicago and Brooklyn, N.Y., on pedestrian and transit malls.

Basically both of these recently funded projects will restrict auto traffic in a specified zone while assuring a more convenient, comfortable and safer environment for public transportation to the downtown shopping areas. The projects are joint ventures of the private interests, principally retail operations, and public government agencies, in planning and designs.

In the case of the State Street Mall in Chicago, the U.S. Secretary of Transportation said, "We believe it will not only provide adequate movement patterns for vehicular traffic and improved movement of public transit, but will also provide a pleasant pedestrian environment and stimulate retail activity."

The Chicago project will encompass nine blocks in the Loop between Wacker Drive and Congress Parkway and will be known as the State Street Mall.

In Brooklyn, the mall project will be along Fulton Street, where the borough's principal department stores are located.

Last fall, the federal transportation agency also approved $600 million for a rapid transit system in Detroit, but with the requirement that the private sector invest an equal amount in development along any proposed routes. Local officials had been pushing for a 20-mile heavy rail system, some of which would be constructed as a subway. At press time no final decision has been made.

Another major development in the Motor City is the Renaissance Center on a section of the city's riverfront. The redevelopment is being financed entirely by private capital and has as its center a new 70-story hotel circled by four 30-story office buildings, to be linked by covered walkways. Some critics, however, say the new Center will do little to help revitalize the central downtown business district, some distance away.

Edmund C. Bacon, a designer of downtown development from Philadelphia, suggests "redevelopment of downtown projects does not necessarily mean revitalization will follow." He expresses doubt that the Renaissance Center will be helpful to the retail business in the city's central business district.

Participating in a symposium on a new approach in design for reviving downtown, Romaldo Girurgola, a designer, described the redevelopment and revitalization project he had worked on in the downtown area of Seattle.

First, he explained, was to develop a "magnet" to draw people to the area. This was achieved by rebuilding the old Times Square building there, which had been a terminal, into a museum, and the station, for a monorail system. From the building people will be able to go into any of the three department stores in any kind of weather, using the walkways.

By using a monorail transit system, he continued, the city was able to establish a public transportation system without disrupting the automotive traffic patterns to any great extent. There was some re-routing of traffic at the central point near the Times Square building for the mall and walkways.

The monorail, subway and other rail systems are not the only means that many of the nation's cities are considering to update their public transportation to revitalize CBD.

Transportation experts such as Arthur Saltzman, who has studied the needs of urban poor, says the emergence of gypsy taxis and illegal jitneys in many of the major cities of the nation is evidence of increasing need of public transportation.

He notes, however, that legal resurgence of jitney operations will require changes in restrictive legislation which was enacted in the late 1910's in many municipalities at the insistence of more conventional transportation operators.

The alternative transportation methods, which Saltzman labels "para-transit," are dial-a-ride, subscription buses, minicars, jitneys and taxi pools, which do not require development of sophisticated equipment or construction of new roadways.

Admittedly, most of these transportation methods have been studied as a means of providing the car-less poor in the inner cities transit to places of employment. The side effect is one of also enabling them to travel to the CBD for the purposes of shopping. However, public transportation and parking is essential not only for customers to the inner city retail business but also for the employees of those businesses.

Here another conflict arises with the employees of the downtown business. Many live outside the city and commute by car, thus overburdening the existing facilities. The result is to discourage customers from trying to use the parking facilities.

21

NEW SENSE OF MOVEMENT TO
OLD BALTIMORE SHOPPING AREAS

ROBERT KANIGEL

Honking horns and the stench of exhaust fumes are gone from Lexington Street these days. A two-block, 600-foot stretch of this heavily-trod shopping street has been blocked off to cars, paved with brick, stocked with comfortable benches, and planted with bushes and trees. And most affected retailers—some initially had doubts—seem won over by the transformation.

"We were concerned at first," concedes Joel Winegarden, president of Brager-Gutman, the promotional department store that ranks as the mall's second largest retailer. "But the absence of cars had done us no harm. In fact, business has picked up each year since the mall opened in 1974."

Says Alice Ivey, vice-president for marketing and sales promotion at Stewart's, alone among downtown department stores with an entrance on Lexington Mall: "It's worked out well for us. It's drawn excitement to downtown—and I think that's just what we need."

Not all retailers share her enthusiasm. Dee Gabiger, for instance, manager of a Forsythe shoe store, has heard complaints—particularly from older customers—about rowdy youths who hang out on the mall. And while she generally views the $850,000 project as an improvement, she doesn't think it's brought the sales jump merchants had anticipated.

But the mall has, without question, achieved one of its prime goals—that of attracting some of the thousand of Charles Center office workers to the retail district for lunchtime shopping.

One survey by the architectural firm of RTKL Associates found a jump in pedestrian traffic, compared to pre-mall days, "which can be safely estimated to range between 25 and 50 percent." And that came, the report stressed, at no expense to pedestrian activity on adjacent streets.

"We're seeing faces we never saw before," says Martyn Grieg, general manager of the downtown branch of Lann's, a women's and children's apparel store with two suburban branches. "We're definitely beginning to lure the Charles Center crowd."

The mall's completion in June 1974 moved Lann's to remodel its main store extensively. "We went about it so as to tie into the mall," explains Grieg. "For **159**

SOURCE: Reprinted from *Stores* Magazine; ° National Retail Merchants Association, March 1977.

example, the mall uses bronze-finished lamp posts. So we used a similar finish for our show windows." The $100,000 job extended Lann's street-level selling floor—one of three—by eliminating a U-shaped area out front, thus picking up 20 percent extra selling space. Also part of the new look were painting and wallpapering, new carpeting, fitting rooms, and lighting.

The mall's success in drawing better-heeled office workers, coupled with the remodeling, has yielded what Grieg terms "a healthy increase in volume." The store has also begun stocking better lines of merchandise.

A mile northeast of Lann's stands what is said to be one of the first inner city pedestrian malls outside the confines of a central business district—Oldtown Mall. Back in the 1880s, Oldtown was the city's principal shopping area. By the 1920s, however, it had begun its long downward slide. And by the 1960s, it had become an almost exclusively black slum, one with the lowest average family income in the city.

Yet its Gay Street shopping area retained hints of health; the city viewed it as worth saving. So as part of a $17 million urban renewal project, Gay Street—clogged with auto traffic, visually polluted by tawdry, overhanging signs, and beset by increased vacancies—became Oldtown Mall.

$2.4 million worth of public amenities were pumped into the once-fading commercial street. Benches, kiosks, fountains, a public stage for outdoor concerts, modern light standards and street furniture were installed along the bricked-in promenade. Two hundred metered off-street parking spaces were provided, with another 150 planned.

Merchants, who were involved from the very beginning, were required to remodel their street frontages—the idea being to exploit the 19th century flavor of the two and three-story row structures that lined the street. All told, merchants have invested $1.7 million in their men's shops, drug stores, record shops, bakeries, liquor outlets, and shoe stores.

Arnold Swain, owner of Braun's Jeweler's, has renovated his 3,000 square foot store to the tune of $35,000. Since completion of the mall in mid-1976, he's noticed a decided upturn in pedestrian traffic—though during construction itself business dropped.

"At this point," he says, "I've got a very positive outlook." He points out that the average driver won't go to the trouble of parking just to check out an alluring window display, whereas a pedestrian can duck in on impulse.

Hard hit by the 1968 riots that rocked Baltimore, Oldtown hardly yet ranks as a thriving retail area. But even now only five of the mall's 84 properties remain vacant. Almost 40 percent of the businesses are black-owned.

Many Oldtown retailers lament the loss of housing torn down for urban renewal. While a modernistic 187-unit high rise has already been occupied, and other housing is under construction nearby, much surrounding land once a source of Gay Street patronage remains vacant. When it fills up, merchants agree, business will rebound.

"So far," say Ellis Rosen, manager of Seif's Corner, a men's shop located in Oldtown since 1892, "the mall hasn't meant anything good or anything bad" in terms of business volume. But its psychological impact has been great.

"For years this area had a bad reputation," he explains. "But now things are changing." And his store's elaborate renovation, spurred by the mall's construction, has garnered him a steady stream of thank-yous from appreciative customers.

Pedestrian malls are no panacea to the ills besetting urban areas. But coupled with spruced up storefronts, brightened interiors, and vigorous promotion, they do create excitement—and a sense of movement. And they offer a setting free from the roar and smell and hazards of vehicular traffic.

Which to judge from the RTKL survey of Lexington Mall, shoppers appreciate. Asked what they viewed as the mall's most desirable features, "freedom from traffic" came out at the very top of the list, cited by 91 percent of those questioned. 85 percent said they favored an extension of the mall, and 77 percent said they wanted to see other streets similarly converted.

"It used to be," says Martyn Grieg of Lann's, "that shoppers would come down here, get whatever they'd come to get, and hurry off. Now they linger. They bring their children. In good weather, they eat lunch on the mall. And they stay to shop some more. Yes, for us it's been a real blessing."

COMMERCIAL REVITALIZATION

In most big cities, it's not just downtowns that are hurting.

Neighborhood shopping areas, bypassed by the big push to suburbia, have witnessed physical deterioration, static or declining sales, and rising vacancies. But now in Baltimore, such areas are starting to get some help.

"Commercial Revitalization" is what this city-sponsored frontal attack on the problems facing older retail districts, is called. Here, merchants get in on the act from the beginning, working with city-paid architects and planners to pump new life into their neighborhoods—and their businesses.

New sidewalks, street plantings, off-street parking lots, and covered arcades are among the city-furnished payoffs when merchants agree to bring their storefronts up to specified architectural standards.

The financial fuel for the program flows from bond issues approved by Baltimore voters in 1974 and 1976. One provides a total of $4 million for public amenities in commercial districts. Another makes $3 million available to aid merchants in bringing their properties up to snuff. Both bond issues mature in 20 years, with a relatively low interest rate of 7 percent.

Part of the problem facing these older areas, explains Herman Katkow, director of the Mayor's Advisory Committee on Small Business, is that banks have made loans to inner city businesses only reluctantly. And when they have, they've demanded five, three, sometimes as little as two-year pay-back terms. In the Baltimore program, merchants benefit both from city investment in their neighborhoods and the attractive loan terms made available.

One of first areas to get in on the program was South Baltimore—a mostly white, blue-collar neighborhood just south of the city's massive Inner Harbor redevelopment area and adjacent to its Federal Hill historic district. Here, some 200 businesses of all kinds, most housed in narrow row structures, were clustered on two main streets around a nineteenth century public market.

The area was stable compared to some other Baltimore shopping areas, although vacant storefronts were beginning to appear. The attitude of most merchants was, as one puts it, "skeptical and cynical." For years they'd been ignored by the city, explains Katkow, who had functioned as a kind of ombudsman to the merchants. They'd watched the neighborhood deteriorate around them. "The prevailing attitude was one of disbelief that this new program would ever amount to anything more than words."

Yet now, according to Irwin DuBois, vice-president of Sherry's Shoes and president of the South Baltimore Businessmen's Association, "the mood has changed considerably. I myself am very high on the area." With the help of city architects and designers, the neighborhood is due a "period look." Merchants get up to two years—a city urban renewal ordinance makes it law—to replace corrugated metal fronts, restore boarded up windows, install shutters, and pull down overhanging signs. Already 60 businesses, according to project coordinator Paul Gilbert of the city's Housing and Community Development agency, have completed or begun work. Loans have ranged from $3,000 all the way up to $250,000.

Though the program can't reach into a neighborhood unless its business community supports it, a few merchants invariably resist compliance, notes Herman Katkow.

One variety store owner, he recalls, "vowed never to spend a nickel." When Katkow—himself a former women's wear retailer—reminded him he'd be in violation of the law, the man swore he'd take it to the Supreme Court. Katkow gently pointed out that legal fees alone would far exceed the modest cost of renovations. The merchant relented. Now, according to Katkow, he's one of the program's biggest boosters.

South Baltimore businessman Alvin Cherry, owner of Delly's Card and Gift Shop, is likewise enthusiastic about the program. After $30,000 worth of renovation, Cherry reports: "There's no doubt about it. Business has increased. And there's not a day that goes by when I don't get a good word from a customer."

Irwin DuBois notes that he and his fellow merchants are "beginning to see new faces around here. And some of us are beginning to stock higher-priced lines of merchandise."

And the best is yet to come. As Paul Gilbert sees it, the old neighborhood bears a surprising, if superficial, resemblance to suburban shopping malls—where two department stores at either end build trade for smaller shops in the middle.

In South Baltimore, the two key shopping streets are linked by Cross Street and its long, narrow public market. Capitalizing on this geographical quirk, the city—with the backing of the merchants—has committed $300,000 to a sidewalk-widening along Cross Street, making it into a semi-mall. Benches, bollards, plantings, and distinctive paving bricks will thus help tie together the two elements of the H-shaped district.

On Cross Street, rents hover around $150 a month for a 15-foot frontage, compared to $250 on adjacent blocks. Gilbert foresees rent hikes there, and concedes that might drive out some marginal businesses. But as the natural outgrowth of a healthier business climate, he admits he'd like nothing better than to see rents rise.

Initially greeted with skepticism among hard-bitten urban retailers, Baltimore's commercial revitalization program has already won acceptance in four neighborhoods, with eight more in the works. Other areas, according to Herman Katkow, are clamoring to get on board.

Meanwhile, back in South Baltimore, a private developer lured by the neighborhood's enhanced prospects has announced his own $2 million, bank-financed commercial rehabilitation venture—one that takes Washington, D.C.'s vibrant Georgetown, no less, as its model.

PART FOUR
DISCUSSION QUESTIONS

1. Why do you think Procter & Gamble has had such a successful marketing program over the years?

2. What changes in retailing has Carter Hawley Hale pioneered?

3. What are the contributing factors to Leslie Wexner's wealth?

4. What changes are occurring in the marketing of cosmetics?

5. What changes in parking and mass transit are likely to affect downtown shoppers in coming years?

6. What might attract shoppers back to the downtown areas?

PART V

FINANCING THE ENTERPRISE

The cost of money—whether borrowing or lending it—has an ever-changing effect on all businesses. The cost of that money must withstand bureaucratic edicts from all phases of government almost on a daily basis, thereby making the job of money management an extremely difficult one.

The two sources for funding enterprises, equity or debt, require businessmen to be increasingly aware of the changes that take place and to know what decisions to make as conditions change.

As a method of controlling inflation, regulatory agencies change the price paid for money through movement of the prime rate. Stock prices on all the exchanges are affected by numerous conditions—some real, some psychological. All these factors have to be taken into consideration by the business person when analyzing appropriate sources of funds.

Not to be forgotten is the insurance industry, which affects the cost of operating many types of businesses. As is evident by the recent publicity received by various professions, insurance costs can greatly hamper the flexibility desired in operating a business.

22

COPING WITH A TUMBLING DOLLAR

SANFORD ROSE

All that loose talk about a fall in the value of the dollar has obscured one relevant fact: namely, that the dollar has actually been rising rather than falling. It has depreciated, to be sure, against two strong currencies, the deutsche mark and the yen, but it has gained ground vis-à-vis many others. Measured against forty-six leading currencies, weighted according to their importance to U.S. trade (and together they account for about 90 percent of it), the dollar has appreciated by almost 2 percent in the first eight months of the year.

It is just as well, however, that the subject has been broached. Though the dollar may be holding up well for now, our foreign-trade balance has fallen off a cliff, tumbling from a surplus of $11 billion in 1975 to a deficit that may reach $26 billion this year. So far, foreign holders of all those surplus dollars have been quite content to reinvest them in the U.S.—hence the dollar's strength. But such capital flows can reverse course even more quickly and remorselessly than the tides of foreign trade. Many high officials in Washington, whatever they say in public, are deeply worried that the dollar may be on the verge of taking a dive.

At a more fundamental, policy level, it is clear that the public at large, and many public officials, aren't at all sure what such a turn of events might mean for the U.S. economy. They are not yet at home in the world of floating exchange rates—witness the confusion in Washington last summer when Treasury Secretary Michael Blumenthal apparently tried to "talk" the dollar down against the D-mark and yen, and Arthur Burns, chairman of the Federal Reserve, tried to bolster it. Sundered from the solid pillars of Bretton Woods, opinions about currency questions, like currencies themselves, have tended to fluctuate.

HOW VICIOUS IS THAT CIRCLE?

The devaluations of the dollar in 1971 and 1973 were generally acclaimed—with our goods more competitively priced, we could at last compete with the Germans and Japanese. Since then, however, there have been a number of other currency **167**

SOURCE: Reprinted from the October 1977 issue of *Fortune* Magazine by special permission; © 1977 Time, Inc.

depreciations that have appeared not to work. The Italian lira, for example, declined steadily with no apparent beneficial effect until just a few months ago, when it began stabilizing.

A theory, somewhat debased in the descent from its various economic authors to the daily press, describes the sequence of events in such depreciations as a "vicious circle." This doctrine holds that the fall of a currency stimulates the domestic economy but also sets off an inflationary spiral that eventually causes a further depreciation of the currency. Since some economists fear that the "vicious circle" may even apply to the U.S., it is worth examining what exactly would happen if the dollar does drop.

HOLES IN THE CONVENTIONAL WISDOM

To put it most charitably, the commonly held opinion—that a fall in the dollar would stimulate the U.S. economy—is somewhat imprecise. In both the short and medium term, anywhere from six to eighteen months, a serious dollar depreciation would be depressive, not stimulative. The most obvious and immediate effect of a depreciation is that the dollar loses some of its purchasing power. As that happens, consumers typically cut back on their spending. This will tend to hold down rather than increase the growth rate or real G.N.P. That is what happened after the first dollar depreciation in 1971. And it probably happened again after the second depreciation of 1973.

Whether the impact of any prospective dollar depreciation is truly inflationary, apart from the short-term effect, is a somewhat more complex question. The prices of imports do rise, but not by the full amount of the depreciation. This is especially so in the case of the U.S. Anxious to preserve their share of the world's largest market, foreign exporters would almost certainly shave their domestic profit margins in order to lessen the rise in their dollar prices. If the dollar depreciated by 5 percent, import prices might rise by something like 3 to 3.5 percent. Such an increase would translate into anywhere from a .2 percent to a .3 percent rise in G.N.P. deflator, the most comprehensive measure of price changes in the economy.

Dollar depreciation would bring down the prices of U.S. exports in foreign currencies, thereby giving exporters competitive adavantage. Instead of taking the whole price advantage, however, the exporters would probably raise their dollar prices a bit, in order to improve their profit margins; that would, of course, affect their domestic customers. Given a 5 percent fall in the foreign-currency price of computers, U.S. computer manufacturers might decide to raise their domestic price, by, say 2 percent, knowing that the foreign-currency price would still be lower than it had been before the depreciation. Finally, the prices of goods that compete with imports—shoes, cars, clothing, for example—would also go up as consumers gradually shifted their purchases from higher-priced imports to temporarily lower-priced domestic substitutes.

NIGGARDLY ESCALATORS

This catalogue of inflationary effects sounds fairly formidable, but unless the rise in prices leads directly to a speedup in wage increases, an inflationary spiral is unlikely to take off. Wages in the U.S. tend to respond very sluggishly to changes in the price level, in part because the overwhelming majority of workers are not unionized. Even those who are unionized have cost-of-living escalators that, despite some recent improvements, are still downright niggardly in comparison with those won by European labor unions.

In the final analysis, however, whether a depreciation sets off an inflationary spiral that will lead to a second depreciation depends on the behavior of the monetary authorities. Keynesians and monetarists agree on this point.

As the fall in the value of the dollar pushes up the domestic price level, the real value of consumers' liquid holdings—e.g., bank balances—declines. To shore up those liquid assets, consumers buy less and, if necessary, sell off a portion of their fixed-income securities, which pushes down bond prices and therefore pushes up interest rates. If the Federal Reserve tries to offset these effects by increasing the growth rate of the money supply, it will aggravate inflation and defeat the purpose of the depreciation, which is to reduce spending on imports as well as to cut down on the consumption of domestically produced goods in order to free resources for potential overseas sale. That's where the vicious circle comes in. In Italy and elsewhere, the monetary authorities, to avoid short-term pain, have generally nullified the currency depreciation by inflating the money supply.

THE FED MUST KEEP ITS COOL

On the other hand, if the Fed clings to its pre-existing monetary stance, the fall in effective demand will obviously cause some prices to decline or, more likely, to rise at slower rates than they otherwise would have. Inevitably, however, some businesses will respond to a fall in demand by reducing output rather than prices, thus increasing excess capacity and unemployment.

Though the Fed would naturally like to prevent this, it must hold itself in check. If the Fed keeps its cool, the decline in spending will be comparatively short-lived. As unemployment lowers real income, consumers will once again become satisfied with the relationship between their banks balances and the now-shrunken level of their earnings. They will therefore stop squirreling away cash. Meanwhile, spurred by an increase in overseas sales owing to lower foreign-currency prices, U.S. employment will increase, and the depressive stage of the depreciation will give way to the stimulative phase.

But will the price reductions that inevitably occur during the depressive phase offset the initial price increases? Most economists are highly dubious. There are certain circumstances, however, in which the inflationary impacts of depreciation could turn out to be quite ephemeral. A declining dollar will unquestionably improve the trade balance. The combined effects of the 1971 and 1973 depreciations eventually contributed to that $11-billion surplus in the 1975 trade account. Future depreciations may not prove so successful, but they will strengthen the balance in manufactured goods, especially if other countries' economies start growing more rapidly than that of the U.S., which was the pattern in the Sixties and early Seventies.

It must be emphasized that no one expects the U.S. to run a trade surplus—at least not in the near future. Heavy imports of high-priced oil could keep the overall trade balance in the red for some years. But most of the dollars that go to pay for oil imports are never converted into other currencies and thus do not cross the foreign exchanges to help depress the value of the dollar. The oil exporters simply invest the bulk of their dollar proceeds in short-term U.S. securities. In effect, we are bartering Treasury bills for oil.

Given the understanding that the oil deficit does not threaten the value of the dollar, speculators could respond to a sharp improvement in the manufactured-goods balance by moving back into dollars. The value of the dollar would then rise, reducing the prices of imports and helping to reverse the inflationary impacts of the previous depreciation.

Once the manufactured-goods balance showed substantial improvement, Congress and the President would be in a politically favorable position to take long-overdue actions of a decidedly anti-inflationary nature. They could, for example, begin scrapping some of the import quotas we have been steadily accumulating.

SUBSIDIZING THE UNPRODUCTIVE

When exchange rates are free to float, the folly of retaining quotas becomes obvious. If the U.S. suddenly removed all import quotas, the volume of imports would increase, but the value of the dollar would then fall, eventually stimulating U.S. exports. Although the elimination of quota protection would adversely affect certain industries, total U.S. real income would ultimately rise by a relatively substantial amount.

The reason is that quotas stimulate investment in import-competing industries, which are generally the most backward in the economy. By discouraging imports, quotas also keep the exchange rate artificially high, pinching off export sales and thus investment in the export industries. Since these industries are the most productive in the country, quotas subsidize the least competitive sectors of the economy at the expense of the most competitive. So the elimination of quotas would in time raise productivity substantially and thus lower prices—by much more, in fact, than a 5 percent depreciation would raise them.

No one doubts that the U.S. can cut the value of the dollar through unilateral action, either by talking it down, which is not especially recommended, or by letting in more imports, which *is* heartily recommended. What people are concerned about at this juncture is whether market forces over which we have only limited control will drive the dollar down in the near future—and by some fairly sizable amount.

The answer to that question depends, in the first place, on what causes exchange rates to move. This remains something of a puzzle and is the subject of a dispute between monetarist and Keynesian economists. Monetarist theory focuses on relative rates of money growth, holding that if our monetary growth rate exceeds the rise in U.S. real income by more than foreign monetary expansion exceeds the rise in foreign incomes, the dollar will depreciate in the long run vis-à-vis the currencies of the rest of the world.

When the central bank pumps out an excessive amount of money, dollar prices rise and consumers respond by buying more lower-priced foreign goods and services than they used to. In turn, overseas consumers cut back on their purchases of U.S.

goods by switching to cheaper domestic products. The result is an increase in the supply of and a reduction in the demand for dollars, which precipitates a fall in the exchange rate. According to the monetarist view, therefore, the fate of the dollar lies entirely in our own hands. If the rate of growth of money is carefully controlled, the dollar will not depreciate. Many monetarists are now worried about the outlook for the dollar; they point to the flight of some capital into other currencies in recent months as evidence of excessive money creation here.

The Keynesians argue that exchange-rate movements depend on changes in real income and prices that are not necessarily related to the behavior of the money supply. A strand of Keynesian analysis emphasizes some special structural factors that could work to depress the value of the dollar whenever the U.S. economy grows at the same rate as the rest of the industrial world. Currently our economy is growing at a faster rate, which exacerbates the problem.

GROWTH IS A TWO-EDGED SWORD

The nub of the argument, originally advanced in 1969 by Hendrik Houthakker, a professor of economics at Harvard, and Stephen Magee, now a professor of finance at the University of Texas, is that if all economies grow at the same rate, U.S. exports will rise more slowly than U.S. imports. This, they say, is because world demand for the kinds of goods we export—e.g., grain and airplanes—is simply less sensitive to changes in income than is our demand for the kinds of goods we buy abroad. By contrast, Japan is one of several countries that are in the opposite position. For example, each 1 percent rise in world income increases U.S. exports by about 1 percent, but increases Japanese exports by approximately 3.5 percent. When our G.N.P. rises 1 percent, our imports go up by 1.5 percent. But when Japan's G.N.P. rises 1 percent, its imports grow by only 1.2 percent.

The reasons for this U.S. predicament have never been spelled out in detail. It may simply be that American businessmen, preoccupied with our huge domestic market, are poor international salesmen, whereas foreign businessmen have made much more conscious attempts to gear the mix of their exports to income-sensitive products and to concentrate their marketing efforts on countries that have an above-average potential for income growth.

If the Houthakker-Magee findings are still valid, the U.S. faces a painful choice. We can slow our rate of growth and preserve the external value of the dollar. Or we can grow at a rate comparable with or faster than the rest of the world and depreciate more or less continuously unless capital inflows offset our mushrooming trade deficit.

TROUBLE IN MANUFACTURES

Many high officials in government are genuinely worried about the Houthakker-Magee effect. Their forecasters tell them that for the foreseeable future the U.S. economy is expected to continue growing at least as rapidly as, if not more rapidly than, most of the rest of the world. Evidence of the consequences of this surge in U.S. growth turns up in some depressing forecasts that a number of officials are trying to keep under wraps. First, the 1978 trade deficit is expected to be at least $2 billion higher than this year's $26-billion deficit. Even more important, our surplus on manufactured goods, which excludes oil transactions, is expected to continue falling, from a vigorous $12.5 billion last year to an anemic $1.6 billion in 1978.

During the first quarter of 1978, when our manufactured-goods surplus is expected to bottom out at only $100 million, speculators might begin deserting the dollar en masse, unless capital inflows showed surprising strength. If speculators flee the dollar, it would almost certainly begin depreciating—and not merely in relation to the D-mark and the yen.

The future may not be all that bleak, however. There does seem to be a practically inexhaustible foreign demand for U.S. assets, so capital infusions could indeed stabilize the dollar, perhaps for an indefinite period. And growth rates in other countries could speed up dramatically and quite suddenly, belying the careful projections of government bureaucrats. If neither of these events occurs, however, the dollar, which seems to be in no danger of slipping during the balance of 1977, could come under considerable pressure by early to mid-1978. If the dollar should cave in under this pressure, the effect on the U.S. economy would still be minuscule unless the monetary authorities panic.

23

CHECKLESS BANKING
IS BOUND TO COME

SANFORD ROSE

During the last year or so, assessments of the future of consumer electronic funds transfer have abruptly shifted from unrestrained optimism to equally unrestrained pessimism. Just a short while ago, it was being widely predicted that we would soon become a nation of plastic-card junkies hooked on a group of machines that would satisfy most of our financial needs without ever requiring us to set foot in a bank. More recently, such notions have given way to a spate of downbeat pronouncements, culminating in contentions that the country does not need and possibly cannot afford a nationwide EFT system. As *Business Week* put in in April, EFT "may never arrive at all."

Neither the Pollyannish nor the Cassandran view bears much relationship to reality. The nation needs a consumer EFT system, and it will eventually get one. But the pace of advance will be slower than previously thought, and the ultimate configuration of the system is at present almost impossible to predict. It is clear that many banks and thrift institutions which plunged into ill-conceived EFT experiments a few years ago will soon be dropping out. Some will get back into the business after rethinking their strategies, and they will be joined by other institutions that have profited from the mistakes of their forefunners.

In cooperation with retailers, the Federal Reserve, and Congress, these financial institutions will ultimately create an EFT system that will offer a variety of important benefits. It will save the consumer time. It will provide him with twenty-four-hour access to his money. It will give him a greater choice among competing banks and savings and loans than he now has, as well as protection from the theft and unauthorized use of checks. Perhaps most important, as EFT matures, people will be able to borrow money on more favorable terms. The cost of consumer credit will either fall absolutely or rise much more slowly than it otherwise would have.

THE BANKS HOLD THE LINE

A fully developed EFT system will contribute to a more efficient allocation of the nation's resources. Those who argue that we may not need EFT fail to grasp its **173**

SOURCE: Reprinted from the June 1977 issue of *Fortune* Magazine by special permission.
ᶜ 1977 Time Inc.

ultimate significance. An understanding of the contribution EFT will eventually make to society has been slow in coming. In the late Sixties, EFT was thought to be essential primarily because the paper-based national payments mechanism was in danger of breaking down.

According to John Benton, executive director of the National Commission on Electronic Fund Transfers, a body created by Congress in 1974 to study the development of EFT systems: "The Federal Reserve, the American Bankers Association, and a number of other groups thought that we would have to convert from paper to electronics in order to substitute an inflation-hedged, machine-intensive clearance system for one that was labor-intensive and relatively unprotected from the effects of inflation."

To paraphrase Mark Twain, reports of the imminent demise of the paper-based system proved to be premature. Through the creative application of technology, the banks have been able to hold down the cost of check processing, inflation notwithstanding. According to the Chase Manhattan Bank, the direct backroom cost of processing a check approximates 5 cents, about the same as it cost a few years ago. By contrast, the minimum cost of handling an electronic deposit or withdrawal runs close to 40 cents. Superficially, it would seem that, at the moment, paper holds a decisive edge over electronics.

Such a comparison is dangerously misleading, however, since it ignores, among other things, the amount of time the consumer must spend cashing a check. If a man earns $20,000 a year, every minute eliminated from the working day costs either him or his employer 18 cents. Suppose that such an employee decides to write a check on a Friday in order to obtain funds for the weekend. After writing the check, he presumably would take it to the bank. According to bank-industry statistics, he would spend an average of six minutes waiting in the teller's line to cash his check. Without counting the time involved getting to and from the bank, the cost of this little expedition amounts to $1.08.

IT'S EASIER IN NEBRASKA

But suppose that this transaction could be deferred until the following day. In a few states—Nebraska, for example—there are point-of-sale-terminals (POS's) located in neighborhood supermarkets that are on-line to a bank's central file and therefore capable of electronically authorizing cash withdrawals. So while he is doing the family's Saturday grocery shopping, the consumer can also withdraw the funds needed for the rest of his weekend. It will probably cost the bank at least 40 cents more to process this electronic communication than it would a paper check. Considered from society's viewpoint, however, the electronic transaction is the cheaper of the two—i.e., the one that is least wasteful of scarce human resources.

At this stage of its development, consumer EFT can be likened to a positive "externality"—a benefit that many could enjoy but only a few would be required to pay for. Obviously, neither the consumer nor his employer would volunteer to help defray the bank's EFT costs, even though both benefit from the existence of the point-of-sale terminal. It is the bank that must pay for this facility, and, being a profit-making organization, the bank has to evaluate EFT on the basis of hard-nosed economics.

The economics of full-service EFT—i.e., of providing consumers with the ability to

make deposits and withdrawals from remote terminals—are, quite frankly, rather unattractive at the present time. Such a service requires an enormous initial fixed cost, and most banks already have large investments in check-processing equipment. If a bank could get enough people to use terminals—displacing at least 10 to 15 percent of its existing check volume—it could perhaps sell off a significant quantity of its standard equipment. Failing this, the bank would end up having to amortize two check-clearance systems at the same time—one paper based and the other electronic. The charge to earnings would simply prove too great to support.

Full-service EFT thus poses a troublesome conundrum. Given sufficient volume, the per-transaction cost of electronic banking can be lowered substantially. But before it could reach the required volume, a bank might suffer an unacceptable and perhaps even fatal drain on its earnings.

THE STOCKHOLDER IS NERVOUS

Still, there are a few banks—e.g., the U.S. National Bank of Omaha—that are currently providing full-service EFT, usually justifying their investment on the grounds of "positioning themselves for the future." This oft-repeated but rather nebulous phrase is beginning to make the stockholder highly nervous. Eventually, the stockholder will insist on solid projections of black ink. Unless a bank can demonstrate the capacity to earn perhaps 15 percent after taxes on its EFT investment within a three- to five-year period, management will be placed under great pressure to abandon full-service EFT.

It is possible, then, that the EFT movement will be forced to take a step backward before it can again propel itself forward. There is no doubt that EFT will eventually spread across the nation, but it must progress at an economically sustainable pace. Banks and savings and loans will first have to educate consumers to use plastic debit cards in unfamiliar machines. These cards identify the bearer as an account holder.

In analyzing fifteen case studies of financial institutions that are heavily involved in EFT, the National Commission on Electronic Fund Transfers reached two basic conclusions: first, most of the institutions that are currently making a profit on EFT owe their success in part to the enormous sums they spend on advertising and marketing—between 37 and 43 percent of their annual operating budgets. And second, most of those that are either in the black or on the verge of becoming profitable do not provide full-service EFT. Instead, they sell electronic check-guarantee or check-authorization services.

DUNNED BY THE COPS

If the way to begin making money in the EFT business is to sell check-guarantee services, then financial institutions must go where the bulk of the checks are being cashed. Specifically, they must approach the retailer and spend a great deal of effort trying to understand and serve his needs. The logical place to begin is in the major supermarkets. They cash an estimated $90 billion in checks each year, equal to nearly 80 percent of their sales volume. Some of these checks are obviously duds; however, it would be a major tactical error to try selling EFT services to supermarkets solely on the basis of reducing their check losses. In the Sixties, supermakets found their check losses rather worrisome, but they have since reduced them dramatically, to a mere .04 or .05 percent of the dollar volume of checks cashed.

While the electronics industry was sitting idly by, the supermarkets began taking aggressive action in the early Seventies to curb loss rates. They issued their own check-cashing cards, installed courtesy booths to validate checks, and began accumulating cumbersome but adequate Rolodex files of bad risks.

What's more, they adopted what can only be described as Draconian collection techniques. Says Lawrence Russell, a principal at McKinsey & Co., Inc., who specializes in the food industry: "Since the supermarket manager's income is crucially affected by the amount of his check losses, he will go to almost any lengths to reduce them. I know of cases where store managers have employed uniformed policemen to knock on doors in order to coerce bad-check passers into paying up. Some managers even go to the extent of writing threatening letters on court stationery."

COLUMBUS SHOWS THE WAY

The cost to the supermarkets of drastically paring their check losses has been substantial, in terms of time and personnel. But very few stores have bothered to calculate those costs. To sell an electronic check-guarantee system, the bank marketer must be able to present hard figures on what it now costs the supermarket to control its losses and the savings that the new system will bring.

One of the cleverest consumer-marketing men in the banking business is John Fisher, a vice president of City National Bank of Columbus, Ohio, a highly profitable, medium-sized institution that emphasizes consumer (rather than corporate) business. In the fall of 1976, Fisher kicked off a campaign to sell supermarket managers on the virtues of customer-operated, point-of-sale-terminals. He asked the supermarkets to let him install at least two I.B.M. 3608 terminals per store.

By inserting either a bank-supplied debit card or a BankAmericard into the terminal, the customer obtains approval of a check or a credit-card transaction form. The terminal is connected to what is called a negative file—a continuously updated bank record of bad risks. Since City National is the largest processor of BankAmericard transactions in the Midwest, it possesses a huge negative file, enabling it to guarantee with relative safety any check that is not flagged by the file. If the check or credit-card form passes muster, the terminal prints an authorization on it, and the customer can use it to pay for groceries at the checkout counter.

In selling his system to the Kroger, Big Bear, and Fazio supermarket chains, Fisher emphasized that the bank's self-service terminals would enable the store to economize on high-priced labor. The supermarkets customarily approved checks at either a cash register or a courtesy booth. In the first case, the check-cashing procedure slowed down the checkout line while tying up the services of a checker, who typically earns between $6 and $7 an hour. In the second case, the store had to keep its courtesy booth continuously manned, which also requires the services of fairly well-paid employees.

Kroger calculated that City National's self-service terminals would save each of its stores at least forty man-hours a week, or close to $300. Since the bank's fee, which is based on the volume of transactions, promised to be considerably lower than that figure, Kroger had no difficulty accepting Fisher's sales pitch. In so doing, the supermarket obtained an unexpected ancillary benefit. Before City National came along, Kroger would not let its customers charge any purchases to BankAmericard. Now that the bank guarantees credit-card as well as check purchases, the store has no reason to object to BankAmericard. It is probable that a number of people who like to shop with credit cards rather than checks (in order to take advantage of the three- to four-week float) have now switched to Kroger.

THE BOON OF PRIVACY

Shrewd marketer that he is, Fisher was careful to design his terminals to guarantee maximum privacy. If the shopper's check or credit card is rejected by the terminal, no one need know about it. The consumer does not suffer the embarrassment of a semipublic rejection at the cash register, nor is the checkout clerk required to turn down people, possibly triggering a time-consuming argument. Hence, the consumer benefits from the City National system in at least three ways. First, he gets the boon of privacy; second, he is not restricted to checks or currency in paying for his groceries; and, finally, he can move through the checkout line much more rapidly than before.

Thus far, Fisher has installed 125 terminals in sixty-eight supermarkets. These terminals are now processing an estimated 350,000 transactions a month. When the bank first analyzed its POS venture, it expected to earn enough, principally from merchants' fees and the interest on additional BankAmericard transactions, to achieve a 15 percent rate of return within three years. Since then, Fisher has found new sources of revenue that could raise profits substantially.

Other financial institutions in the Columbus area saw an opportunity to serve their customers by giving them the option of using Fisher's terminals. Credit unions, for example, now have the right to issue share drafts, which are similar to checks, i.e., in that they permit credit-union members to transfer funds held on deposit with the union to third parties. Two credit unions asked Fisher to let their members validate share drafts in his terminals. So for a fee, City National is letting the credit unions share the terminals, thus swelling the bank's earnings while providing credit-union members with another means of paying for their groceries.

In addition, the popularity of the Columbus experiment has piqued the interest of many other banks, both in the Midwest and elsewhere. Fisher has succeeded in franchising his POS system to a number of other financial institutions, some as far away as Albuquerque. The unexpected infusion of fee income has greatly improved returns. Although the City National project is only nine months old, operating revenue already exceeds operating expense, and that three-year target of a 15 percent rate of return may ultimately prove much too conservative.

The meteoric success of City National's system proves that, with careful marketing, EFT-type services can be profitably sold to even the most skeptical merchants. But check-guarantee systems are a long way from full-service EFT. Fisher cannot collect deposits at his 125 terminals because the law says that a deposit-collecting terminal is the legal equivalent of a branch. So even though the I.B.M. 3608 can be easily modified to accept bank deposits, Fisher is precluded from offering shoppers this service unless he obtains a branch permit for each store in which he has placed terminals. To get such a permit, City National would have to incur an estimated $20,000 per store in legal and administrative costs—without any guarantee that the bank regulators would eventually approve its application.

THE CONSUMERS WILL START TO WONDER

Nonetheless, electronic check-guarantee systems represent an important stepping-stone on the way to full-service EFT. If the banks and thrift institutions can market check-guarantee services to the bulk of the nation's nearly 33,000 major super-markets, the consumer will in time grow accustomed to that terminal. He will then begin wondering why the law does not allow it to serve him to the limit of its technological capability.

It is sometimes argued that the consumer is irrevocably wedded to the check, but if a POS terminal is legally able to accept deposits and authorize withdrawals, there is every reason to suppose that the consumer will eventually sue for divorce. That would be especially true if the terminal were capable, as many now are, of printing a receipt for his transaction that can serve the same purposes as a canceled check.

THE NOW REVOLUTION

Ironically, the spread of check-guarantee systems could undermine their own *raison d'être.* For these systems would surely whet the consumer's appetite for even greater convenience—i.e., the ability to spend money without having to use any checks at all.

Convenience may not be the most powerful motive impelling the consumer to demand a change in the laws that circumscribe his use of a POS terminal. The cost of a consumer checking account is about to rise substantially. The reason, paradoxically, lies in the spread of the consumer movement. For the last few years, consumer groups have been promoting the NOW account. The NOW account, or negotiable order of withdrawal, permits individuals to write checks on interest-bearing accounts. Thus far, this type of account has been legal only in New England, but the Federal Reserve is preparing to ask Congress to consider nationwide NOW legislation. If the legislation is passed, the banks will eventually be forced to pay interest on all consumer checking accounts.

Superficially, it would seem that the consumer will benefit greatly from this law. A much more likely scenario is that the low- to middle-income consumer will lose, while the high-income consumer will gain. According to Federal Reserve data, it costs the typical bank with more than $200 million in deposits approximately $63 a year to service an average retail account—one with a balance of about $1,000. But the bank usually charges the consumer only $15 in fees, in effect losing $48 per account.

If banks were required to pay interest on consumer checking accounts, it is a safe bet that they would begin charging the full cost of servicing these accounts. Assuming that the banks paid 3 percent interest, the average consumer would receive $30 in interest income, but would be required to pay $48 in additional fees for account maintenance. The high-income consumer—with an average balance of, say, $5,000—would receive $150 in interest income. And although his service fees would also increase, they would not amount to very much more than those of the middle-income consumer, since the number of checks drawn on a $5,000 account is not much greater than the number drawn on a $1,000 account. The ultimate impact of the NOW account will be to redistribute income in a perverse fashion—from lower- to higher-income consumers.

"GET THE LAWS CHANGED"

As soon as he realizes what is happening, the average consumer will obviously become greatly incensed. He will demand that his bank explain why he is worse off than when he wasn't earning any interest at all. An astute banker could then make a little speech to his retail customers, along the following lines: "A major reason for the high cost of servicing a small retail account is that checks must be individually sorted and stored in our back room until the end of the month. But if you could use our POS terminals and automated teller machies (ATM's) for nearly all your banking transactions, the number of checks would be sharply curtailed."

"To be sure," the banker might add, "it now costs us more to process EFT transactions than it does to handle checks, but that is only because the volume of electronic traffic is still too small. So if you want to cut the cost of account maintenance, get the laws changed to allow us to put up full-service EFT facilities wherever the consumer traffic is heaviest. That's the only way you will end up reducing costs and emerging with a net profit from the interest you now earn on your checking accounts."

Since this logic seems unassailable, the consumer will eventually join the bank in its drive for greater freedom to install EFT facilities without the need to apply for costly branch permits. (In some states, of course, banks cannot branch at all, so unless special legislation is passed authorizing off-premises EFT facilities, they can install full-service terminals only in their headquarters buldings.) With pressure from the consumer, who would now be motivated by both the desire for greater convenience and the need to reduce costs, the states and Congress can be pushed into passing laws that would exempt *all* EFT facilities from the status of branches. In a'sense, then, the NOW account, by contributing to a rise in the cost of paper transactions, may greatly stimulate the consumer's interest in using electronics and in making sure that EFT facilities are close at hand.

If the banks can shuck off the legal fetters that constrain their EFT activities, they will shortly be putting up many more terminals in railroad and bus stations, airports, student and community centers, etc. Since these are essentially unsupervised locations, the EFT terminal would have to be an ATM, a theft-proof box that costs about $35,000—only $6,500 to $8,000 of which represents computing intelligence.

A good deal of the rest goes for armor-plating and other accoutrements designed to ensure security. To reduce their hardware costs, the banks will logically gravitate to retail establishments, where cheaper terminals, costing anywhere from $5,000 to $13,000, can be installed because the store's security system will also protect the bank's equipment.

SEARS WOULD BALK

It is widely believed that the banks will have trouble getting their hardware into any other stores but supermarkets. The general-merchandise stores are expected to balk. A number of them have their own credit cards, which they use as marketing tools and, in the case of a huge merchandiser like Sears, Roebuck, as major income producers. The general merchandiser is not keen on admitting card-activated bank equipment that can, among other things, authorize overdrafts to shoppers who are temporarily short of funds.

This argument is a bit overworked, since a growing number of medium-sized general merchandisers have actually asked banks like Wells Fargo and Citibank to take over credit-card systems that have proved costly and unworkable. Nevertheless, it contains more than a grain of truth. It is probable that, in many cases, the banks will have to pay the general merchandiser a substantial fee in order to install full-service POS terminals. The banks can hardly object, however, since they will be able to collect deposits in retail stores rather than at high-cost ATM's or in bank branches. Indeed, some banks may even be able to shut down branches or at least avoid opening new ones.

UP AGAINST A POSITIVE FILE

As soon as a significant number of supermarkets and general merchandisers do accept bank terminals, others will be forced to follow. The reason is that unless they do, their check losses could easily wipe them out. A potential bad-check passer will not bother with a store that has a full-service bank POS system (assuming that such a store still accepted checks). He would be running too great a risk. The bank system would probably be on-line to its central records, and possibly, through a switching mechanism, to the records of other banks as well. So the bad-check passer would come up against what is called a positive file—one that could unequivocally determine that he couldn't cover his check.

Instead, the bogus-check passer would try his luck at the store without a bank system, where he would generally be working against a comparatively small negative file of known risks. With these stores getting all the bad checks, they would eventually have to beg the banks to install terminals, however unpalatable the idea might be.

At least one store in Atlanta has already been virtually compelled to purchase an EFT service that management originally thought it did not need. First National Bank of Atlanta developed a check-guarantee system that it calls the "Honest Face." The program has already achieved widespread acceptance, so the bank has been able to put together an enormous negative file, composed of the combined records of all the stores it serves. At first, the Winn-Dixie chain was reluctant to join the program.

According to Robert Cady, a vice president of Payment Systems, Inc., and one of the designers of the First National system: "Winn-Dixie held out for a long time, but it's an open secret in Atlanta that the store eventually capitulated in part because its check losses were significantly higher than before the Honest Face program was instituted."

In effect, once a critical mass of stores accepts bank terminals, EFT will explode, dragging reluctant and even some die-hard opponents into the program. The upshot is that the consumer will get thousands, and perhaps even hundreds of thousands, of convenient outlets where he can do his banking. The volume of electronic transactions will soar, reducing unit costs below the level of those for paper transactions.

Benton of the National Commission on Electronic Fund Transfers estimates that if a large financial institution or a group of institutions were to install 3,000 to 5,000 EFT terminals, each of which processed 5,000 or more transactions per month—the most heavily used EFT facilities are already handling 8,000 to 11,000 per month—the cost per transaction could be driven comfortably below a nickel. That is, it would get to be less than the average back-room cost of processing a check at a highly efficient bank. And if the comparison is with a check brought to the bank by a customer, the cost of teller time would have to be added to the back-room cost—which would make it even more attractve to use EFT rather than the traditional check.

Ultimately, the consumer will be able to perform nearly all essential banking transactions through the use of POS terminals. He will be able to deposit and withdraw money in whatever form he likes. He will be able to debit his account to make a retail purchase or to pay an outstanding bill, such as the mortgage. He will have the capability of transferring funds from one type of account to another or of getting a cash advance from his bank.

Nor will he be restricted to performing these transactions with banks that are located in his particular geographic area. The National Commission is recommending that terminal owners be compelled initially to transfer the customer's deposit to any bank or thrift institution of his choosing, provided that the transfer takes place within the same state or in what the commission calls a "natural market area," e.g., the New York, New Jersey, and Connecticut metropolitan area.

Advocates of competition hope that the National Commission will eventually recommend complete interstate terminal banking, meaning that a New Yorker, if he wishes, will be able to do all his banking with a California institution by manipulating the buttons on a POS terminal located in a Manhattan supermarket. In this way, the consumer will be guaranteed the best banking deal he can get—in terms of rates, services, and fees—from any depository institution in the country that cares to compete for his business.

TERMINAL BORROWING

Perhaps the greatest potential benefit of electronic banking to the consumer will be a decline in the cost of credit. Banks perennially assert that they have to charge the consumer high rates on installment loans, in part because processing costs are so great. Every time a monthly payment is made, a clerk must open an envelope, verify that the amount of the check equals the amount due, and then place a record of the payment in the bank's central file. If, instead, the consumer authorized his bank to debit his account automatically for the amount of his monthly bill, the transaction would obviously be much less time consuming.

Costs could be further reduced if the bank was able to convert an installment loan into an overdraft facility. Eligible customers can arrange for such facilities by visiting the bank. After the initial visit, however, the consumer would not have to fill out forms or take up the time of a bank lending officer when he wished to borrow money. He would simply initiate a loan by debiting his account, via a POS terminal, for more than the amount of his balance. Unlike the bad-check passer, who would get a "stop" order from the bank's computer, the legitimate overdraft borrower would get the same "OK" he would have received if his checking-account balance had been large enough.

But how would the bank know whether the habitual borrower was still eligible for the overdraft? First, the bank would have accumulated an enormous data base containing the records of all purchases made by the consumer at various points of sale. So it would have a fairly good fix on the consumer's expenditure pattern. The next step would be to obtain on-going records of the consumer's income. Such records could be compiled more easily if employers were willing to make checkless payroll deposits.

A number of companies are already eliminating checks and instead transmitting payroll information by magnetic tape to an automated clearinghouse (ACH)—an organization that combines, sorts, and distributes payment orders in machine-readable form. The employee provides his company with the name of his bank, and a day or so before every payday the company sends a single magnetic tape, containing all payroll information, to the ACH. The ACH then dismantles the tape, delivering to each bank in the clearinghouse that portion which contains credits to its depositors' accounts. Eventually, of course, the companies will be able to communicate with the clearinghouse directly by computer, and the various ACH's—there are already thirty-two around the country—will be able to communicate among themselves in a similar manner.

It is often argued that the majority of employers will never agree to direct payroll deposits because they would thereby lose substantial float—that is, money would be credited to employees' accounts much sooner than it would if payment were made by check. Nonetheless, companies like Xerox, I.B.M., and NCR have discovered that they save more money in clerical costs by eliminating check-based payrolls than they lose in float. As a result, they are funneling at least a portion of their national payrolls through regional ACH's. It is likely that, prodded by eager employees and equally eager accountants, other companies will shortly be following their example.

Armed with up-to-the-minute records of both the consumer's income and his outgo, a bank can monitor his eligibility for overdraft loans at a fraction of the current cost and with minimal risk of default. Inevitably, competion will force the banks to pass their savings on to the borrower, substantially reducing the consumer lending rate. Many more consumers would then find it advantageous to borrow from banks, and, as a result, the business customer may face increased competition for a given supply of lendable funds. Although the business borrower is in no danger of being crowded out by the consumer, business-loan rates might eventually rise in relation to consumer rates.

MONEY IS COMMUNICATION

The nation is a long way from reaching what used to be called the cashless society. There may come a time when the consumer who pays his bills with cash will be looked upon with suspicion and distrust, but that time is still many years away. Within the next ten years, however, the use of electronic money will greatly increase, while the use of checks, and eventually cash, will begin to level off and decline.

Money is basically a form of communication, and people are gradually realizing that it makes little sense to communicate with checks when technology is making it much more economical to use electronics. Although there are atavistic attitudes to be overcome, groundless fears to be put to rest, and obsolete laws to be swept aside, the spread of electronic banking cannot be halted. EFT simply promises too many benefits for too many people.

24

CUSTOM CHARGE: EVALUATING ALTERNATIVE CREDIT PLANS

MARIAN BURK ROTHMAN

Customers are saying "Charge it!" with increasing frequency in virtually every major department, discount and specialty store in the country.

And when they use the card with the store's name, they probably don't know who is extending the credit—retailer, banker or outside agency.

The terminology differs from store to store—private label, in-house, proprietary, or custom charge program—but the intent is the same: to provide alternative payment arrangements for as broad a customer base as is practical.

A check of the STORES Top 100 Department Stores listing (July 1977), shows that only three—Alexanders, J.W. Mays, and Crowley-Milner—do not offer any store charge plates. Of the remainder, all but three operate their own in-house credit plan. (Sattler's has sold off its receivables, Korvettes and Richard's of Miami have contracted with Citibank for private label credit.)

Yet, caught in the economic crunch, with mounting receivables and growing back-office expenses, many retailers are taking a hard look at their own credit operations.

The figures are staggering: at the end of 1976, retail installment credit receivables outstanding were over $19 billion. Non-installment receivables outstanding in the retail field stood at $8.6 billion, according to Federal Reserve Board estimates.

In study after study, such as the NRMA-sponsored Economic Characteristics of Department Store Credit (1969) and Economics of New York State Retail Store Revolving Credit Operations (1973), the conclusion is the same: extending customer credit is costly to retailers.

Though balanced against revenues from finance charges, the expenses of borrowing against receivables and costly labor-intensive credit administration rarely allows the merchant to break even.

Weighing the advantages of independent credit plans in retail stores—close contact with customer base; prestige of name; selling and marketing tool; convenience for customer—against the alternatives of third-party credit arrangements, merchants respond differently.

184

SOURCE: Reprinted from *Stores* Magazine; ᶜ National Retail Merchants Association, December 1977.

K mart and the now-defunct W.T. Grant chose to discontinue their own store cards entirely, in favor of bank cards, though Grant carried more than 2.2 million accounts.

Other retailers, like Dayton-Hudson, determined to maintain long-established image and service to their charge customers, have opted for more efficient account procedures in service and authorization.

But other alternatives do exist.

In recent years, several major banks have aggressively marketed private label programs which permit the retailer to offer his own card, with the bank handling the details.

This may be due to the fact that these larger financial instituions have moved their own card programs into the black, aided by technological advances and hard-earned experience. With the big banks' ability to economize costs comes the ability to acquire new receivables on a profitable basis.

Citicorp, considered the giant in the field (see p. 34), entered the private label market in 1973. But others, including Wells Fargo and Bank of America, have made their own bids for the retail market of late.

Custom Charge, Wells' name for its program, was introduced in April, 1976. Sixteen months later, its receivables topped $70 million on over 700,000 accounts, with nearly 50 merchant-chains participating.

The John Breuner Co., RB Furniture, both based in California, and the Furniture Guild Association are among those who use the program.

Whether the retailer is beginning an in-house program, or redefining an existing operation, Custom Charge offers a variety of options.

Among the features available: daily purchase of receivables on a non-recourse, full recourse or modified recourse basis; credit application, processing and authorization services; personalized card and promotion design; collections, and customer inquiry service.

Once a retailer has decided on Custom Charge, the start-up or conversion period averages 120 days. It's a matter of defining the exact services to fit the individual store's needs, implementing the training and materials necessary, interfacing systems where applicable, and informing customers—through disclosure procedures—of the change.

"One of our responsibilities to the merchant is credit card promotion," indicates Robert A. Rodriguez, vice president of Wells Fargo Bank and manager of Custom Charge.

Because retailers value the store charge as a market research tool, adds Custom Charge's Al Dayton, provisions for maintaining specified information, such as mailing lists, are included in the service. In addition, breakouts of sales by department can be extracted for the merchant's use in such support programs.

For point of sale support, Custom Charge offers WellService (STORES, August 1977) as part of the private label package.

"At present, it's the only authorization service which can verify not only in-house, but also the other major credit cards, as well as checks," states Rodriguez.

The future of private label, he continues, lies in the capacity to interface with electronic checkout devices without disturbing the total operations of the store.

While Custom Charge has made its greatest inroads in the home furnishings area, Rodriguez views regionalized department stores and large specialty outlets as "a very viable market."

"We can deliver a private label package to a retailer at a cost less than his present in-house program, with increased efficiency," he says.

Bank of America recently launched its own Retail Services division, offering private label credit with a tailor-made approach. Though the bank has, in the past, provided such services on a limited basis—White Front Stores were customers—this newest program is the bank's first formal bid.

Steve Yotter, vice president of processing and service, Bank of America, is reluctant to disclose names but says negotiations are underway with several retail firms.

As in the Wells Fargo program, Bank of America offers immediate cash conversion of receivables; application, collection and authorization procedures, and customer relations services. Store name and logo are incorporated on statements and other forms to preserve the integrity of the operation.

"We use a modulized approach to each merchant's needs," notes Yotter. If the retailer wants to handle his own billing, for example, this is considered in the overall design.

Yotter acknowledges the retailer's concern over personalized service, and the resulting reluctance to relinquish control over customer accounts. At the same time, he adds, "legal and financial entanglements of credit cards can prove costly, especially for smaller merchants."

Meanwhile, in an unusual move, VISA USA (formerly BankAmericard) introduced its own version of a retailer-identified credit card in July.

Tom Honey, vice president of VISA, describes the theory behind this new program: "The option of placing a merchant's name in the blue band, above the VISA logo on the face of the card, allows retailers to gain the psychological edge of a loyal customer base while combining wider acceptibility of VISA cards."

The card itself is actually issued by a VISA member bank, through a contract agreement with the individual retail business. Other nonfinancial institutions, such as shopping centers, may also participate.

Honey emphasizes that the member bank and retailer are free to build any type of program around the card.

Potential benefits include purchase and funding of receivables, sharing of credit risks, and the opportunity for cross-selling various financial services to customers. For example, the retailer may arrange through the member bank to provide customers with a major purchase plan, as an alternative financing option to the regular charge.

There are other areas which may be negotiated between bank and merchant. Among these are flexible billing arrangements, processing and authorization.

Another approach is the umbrella shopping center card.

The White Flint Credit Card, introduced for use in the White Flint Mall, North Bethesda, Maryland, in March, provides yet another credit alternative to local mall merchants.

The prestigious shopping center anticipates a total of 100 stores when fully occupied. At present, 65 stores currently operating honor the mall card. However, the three anchors—Lord & Taylor, Bloomingdale's and Raleigh's—are not participating.

The Citizens Bank & Trust Company of Maryland administers the program and handles credit arrangements, with authorization and processing through the Atlantic States Bankcard Association.

"The White Flint Program is run about the same way as any nationwide credit card," explains one bank official. For instance, issued cards are valid for 18 months; but no cash advances can be obtained.

Prior to the White Flint mall opening, the bank promoted the new charge plan with a computerized direct mail campaign. To date, 14,000 accounts using 25,000 cards are on record. Although the transaction volume is not as high as expected, the average ticket, says the bank, is in the $35-45 range.

In at least one retailer's opinion, though, the mall card's future may depend upon the willingness of major store tenants to honor it.

"The program would do better if the three anchors accepted the card," admits H.A. Swiger, vice president of Citizens Bank & Trust. "But they won't stand by for too long and see customers shop stores which honor the White Flint Card."

Washington, D.C., customers of four stores, Garfinckel's, Hecht's, Raleigh's, and Woodward & Lothrop, can charge their purchases on the Washington Shopping Plate. Though each store requires individual application and grants its own credit, the group plate association enables members to economize on common costs.

One of the oldest plans of its kind in the country, the Washington Shopping Plate Association—WSPA—dates to pre-war years.

The program uses a common numbering system, with a check digit identifying which members are granting credit on an individual plate. Originally, seven stores participated; today, even with the membership diminished to four, the program boasts 2.2 million accounts, with an average of 2.5 members assigned per number.

The WSPA represents a convenience to the customer, says Bob Holbrook, credit manager for Hecht's. "Instead of carrying four pieces of plastic, the shopper need only carry one," he explains.

Further, the customer need only notify one central office, operated by CBI (Credit Bureau Inc. of Georgia) for the WSPA, in case of stolen/lost cards or changes in address.

Through a recently upgraded computer system, with CRT stations in each store, such file maintenance material as new account information and special statement instructions are funneled to CBI each night for processing and returned to the proper stores on tape the next morning.

Paul A. Luttkus, credit manager of Garfinckel's, emphasizes that each store holds its own receivables, with its own automated internal accounts receivable system. Credit promotions are handled independently by individual stores. And if the customer has an account at all four stores, she will be billed by each store separately.

The system has been so successful, says Luttkus, that the WSPA is considering the approaches of another plate association, as well as a large retailer, with offers to buy the EDP package.

The concern over retail credit has heightened with the advent of recent technological advances which threaten to blur the traditional definitions of credit, debit, bank branch and retail outlet.

In hearings before the Subcommittee on Consumer Affairs of the Committee on Banking, Finance and Urban Affairs of the House of Representatives, as well as in hearings before the National Commission on Electronic Fund Transfers, a number of pertinent issues which influence the granting of retail credit have been raised.

Dolores Marunyak, credit manager of S.W. Metzler Stores, Uniontown, Pa., in testimony representing the NRMA, outlined one major reason why merchants, prefer to handle their own credit:

> ". . . Retailers do not view their credit operations as a profit-making activity itself, and consequently, utilize a liberal, but reasoned, credit-granting philosophy. Third-party financiers, on the other hand, must be concerned with the profitability of each account from a purely credit point of view. In short, retailers prefer an independent credit operation, because it permits them to make credit available to as many customers as possible."

A related point, raised by Paul Luttkus of Garfinckel's, is that merchants risk less when extending credit than outside agencies. While the store stands to lose not the retail value but the wholesale cost of the article, the bank would bear the loss of the full retail price.

Further, in turning over their credit programs to a third party, smaller merchants fear possible cost-pricing abuse, should discount rates be raised.

A developing problem is that of the multipurpose bank card, which may offer customers access to funds on deposit, as well as lines of credit, and/or check guarantee functions. VISA is the most visible nationwide version of this card today, with its combination debit-credit cards.

In combining several payment functions triggered by a single piece of plastic, financial institutions may have made money management more convenient for the consumer, but the retailer's headaches have just begun.

NRMA has taken the position that the merchant must have the right to select and decline the types of payment methods which he will honor.

Where payment services are not separated or clearly identified on the card, the retailer loses the ability to discriminate between credit and debit transactions—and he may unknowingly embark on third party credit.

Taking this a step further, as multipurpose cards gain acceptance in the marketplace, the retailer will face mounting pressure to accept all aspects of the cards' functions; at this point, third party credit may cease to be an option, and the store's own credit plan may be threatened.

Bank card officials such as D.W. Hock, president of VISA USA, Inc. insist that retailers risk invading cardholders' privacy by delving into their financial arrangements. They further note that the customer is free to choose other payment alternatives at the point of sale. Only legislation will settle this debate.

Another key issue is the use of credit files for marketing promotion. With existing and proposed legislation governing consumer privacy, it is doubtful that a third party credit grantor would be allowed to release information concerning store accounts, although certain portions—names for mailing—may surface.

For example, some stores isolate those accounts purchasing in specified departments and mount mail promotions on this basis.

And inactive accounts may receive personalized mail, even discount privileges, to draw the customer back into the store. If the merchant relinquishes his credit program, this important marketing tool may lose its effectiveness.

Then there is the touchy question of store name and reputation. With an in-house charge program the retailer builds loyal customers with service and personalized attention.

Will standards be maintained, when a third party financier takes over?

For their part, the banks and outside agencies are working with retail clients to offer a variety of customizing features. Envelope stuffers, deferred payment plans, holiday credit promotions, specialized service—all are available, at a price.

By prior arrangement, stores may continue billing or other credit functions while turning receivables over.

This is the arrangement at Korvettes, where the store retains control over authorization.

Although for many retailers the main attraction of third-party credit is getting out of the credit business and returning full attention to merchandising, with improved cash flow, for others the decision involves a factor not even considered a decade ago: computerization.

Electronic point-of-sale equipment is on its way to becoming the industry standard at checkout, creating a need for sophisticated back-office computer support.

For many retailers, it is simply less expensive, and less complicated, to allow a bank or third party to set up electronic interchanges.

Retailers with independent credit plans may not feel the brunt of EFT programs for some time to come, while those who honor bank cards may become involved sooner.

The American National Standards Institute, anticipating electronic interchange on national and international networks, has devised a voluntary, internationally adopted standardized numbering system to distinguish between various categories of credit cards. A different initial digit identifies each charge group: for example, 3 is for T & E cards, 4/5 are bank cards, 6 is retailers.

There are no plans at present for the retail industry as a whole to conform to this voluntary standard. The expense involved in reissuing new plates and changing account numbers would be enormous. Today, the possibility of interchange between retail label charges and banks or other credit grantors seems remote. But future developments in payment systems or retail philosophy may change this.

25

CHARTING THE COURSE
OF STOCK MOVEMENTS

PAMELA ARCHBOLD

"The fall through the 43 level resulted in a significant support breaching, and last week the stock was probing into the next area of underlying resistance visible at approximately 27–31. Working off the July-September distribution pattern, an objective into the mid-20s is also readable."

That may sound like talk from outer space, but isn't. It's the carefully researched conclusion on the future price of a stock, calculated by a leading technical analyst. In reaching such a conclusion the usual research factors, such as earnings, sales and the company's financial condition, are disregarded. Instead, the technical analyst uses terms such as: support, resistance, breadth, trend line, volume—along with, of course, a chart that plots all their courses. This diversity of research techniques characterizes the basic difference between security analysis and technical analysis.

The security, or fundamental, analyst studies an industry and the companies within that industry. Comparisons are made of the companies' earnings, as are predictions of the companies' future earnings.

On the other hand, technicians use the history of a stock price to predict that stock's future price movement. This historical information is, of course, interpreted in relation to the general trend of the stock market as a whole.

As a group, the technicians don't have the visibility and consequent recognition that most security analysts are accorded; in some people's minds, even, the technicians are simply not useful at all. "The most popular misconception about us is that we are using a crystal ball, but the fundamentalist is using a slide rule," comments Philip Roth, one of the 15 technicians at Merill Lynch.

Technicians must be doing something right, however, because over the past two years literally hundreds of security analysts have been laid off from Wall Street firms—usually as part of a cost-cutting move—and proportionately fewer technicians have suffered the same

SOURCE: *Exchange*, December 1974. Reprinted by permission.

fate. One reason for this was suggested by technician Ralph Acampora, Jr., of Harris Upham: "People on the Street rarely tell an investor when to sell. A security analyst should give the caution points, but usually he doesn't, so a technician becomes invaluable—particularly in a bear market."

One successful technician is William X. Scheinman of Weisenberger Services. The number of customers is usually a good sign of success in this line of work, and Scheinman has a large number of institutional clients, each of whom must trade at least $50,000 worth of commissions per year through Weisenberger to remain on Scheinman's mailing list. Of course, these clients follow Scheinman because he has been calling many of the major market moves correctly over the past few years.

The crux of technical analysis for individual stocks is simply the supply and demand for each stock. Thus for the technician the word demand becomes "latent support," because from his viewpoint there are investors willing to buy at a certain lower price level for every stock that trades. Similarly, the word supply becomes "potential resistance," because there are always investors willing to sell when a stock reaches a certain higher level.

Most technical analysts have stock-price charts covering the past 40 years, usually with the last few years done on a day-to-day basis. The charts detail the high, low, close and perhaps shares traded. (Volume is not a factor in all types of technical analysis, however.) From this information, a technician tries to determine at what level an investor should buy or sell a given stock. Since a decision of this kind requires a certain amount of interpretation as well, some technicians fare better than others. Insofar as calling the right moves is concerned, however, technicians are usually compared to professional economists, who are constantly making predictions and seemingly are always half-right. "I may not get you out at exactly the top, but I'll sure save your shirt from the bottom," explains Harris Upham's Mr. Acampora.

Sometimes a technician makes a recommendation that has no fundamental reasons whatsoever. When this happens at Merrill Lynch, the security analysts for the stock are consulted, but they don't have veto power over the technicians, and the decisions are usually fairly mutual.

Analyzing stock movements as a whole is a slightly different matter for the technicians who, like the economists, are themselves divided into different schools of thought, such as the Dow Theory, Intra-Day Intensity, Divergence Analysis, Relative Strength and Moving Averages. Each of these concepts approaches the market from a different angle, but all draw upon the same basic market information.

These various indicators are an attempt to pinpoint the psychology of the market and investors' behavior. Among the 20-odd main indicators used by technicians are advance-decline ratios, mutual fund cash, margin debt, new equity financing, short interest ratio, odd-lot balances and specialists' short sales. Naturally, following 20 different indicators means a lot of charts, and a typical technical department is inundated with a variety of them. At Harris Upham an entire 20-foot wall is covered from floor to ceiling with charts on many levels, and in different color inks. Weisenberger's Mr. Scheinman has his entire office papered with them, including some pinned to the drapes. This love of charts and numbers is a key personality trait among the technicians; that, and their easy use of their own special language, have been factors hindering their acceptance.

It is ironic that the technicians have come to be known as the "other" analysts, because actually technical analysis was done long before security analysis was even thought of. The father of technical analysis was none other than Charles Dow, co-founder and for many years editor of the Wall Street Journal. Dow was a stock market follower and writer who began the D-J average in 1884. In those days, companies were not required by law to release any financial information—and most did not. With no actual financial data to work from, therefore, Dow watched stock prices and noticed that if a stock hit a certain low, buying interest was stimulated. From there, Dow went on and developed many theories, some of which are still being used.

Since Dow, many technical analysts have added to his work and refined the process, which computers have made considerably easier in the recent past. Now technicians have an enormous amount of information at their fingertips; Merrill Lynch has a computer that can draw a chart on any stock for a day, week, month or even several years. The computer takes about a minute to put the completed chart into the hands of the technicians. This type of equipment enabled David Bostian, of Loeb Rhoades, to develop his theory of Intra-Day Intensity, which measures stock movement hour by hour.

Today's institutional-dominated market is the first such market in history, and this fact isn't lost on the technicians. "Most technicians are now using several different approaches, because to hang your hat on one today is too risky." says Harris Upham's Mr. Acampora. This type of market is difficult for the technicians to operate in, because of large-block institutional trading.

One individual investor who is a believer of technical analysis explains why: "In this musical shares market, nobody can be right all the time, but the technicians see a lot of things before they happen, which is a great help. Of course, it takes a little effort to understand their language, but it's worth it."

The technicians are well aware that they are more difficult to understand than security analysts. Recently a number of the Street's leading technicians banded together to form the Market Technicians Association of New York. This is the first formal association of technicians, and the aim is to explain technical analysis to the general public, and in some cases to each other. The association is also starting a library at the New York Institute of Finance, at 2 New York Plaza, in downtown New York, which will be opened to the public soon.

Investors who are interested in technical analysis can ask to be put on the mailing lists for technical market letters issued by brokerage houses. With some exceptions, they are free to customers. Both Forbes and Financial World have technical columnists whose writing is to the individual investor. If interest is deeper, Mr. Acampora of Harris Upham, who also teaches the subject at the Institute, suggests reading "Technical Analysis of Stock Trends," by Edwards and Magee. There are a number of other worthwhile books as well, and many standard stock market texts contain chapters on the subject.

To develop charts, the high, low, close and number of shares traded are listed in most daily newspapers, and the more advanced indicators are published weekly on the next-to-last page of Barron's. True to form, the technicians have renamed the page; it's now called the Laundry List (among technicians, that is).

26

SOME REASONS WHY PRICE OF
A STOCK CHANGES SUDDENLY

JAMES P. ROSCOW

The late Gerald M. Loeb, whose books and newspaper columns over his 50 years in Wall Street may have provided more down-to-earth guidance to investors than any other single source, was adamant about the need to give time to your stocks. "Just write down the prices once a week, which doesn't take much time," he used to counsel. "And you should ask your broker or your financial advisor: '*Why* is it up,' or '*Why* is it down?' "

Indeed, a great many investors do precisely this, setting aside a regular time with the Sunday newspaper business section to bring their stock records up to date. And for most investors, even if they do this on a daily basis, there will come those moments when a stock they are following suddenly abandons the quiet ebb and flow of its usual market action. Abruptly, there has been a startling price jump or drop, or a radical change in trading volume. What happened? What's the reason for this sudden activity?

Stock market professionals—and those who mind the marketplace—are just as interested as any individual investor in the whys and wherefores of rapid and abnormal stock price and volume movements. The guiding principle of any securities market is that it should be fair and orderly. It should be a place where the supply-and-demand equation for any stock, bond or other security can work itself out in an organized way. It should be a marketplace that is open to all comers on a fair and equal basis, where all can trade under conditions of full disclosure: access to the same information at the same time. Unexpected and excessive trading action violates this orderliness. It also bruises public confidence in the marketplace. Nor is it very reassuring to the company whose stock is behaving strangely.

What is "unusual" activity? This is not a simple question, because the answer will vary from stock to individual stock. Each stock has different characteristics: its price level, its distribution, its popularity—and these will also vary over time. But in any given period, these characteristics will combine to produce normal trading patterns. Any deviation from these patterns is "unusual" for that stock at that time. There may be a singularly large price

SOURCE: *Exchange,* December 1974. Reprinted by permission.

movement up or down on volume, or a sudden spurt in volume. The stock may be moving inexplicably against its own recent trend, or its industry's trend—or the over-all market trend.

At the very least, the reasons for abrupt stock action must be learned and explained. Investors have a right to know. This has been true for a long time, and as a result a good deal of effort has gone into market surveillance procedures. In some of the "thin" and volatile markets of recent years, both the problem and the need to explain it have increased. But the need is also critical today as our world contracts and becomes more of a piece economically, financially and from an investment standpoint. The markets—and the interests of their investors—are vulnerable to virtually everything that can happen close at home or anywhere around the globe.

What can cause a company's stock to make a sudden and unusual move? A general rule would be: Anything that might affect the assets or earnings of the company. Briefly summarized, here are 10 kinds of reasons.

1. Favorable or unfavorable news from the company itself. Usually this will be an unexpected development—or at least one that has not previously been known outside the company.

2. A favorable or unfavorable research report on the company from a brokerage firm or an analyst elsewhere in the investment community.

3. A simple "buy" or "sell" recommendation from somewhere in the investment community, not part of a detailed research report.

4. A block trade of a large number of shares in the company, usually by a large institutional investor.

5. A news story on the company. This will probably have the most impact coming from the financial press. But it might also appear in the general press, or on radio or television, or even in a scholarly or technical publication that is usually seen only by a limited audience.

6. An economic development affecting a company or its industry. The possibilities are virtually infinite: a steel strike that affects the auto makers; an auto strike that affects steel consumption; a coal strike that affects both. Another example would be a change in the supply or price of a commodity —oil, or a metal, or sugar—that affects the companies whose business depends on that commodity.

7. Government action. The possibilities are also infinite; Federal Reserve policy; the imposition of oil import quotas, or their removal; the devaluation of a currency; curbs on foreign investment.

8. Regulatory action. This could be a suit filed by the Federal Trade Commission, or a new gas-price policy from the Federal Power Commission or the approval or denial of an airline route by the Civil Aeronautics Board. An action by the Securities & Exchange Commission against a company will almost certainly have a negative effect—while the resolution of an SEC matter will probably have a positive effect.

9. An international development. Once again, examples abound. They may be economic: a poor balance-of-trade or balance-of-payments report, or a

good one. An oil embargo. The nationalization or expropriation of foreign assets. These events may also be political or military: a dramatic or unexpected outcome of an election; the overthrow of a government; the outbreak of a war; or the success or failure of peace talks.

10. Rumors. Factual events are capable enough of affecting stock prices. But so, unfortunately, are hints at things that can't for the moment be verified. By their very nature, rumors can often have the most troublesome impact of all on the market action of a stock.

There are times when the reason for a stock's sudden activitiy is elusive—at least at first. "Stocks can move for no apparent reason at all," says A. Barry Witz, an assistant vice president of the New York Stock Exchange. "Sometimes it is just hard to tell why, and one may never know the real reason, because one can't look into people's minds." However, he adds: "I can't recall the last time we could't find a reason."

It is, in fact, part of the professional mission of Barry Witz and his associates to find the reason or reasons behind unusual stock movements. Within the NYSE's Market Surveillance division, headed by J. J. O'Donohue, is the Trading Surveillance Department, which Witz heads. And part of Trading Surveillance is the Stock Watch program. It is the job of Stock Watch, no more and no less, to monitor the trading activity of every issue on the New York Stock Exchange—common stocks, preferred stocks, warrants and bonds—and to look into every deviation from normal trading patterns. Further than that, Stock Watch has an enforcement role that is part of the NYSE's self-regulatory powers of discipline over its members and member firms.

"Stock Watch is tied closely into the policy of timely disclosure—which says that all investors should have access to all pertinent material about a company so that everyone has a chance to participate in the market at the same time and under the same conditions," says Mr. Witz. The press for timely disclosure is not news: the NYSE began requiring regular financial reports of its listed companies at the end of the last century, and Stock Watch itself was born as a monitoring program during the securities market reforms of the 1930s. Most recently, within the past year, the trading surveillance and enforcement functions of Stock Watch have been integrated by pulling together components from three NYSE divisions: Stock List, Member Firms and Floor Procedure.

Today, despite all the complexities of current markets, Stock Watch keeps pace by means of the computer. "We do our job with people, and with machines," says Mr. Witz. The people of Stock Watch, besides Mr. Witz and Arthur Huttick, manager, include chief counsel James Rothenberg and two other attorneys, plus seven investigators with backgrounds ranging from security analysis and brokerage operations to securities regulation.

Two of Stock Watch's surveillance analysts remain "on line"—observing the action of the entire market as it happens, which they are able to do effectively with the aid of electronics. Scantlin display units are tied into the NYSE mainframe computers, and the on-line investigators can monitor simultaneously a variety of trading activity. Across the Scantlin screens marches the complete tape of all trades on the floor of the NYSE, plus a selective tape of 30 to 40 stocks that Stock Watch wants to follow that day, plus the Dow-Jones news ticker, plus the running record of the day's block transactions. And there is still room on the screen for the investigator to summon up current transaction data on any single stock or group of stocks he may want to see at a given moment.

Meanwhile, the NYSE's computers are also supplying a continuous flow of the information that lies at the heart of Stock Watch's job. Every listed issue on the NYSE is programed into the computer with parameters relating to its normal trading patterns. When a stock exceeds those parameters, the computer "kicks out" in printed form the stock's symbol and price, and the minute in time that the abnormal activity occurred. This can happen several dozen times a day, and the task of Stock Watch is to find out as quickly as possible the reason for each abnormality.

This usually involves, to begin with, phoning the company. Is there some current news or development that might be causing the unusual price or volume activity? Has a premature earnings report leaked out, or news of a merger negotiation? Stock Watch may also contact the specialist assigned to the stock to find out who's in the market for that stock: Who is buying it, and from whom? It may then go to those brokerage firms or to the institutions, fund managers and analysts who have an interest in the stock. Unusual trading action— or an impending development that could lead to unusual activity—may prompt the staff to contact the NYSE floor governors and recommend a trading halt in the stock until the reason for the abnormal activity is learned, or until a piece of corporate news has been released and given sufficient time to be absorbed by the investing public.

Most of the unusual activity can be quickly explained, often within the same day it happens, and Stock Watch is serviced by the major newswires to help with this. It also keeps its own files of brokerage research reports, financial publications and other information sources that may explain a change in trading patterns—or even anticipate it. If the explanation isn't found right away, the investigation broadens. Stock Watch can go back through the Exchange's permanent records of all trades for any length of time to trace the origins of any unusual activity. Beyond that, it will go to any logical source for the explanation. "We'll call everyone who might know the reason, or a reason," says Barry Witz. "We'll call foreign governments; we called Indonesia not long ago on an oil development."

The explanation, when it is found, can range from something obscure and quite innocent to something that may require legal action and discipline. Sudden activity in one stock was finally traced to a technical article on one of the company's products that had appeared fully a month earlier in a learned foreign journal—it had taken that long to surface in the consciousness of the marketplace. At other times, information can move too quickly: Two companies involved in merger discussions will have their own executives, their attorneys, their accountants and perhaps some consultants all sharing the secret. The circumstances may make it difficult to avoid a leak that might find its way into the stock market.

Inevitably, some Stock Watch investigations will reveal improper conduct by one or another party in the long chain of a securities transaction. This is where the enforcement role of Stock Watch comes into play, as a part of the NYSE's self-regulatory structure.

In these cases, and also on cases that involve parties who are not members or member firms of the NYSE, a close liaison is maintained with the SEC. "We work closely together with the government on this," says Barry Witz. "And if we find something, the machinery is there . . . the law is there. But beyond the law, there is the more important question. Is the market fair? Is it working for the benefit of everyone? Stock Watch is here for the protection of all investors."

27

EXAMINING THE CASE FOR "UNIVERSAL NO-FAULT"

JETHRO LIEBERMAN

No-fault, that elegant solution to climbing auto insurance rates and congested court calendars, was put forth 10 years ago by Robert E. Keeton, a professor at Harvard Law School, and Jeffrey O'Connell, now a professor at the University of Illinois Law School. Their idea: Eliminate the law's requirement that the victim prove that his injury was caused by the fault of another, but also limit the victim's right to recover for pain and suffering. After years of debate and denunciation, the battle for no-fault auto insurance has largely been won; 23 states have adopted it in some form. Now the argument is whether no-fault laws should be enacted individually by the states or nationally by the federal government.

Heartened by the success of the system he codesigned, O'Connell wants to shake up the insurance and liability industries again. In a new book, *Ending Insult to Injury,* O'Connell calls for "Universal no-fault" for all the non-auto accidents that befall Americans each year, including 20-million injuries in the home connected with consumer products (30,000 are fatal and 110,000 lead to permanent disability) and the rising numbers inflicted by doctors that have precipitated the current malpractice insurance crisis. O'Connell would replace the huge, headline-grabbing recoveries with a method to pay·promptly many potential claims not now reimbursed.

EVENING THE AWARDS

Under his system, which he calls "elective no-fault," a manufacturer of power tools, plate glass, or any other product that accounts for large numbers of injuries, or a doctor or supplier of other services, would not have to pay for the pain and suffering caused by a defective product, faulty servicing, or negligent professional work. Claims for astronomical sums based on subjective judgments about the "worth" of such pain would be eliminated.

In return, however, litigation over the question of fault would also be eliminated. The supplier of goods or services would be required to pay for all out-of-pocket losses even if

SOURCE: Reprinted from the April 28, 1975, issue of *Business Week* by special permission. Copyright © 1975 by McGraw-Hill, Inc., New York, NY 10020. All rights reserved.

the product was not defective or the medical operation was performed in a textbook-perfect manner.

O'Connell recognizes that if such a system were mandatory, the cost would be enormous. Accordingly, he would not impose this no-fault system on anyone. He proposes simply that state legislatures permit manufacturers and professionals to opt for such coverage individually.

A BETTER CHANCE

If this sounds radical, it is. But it is a proposal that deserves to be taken seriously—not only because O'Connell is a formidable advocate but also because the premise underlying automobile no-fault applies to other injuries as well: that the present system of compensation for injuries caused by others is wasteful and cruel.

How many people would choose to earn a living by hiring an agent to place a bet now on a horse race to be run in five years? If you win, you get a large payoff (though your agent gets from half to a third); if you lose, you get nothing and may have to pay.

In essence, this is what the present sue-for-damages legal system amounts to. Winning calls for persistence, money, and luck. Product and medical malpractice cases are more complex than auto cases. Preparation is costly. The cases take years, and are often won or lost not on their merits but by an attorney's ability to gain the jury's sympathy.

Moreover, the distribution of compensation is badly skewed—a few recover million-dollar verdicts, but thousands get nothing. It is not economically feasible to sue for medical injuries for less than some $25,000 or product injuries of less than $5,000 to $10,000. In the big cases, there is strong incentive for the victim to exaggerate his injuries and to inflate his medical bills by undergoing all sorts of useless tests because he will recover these costs even if his own insurance has already paid for them.

DRAWBACKS

Elective no fault would eliminate many of these problems but at the cost of introducing several others. First, universal no-fault might well cost more, not less. San Francisco attorney Robert E. Cartwright, president of the Assn. of Trial Lawyers of America, says that it would be "prohibitively expensive," but the trial lawyers' view is not a disinterested one. Still, Keeton, who as cocreator of no-fault is hardly an antagonist to the idea in general, thinks premiums would undergo a "sharp rise." He believes that, unlike the situation with automobile accidents, the elimination of pain and suffering as a reimbursable loss would not offset the large increase in the number of accident victims who would be compensated for the first time.

Second, pain and suffering, though they can doubtless be exaggerated, are nevertheless real. No legal system can fairly prohibit a person who loses an eye or a limb because of another's carelessness from seeking compensation. O'Connell recognizes this and thinks legislatures can set limits above which victims can pursue traditional remedies.

Finally, any arrangement that does not deter doctors from malpractice, or manufacturers from negligently producing faulty products, or that fails to punish them when they do so cannot gain public support. A driver is not likely to be less careful in states with no-fault insurance, but that is because all injurers are also potential victims. This is manifestly untrue for other kinds of injuries.

HALF A REMEDY

O'Connell agrees that deterrence is necessary, but he argues that reliance on insurance as a mechanism is misplaced. "It doesn't do it now," he says. Indeed, liability insurance rates of particular professionals or corporations are unaffected by specific acts of negligence on their parts.

This means that the problem is deeper than it is usually thought to be, and that universal no-fault is only half a remedy. O'Connell's plan is a sensible alternative, as far as it goes, to the present unfair and antiquated tort system.

But it does not go far enough, and legislators must also create the means of ensuring more responsibility for the safety of goods and services than presently exists. This will not be an easy task, but it is one that no preoccupation with insurance should cause them to ignore. Until it is solved, all insurance plans will be only temporary solutions.

DISCUSSION QUESTIONS

1. Discuss the major causes of the fluctuating value of the dollar.

2. What is E.F.T.? Discuss its impact on individual money handling and business decision making.

3. Discuss how the words "charge it" may change meaning in the not-too-distant future.

4. Describe the technical analysis of stock market prices.

5. What factors can cause the price of a stock to change suddenly?

QUANTITATIVE TOOLS OF MANAGEMENT

Top management personnel hold a high regard for accurate, informative quantitative data. All enterprises must have quantitative data for continued prosperity. Accounting plays a major role in many business and governmental decisions. Frequently changing tax laws also make the accountant's role extremely important.

With this increasing need for faster, more accurate data, the computer is playing an increasingly larger part in the analysis of data. Speeds of computers are increasing with each new generation, and companies are continually modifying their current operations to keep up to date. Computers are even being introduced in the home to improve household management.

Management information systems (MIS) is one of the newer concepts making an impact on all levels of management—from the top to the lowest level. The handling of information can spell the difference between success and failure for business.

The following pages contain articles taken from current magazines and journals that discuss some of the problems related to accounting, computers, and management information systems.

28

OBFUSCATION, INC.

Clarity in the written word is almost a lost cause today. Just ask any English teacher. It's a good thing most English teachers don't read financial statements; then they would really throw up their hands in defeat.

Is all that jargon really necessary? All that obfuscation? Those circumlocutions (otherwise known as beating around the bush)? Those technical terms for common-sense concepts?

Not at all, drawls Delmer P. Hylton, professor of accounting at Winston-Salem, N.C.'s Wake Forest University. Hylton sees no reason why companies couldn't produce financial statements that even an English teacher could love.

Take the term "treasury stock," says Hylton. "What is the treasury, and where is it? Why not just say: Shares of our common stock reacquired from stockholders?"

The word "accrued" is another term Hylton would like to do away with. "Accrued wages payable" means exactly the same as "wages payable." What does "accrued" add—besides a tinge of technicality? Not a thing.

Hylton says that a great deal of the jargon has been passed down from generations of accountants in its antiquated form. Perhaps, says Hylton's associate, Professor Leon Cook, the accountants should have done what the lawyers did: use Latin. Better good Latin than bad English.

Getting back to the existing jargon, Hylton takes aim at terms like "retained earnings" and "reserve," both of which imply the existence of money stashed away somewhere. One of the reasons the Penn Central bankruptcy surprised some people was that the railroad had a retained earnings figure of around half a billion dollars. Those earnings, of course, had long since been sunk into track and roadbed—and they weren't available to pay bills with. Why not substitue "earnings invested in business assets" for "retained earnings," and help eliminate the confusion? (Just as a note of historical interest, "retained earnings" replaced the even more misleading term "earned surplus" about 30 years ago.)

Some other terms the professors feel we could do without: "net sales," which is sales after deducting discounts and allowances; why not just say "revenues"? Then there's "goodwill." Some firms have taken to substituing "excess of cost of acquisitions over net asset value." You have to stare at that one for a second, but at least the phrase means something, whereas "goodwill" doesn't.

Financial statement footnotes, of course, make most insurance policies look like nursery rhymes. Fortunately, the Securities & Exchange Commission is working on **203**

SOURCE: Reprinted by permission of *Forbes* Magazine from the February 15, 1977, issue.

that problem: It is exploring the possibility of introducing "differential disclosure," whereby arcane items required in footnotes would be simplified or summarized for individual investors who haven't the patience or expertise to sift through the clutter. For more exacting financial analysis, the information would still be available in all its jargonistic splendor.

What do the accountants say to all this? They are drafting a "constitution" defining all accounting concepts, but they say the companies themselves have final say over financial statement wording.

Maybe the accountants could improve their image by pressing their clients for the elimination of unnecessary technical language. "You can't convey technical information to someone who has zero knowledge," Professor Hylton concedes, but he adds—and we agree—that there is a lot that can be done to make financial statements easier for the informed layman. Isn't that, after all, the sort of thing democracy is all about?

29

NEW LIFO STYLE CHANGES
COMPANY REPORTS

PAMELA ARCHBOLD

While American consumers have been struggling to maintain their standard of living in the face of intensive inflation, some corporations have been making huge profits because of the pace of price escalation, at least temporarily. What is more, the corporations are unhappy about the situation and are taking steps to "correct" it.

This may seem confusing to some investors, but to an accountant it is elementary. What the companies have been doing increasingly over the last year or so is changing their method of accounting for inventory to the last-in, first-out method, known as LIFO, from the first-in, first-out method, known as FIFO.

Say a manufacturer uses thousands of tons of a particular chemical in producing a cleaning product. The manufacturer keeps a large supply on hand at all times. The cost of the chemical has skyrocketed in recent months, and the price of the cleaning product has been increased accordingly.

Question: Was the cleaning product that is now selling at increased prices made with the recently bought, expensive chemical, or the otherwise identical but much cheaper chemical bought a year or so ago?

Regardless of physical handling of the chemical, the company has its choice. If it has chosen the first-in, first-out method, then in a period of rapid inflation, it makes large profits because it is charging higher prices for goods made with relatively cheaper materials. And accordingly, it pays a large amount of tax on these profits. But when inflation levels off and the company has exhausted its supply (on the books) of cheap materials, its profit picture suddenly darkens.

To reduce this tax burden, and avoid unpleasant surprises to its investors in future quarters, many companies are changing to the last-in, first-out method of accounting, which considers the cost of materials as the price most recently paid.

The LIFO method was approved by Congress way back in 1939, but had been adopted by relatively few companies. The main drawback was that the lower earnings made the LIFO corporations' performance look bad—particularly when compared with FIFO competitors.

SOURCE: *Exchange,* April 1975. Reprinted by permission.

205

As long as investors used earnings as the primary investing measurement, and thereby bought stocks with higher earnings, LIFO remained unpopular.

Beyond that, the difference in the methods was not substantial for many companies because of relatively stable costs. And finally, many companies felt the IRS disclosure rules were inadequate and that the IRS generally regarded LIFO as a loophole.

The situation changed in 1974, because by then investors were paying less attention to corporate earnings, and many stocks reached new all-time lows despite excellent reports. The trend developed because with low stock prices, corporations didn't have anything to lose in terms of investor attention, and lots to gain. The case of Sucrest Corp. is a good example, because in 1973 the company had a loss, and therefore didn't pay taxes. In 1974, however, Sucrest was showing huge "inventory" profits. It changed to LIFO when sugar prices rose 165 percent, pushing earnings to an all-time high.

If Sucrest had stayed on FIFO, taxes would have been $5.5-million in 1974, and Sucrest would have had to pay another $5.5-million over the next 12 months. The switch not only saved the company $11-million in taxes, but also saved it from having to borrow to pay these taxes. The borrowings to cover both years would have added $1-million in annual interest costs, so in effect the switch saved $13-million in two years.

So corporations switch to LIFO because of the tax savings, which in turn allows them to use the money saved for other purposes. They thus lower their borrowings, which is a particular benefit when interest rates are so high.

The savings can be enormous. Du Pont, for example, estimates it will save $150-million in 1974 taxes, and the same amount in estimated 1975 taxes. This will mean a savings of about $6-million in interest cost.

Estimates on the amount of revenue loss to the United States Treasury created by LIFO switches during 1974 vary from $4-billion to $9-billion. The real numbers won't be settled until all the corporations that switched to LIFO file annual reports, but even the lowest estimate has upset the IRS.

The IRS attempted to curb the trend by ruling that corporations could only mention the change in a footnote and not explain the effect on earnings per share at all. The SEC, however, objected strongly and the ruling was amended in late January. The new ruling will allow corporations to explain the change, and the effect on earnings, but only during the first year. After the initial switch, the IRS will allow only a footnote in the financial statements of the annual report. Since the IRS has the power to disallow such changes, most corporations are expected to follow its ruling.

During the first year, shareholders will have little difficulty seeing the effects of the change, but after that some calculations will be required. Given the information that the IRS now makes available, it is possible for investors to approximate the effects of the LIFO change.

The key lies in the footnote, which by IRS decree must read: "If the first-in, first-out (FIFO) method of inventory accounting had been used by the company, inventories would have been $——— and $——— higher than reported at December 31, 19— and December 31, 19—, respectively."

Say the 1974 figure is $1-million. This means inventory value was reduced by $1-million because of the switch, and product cost raised by a million. So earnings were $1-million lower as a result. Reduce this by the company's tax rate from the annual report—say 50 percent. This leaves $500,000 available for earnings per share. Divide by the number of shares outstanding—say 500,000. This means the accounting change reduced earnings by $1 a share.

The adoption of LIFO changes that year's cost of doing business. It is impossible to make the change retroactive. Therefore, only the year of change and following years will show the effects. This creates some confusion on the balance sheet, particularly after the first year when, due to the new IRS rulings, explanations will not be available.

Accountants believe more and more corporations will switch to LIFO, because inflation seems to be almost impossible to control. Investors should remember that the LIFO figures do hold down stated earnings, but that isn't such a bad thing. It is essentially a more stable method of depicting earnings, and perhaps a more accurate reflection of performance. There is some evidence that higher price-earnings ratios are awarded in the market because of the higher "quality" of earnings with the LIFO method.

30

ACCOUNTANTS—CLEANING UP AMERICA'S MYSTERY PROFESSION

CAROLINE E. MAYER

Unexpected bankruptcies of major companies, fraud schemes in some of Wall Street's favorite investments, revelations of widespread illegal payoffs by U.S. businesses—all these and other cases of corporate wrongdoing raise some nagging questions for America's 25 million stockholders:

*How accurate is a company's financial statement?

*How reliable and diligent are the certified public accountants who audit these statements to verify their accuracy and completeness?

Repeated with each new disclosure of corporate misdeed, these questions have sharpened the public's awareness of the auditor's importance in the business world.

Stockholders depend on the auditor's ability as an impartial judge when they study a company's reports and try to decide whether to buy or sell its stock. Banks extend credit, and businesses engage in commercial transactions, on the basis of the information the accountants certify.

The questions now being raised attest to an erosion of public confidence in the accounting profession. Hundreds of lawsuits brought against accountants by stockholders and Government agencies, a flood of new regulations from the Securities and Exchange Commission and a barrage of criticism from Congress all point to the accountant's declining image.

Never before have the activities of the conservative and secretive fraternity of CPA's received so much attention from the public. Uncomfortable with this exposure, the profession has started a two-pronged effort to clean its tarnished image.

It is drawing up new rules for firms that audit publicly held companies, and it has hired a battery of lawyers and public-relations experts to inform the public and Congress on what a CPA's job entails.

A senior partner of one of the nation's largest accounting firms contends: "Accountants have done a lousy job in describing the limitations on what they physically can and cannot do. Auditing the data that back up a financial statement is only a sampling process. We can't possibly audit every transaction."

208

"The public is relying on auditors too much," says Douglas R. Carmichael, the research director for the Commission on Auditor's Responsibilities, a group set up by the American Institute of Certified Public Accountants, the trade association of CPA's, to study the increasing criticism.

Carmichael explains: "Accountants cannot be expected to stem business failures. If a company fails, it's for reasons having nothing to do with an auditor."

Unfortunately for the accounting firms, officials at the Securities and Exchange Commission, many boards of directors and a multitude of stockholders disagree. Lawsuits now pending in the courts charge accountants with failing to detect fraud or to disclose the important financial problems that they found during their investigations.

In separate cases, the SEC and the shareholders of Tidal Marine International Corporation, a shipping concern that defaulted on nearly 40 million dollars of secured and unsecured loans in 1971, have sued S.D. Leidesdorf & Company on the ground that they failed to note that the profits claimed by Tidal Marine were to some extent fictitious. Earlier this year, the SEC and Leidesdorf reached a settlement in which the SEC penalized the firm by prohibiting it from accepting any publicly held company as a new client for 60 days. Leidesdorf is now proposing a $750,000 settlement of the shareholder's suit.

HIGH COSTS OF SETTLEMENT

Settlements of some other claims against accounting firms carry even higher price tags.

Last May, the firm of Elmer Fox, Westheimer & Company agreed to pay 3.25 million dollars into a fund for investors who claimed damages from the sale of Clinton Oil Company securities. In late November, a California State-court jury ordered Touche Ross & Company to pay 30 million dollars in damages to 20 banks and two insurance companies for what the jury called its negligent audit of U.S. Financial, a fraud-ridden diversified real-estate development company that collapsed in 1973. Touche Ross intends to appeal. Meanwhile, still pending against the accounting firm are several other suits by U.S. Financial stockholders and lenders who are seeking a total of nearly 150 million dollars in damages. At present, the International Bank, of Washington, D.C., a diversified financial-service company, has a 9-million-dollar suit against Price Waterhouse & Company, charging it with concealing the insolvency of a subsidiary bank that the company operated in the Bahamas.

Five accounting firms were caught up in one of the largest frauds in Wall Street history—2 billion dollars' worth of bogus insurance policies written by the management of Equity Funding Company of America. To date, four firms—Wolfson, Weiner, Ratoff & Lapin, Seidman & Seidman, Haskins & Sells, and Joseph Froggart & Company, currently owned by Coopers & Lybrand—have agreed to pay a 42.5 million dollar settlement. That leaves one suit—against Peat, Marwick, Mitchell & Company—which is scheduled for trial early next year.

Adding to these woes is increased congressional scrutiny, much of it growing our of the disclosures of illegal or questionable payments made by U.S. companies for political influence here at home and abroad.

Alleged shortcomings of the companies' accountants figured prominently in a harsh 1,760-page report published by the staff of the Senate Governmental Affairs Subcommittee on Reports, Accounting and Management. Subcommittee members followed up with a subsequent report warning the profession that if it fails to make prompt changes that will strengthen its performance and demonstrate that it can call the tune for its clients when they stray, Congress will propose "mandatory reforms."

All of this has accountants, as well as the investing public, wondering what has happened to a profession that was once one of the most highly respected. Melvyn I. Weiss, a New York attorney specializing in stockholder litigation, offers this explanation: "For over 30 years, ever since accountants were required by law to certify the financial statements of publicly held firms, there has been very little questioning of the accountant's role and of his performance.

"As a result, an unhealthy reliance developed between the auditor and the company paying his fee, leading to a situation where the accountant started to forget his real clients—the ones who rely on the financial statements."

New Trends, New Problems

This problem was compounded in the 1960's, Weiss says, by the mushrooming growth in the profession, as demand for accounting services rapidly increased. Many accountants had to be hired quickly, and "this may have contributed to a decline in professional skills," Weiss suggest.

On top of this, he says, "Wall Street in the 1960s and early '70s favored conglomerates and other corporations that seemed to demonstrate an unusual capacity to boost their earnings sharply year after year. The vogue of the "high-performance companies," Weiss says, "placed the accountant in even a more difficult position with his client who wanted good results to get his stock trading at a higher level."

SEC Chairman Harold Williams says the troubles that developed during that era have raised doubts about an auditor's independence.

He explains: "Too often it appears that the auditor believes that he works for the management, not the shareholders of a corporation and other users of financial statements. If hard decisions need to be reached regarding proper accounting, the benefit of the doubt seems to fall inordinately on the side most favorable to the management."

CPA'S AS CORPORATE CONSULTANTS

Doubts about the ability of accountants to deliver fair and objective reviews of their client's affairs have been aggravated by a growing trend among the large firms to provide their customers with a variety of services unrelated to their regular audits. In effect, many of the accountants have transformed themselves into management consultants. They assist in the search for new corporate executives, analyze markets, advise on the most efficient layout for new or modernized plants, study the client's product mix, supply actuarial projections for the corporate pension plan and offer a wide variety of other financial services.

Conflicts Of Interest?

Critics complain that the accounting firm that does these things for a corporate client not only becomes deeply involved in its business affairs but also ends up auditing the results of the steps it advised the management to take. Executive recruitment is particularly worrisome. The accountant who places an executive in a top financial post in a client company has a direct interest in helping that person succeed, and may, therefore, be tempted to compromise when the rules of the profession give any latitude.

And the rules do provide a considerable amount of leeway. The question of how to present financial data fairly is not a simple one. It is often possible—and completely legal—for the same transaction to be accounted for in several ways, all acceptable but sometimes contradictory. That means that a corporation, with the auditor's approval, may on occasion report its affairs—assets, debts, and revenues or profits—according to accepted accounting principles and still leave stockholders and other interested parties with a confusing picture of financial health.

"Company officials have a strong incentive to take advantage of accounting gimmicks or loopholes at their disposal in order to convey the impression they want to make on the public," explains one of the profession's most ardent critics, Adm. Hyman C. Rickover. For years he has charged that the lack of uniform accounting standards has forced the Government to pay more than it should for military goods. He says: "Public accountants are expected to act as safeguards against unreliable financial reporting. But they are under intense pressure to go along with the company's accounting methods, lest they lose the account to a competitor. The CPA's, of course, certify only that all is in accordance with so-called generally accepted accounting principles—which in practice is a euphemism for 'anything goes.'"

Accountants admit that the leeway permitted by accounting principles causes problems. "Audited financial statements cannot be perfectly accurate," the Commission on Auditor's Responsibilities concluded, "because of the ambiguity of the accounting concepts they reflect."

Income, the Commission says, is as vague a concept as health and happiness.

ACCOUNTANTS SOUND SOME WARNINGS

The profession is now cautioning the public that its purpose is not to stamp a "Good Housekeeping Seal of Approval" on any company's financial position. A clean opinion does not mean that a company is financially sound, the Commission says. It merely indicates that the accountant scrutinized the company's records and was satisfied that the statements fairly represent those records. The distinction is one that many investors find difficult to grasp.

Accountants also caution that they cannot possibly detect all frauds. "You can't audit a dishonest person," says Russell E. Palmer, managing partner for Touche Ross. "He will always figure out some way to avoid being discovered."

Kickbacks and payoffs are equally hard to find, accountants say, because the amounts involved usually are small. The illegal and questionable payments made by more than 400 U.S. corporations were, for the most part, not large enough, in relation to the companies' total costs and revenues, to have a "material effect" on profits. Moreover, the cost of making a thorough search for such relatively minute sums would be exorbitant, sometimes more than the cost of the illegalities that would be found, accountants add.

PROS AND CONS OF SERVICES

The Senate subcommittee came to the conclusion that nonaccounting management services "are incompatible with the public responsibilities of independent auditors and should be discontinued."

The large firms stand to lose a great deal of new-found business if they heed that advice. Some corporations, not yet heavily involved in executive recruitment are dropping this service. But most of them balk, arguing that there is no proof that the integrity of any auditor has been compromised by these management services. In fact, they say, consulting is helpful to the auditor beacuse it gives him an opportunity to learn more about his client.

"The accounting business has become enormously sophisticated and complicated," says Norman Auerbach, chairman of Coopers & Lybrand. "An accounting firm needs an enormous breadth of talent and specialties to do its job. These management services help us. Those who say we should get rid of them are thinking too narrowly. They want us to go back to the days of green eyeshades, when an accountant's job was simply making marks on a company's financial statement."

Edwin Mruk, the director of Arthur Young's personnel consulting services, contends that prohibiting accounting firms from offering management services would be like "forbidding your doctor to talk to you about your family problems because they don't have an impact on your physical well-being."

The SEC is considering one solution to this conflict-of-interest problem: a rule that would force all public corporations, in their proxy statements, to disclose all services provided by outside auditors, the fees to them and any company revenues "derived from" them. Such disclosure, says SEC chairman Williams, would "permit investors to decide for themselves whether, in light of these nonaudit relationships, the auditor can realistically be considered fully independent."

Williams also thinks accountants themselves should take steps to guarantee their independence. If they fail, he promises that he, along with Congress, will be prepared to impose federal regulations.

That threat has pushed the profession's trade association, the American Institue of Public Accountants, into action. In September, it rushed to adopt a self-regulation plan for firms that audit publicly held companies registered with the SEC. The plan calls for mandatory three-year reviews of each company's auditing work by other auditors as well as sanctions—suspensions, expulsions, fines and public censure—for any firm whose work is found to be deficient.

Publicly, Government officials say it's too early to predict how successful the self-policing plan will be. Privately, many say the approach doesn't go far enough.

Division In the Ranks

Furthermore, the Institute's plan divides the profession into two sections, one composed of the larger firms that audit companies registered with the SEC, and the other composed of the smaller firms that audit privately held firms. The smaller firms contend that the effect is to create first- and second-class memberships that could substantially hurt their business by building up the prestige of their major competitors. The rules for membership in the SEC division, they say, could be so onerous and costly that they would be prevented from successfully competing, for the lucrative business of auditing public companies.

A greater drawback in the eyes of some federal officials is the failure of the plan to require all corporations to use audit committees, composed of outside directors. These committees would have sole responsibility for selecting, paying, evaluating and, if necessary, firing the auditors. Since the auditor would no longer be hired by the management that is directly affected by the auditor's report, his independence would be enhanced.

Already a requirement to that effect has been laid down by the New York Stock Exchange for all companies whose stock is traded there, effective next July. The response of the accounting firms has been enigmatic. Many applaud the concept and even ask the SEC to require them to deal only with audit companies. But at the same time, they refuse to take the initiative in imposing the rule on their clients, many of whom are opposed to the whole idea.

Officials also doubt that self-regulation in the profession will carry much clout. The CPA Institute has been sharply criticized in the past for being reluctant to impose sanctions on derelict accountants. Furthermore, officials point out, the Institute cannot keep an accountant from practicing, even by expelling him from membership. Only State agencies can do that by revoking licenses.

Two congressional committees already plan hearings on the problems of the profession next Spring. Chairman Williams of the SEC has promised to submit a progress report on accounting to Congress next July.

In the meantime, can the investor place greater faith in the financial statements that are submitted to him with the usual auditor's endorsement? According to Herbert A. Morey, Jr., a partner in Arthur Young & Company: "You can expect your auditor to be looking over his shoulder more often than in the past, to be more concerned with dotting those i's and crossing those t's, to be consulting more with his colleagues, to be staying off the end of the limb for fear of the man with the saw."

That suggests greater honesty, but no relief from the complications that have made it more and more difficult for the typical stockholder to understand, let alone trust, what he reads.

31

MANAGEMENT CAN HELP MAKE DP MORE OF AN INSIDER IN THE COMPANY

BELDEN MENKUS

Usually, a data processing (DP) operation does not create basic products or bring in cash needed to keep an organization functioning. Instead, DP is employed to help the organizational units that do carry on the basic business. (This is true, even when a data center sells a portion of its processing capabilities and services to other organizations.)

The data processing organization's role is unlike that of the other company support services. Its stance is not totally passive; its main goal is not survival. There should be a constructive tension between DP and other revenue generating segments of the organization. (DP must subordinate its goals and priorities to theirs. Yet, it must continue to enhance its mastery of rapidly evolving data processing technology.)

The way in which this complex tension is balanced determines overall data processing effectiveness. (Equipment utilization, staff productivity, error rates and the like all are important, but the quality of DP's relationships with the rest of the organization determines the ultimate value of everything it does.)

This tension creates a continuing dilemma for those DP operation staff members who must work with the users of computer services. Yet, even though DP people know best how to use the computer, they may not fully understand the environment in which it is to be used. What's more, they participate as *outsiders* in a decision making process whose outcome they can do little to influence. Results: residual frustration among the data processing staff; continual friction between these individuals and others in the organization.

Three things can be done to improve this situation.

Help staff members grasp the user's viewpoint. Assign different persons from the DP staff as liaisons with each major computer user group in the organization. Mission: Learn to understand that group's goals, needs and operating constraints through direct involvement in what it does.

Use these key people to keep the data processing staff aware of user problems and needs, and to keep users aware of developing new computer systems.

Introduce key user executives to data processing realities. Help participants understand *what* the computer can do; avoid involvement in *how* it does it. Encourage realistic plans for computer resource use. Mission: Create enlightened consumers, not technicians.

Some executive involvement with data processing could take place through a special non-technical briefing that might be titled "What the Non-DP Manager Needs to Know About Data Processing." You may find that continuing education people in your area can help here.

Reappraise data processing project review and approval practices. Emphasize both the impact of the new application on user operations, as well as enhanced cost effectiveness. Mission: Maintain a more effective joint decision process.

32

THERE'S A COMPUTER IN YOUR FUTURE

LAWRENCE C. LEVY

The snow had already begun to fall and she knew she'd be pressed for time in the morning. So the night before, she went to the kitchen to give herself a head start.

She filled the percolator with coffee and plugged it into a socket. She put two fresh eggs into a pot of water on the stove and a slice of frozen bread in the toaster. Then she sat at a counter-top console that resembled a tv set and a typewriter keyboard.

Leafing through a box nearby, she selected a flexible disk the size of a record, but square, and slipped it into the disk drive console. After she tapped out a few words, the screen came alive:

"What time would you like to get up?" it flashed.

"7 a.m.," she typed. But, remembering the snow, she deleted the entry and put in its place "6:45 a.m."

"Alarm at 6:45 a.m.," the ever-careful machine repeated. "Is that correct?"

"Yes."

"What else can I do for you?" it flashed, listing a dozen words, such as coffee, toaster, oven alarm—each with a number next to it. She immediately typed the number next to "coffee," and the machine replied as it always did:

"Good to the last drop! What time do you want your coffee perked?"

"7 a.m."

"Coffee perked at 7 a.m.," it said. "Is that correct?"

And so it went with the eggs and the toast. And with the instructions to the engine heater in the car in her garage. She asked the computer to turn on the heater at 6 a.m.—enough time to warm up her car so it would run smoothly by the time she'd be ready to leave. As smart as the computer was, she mused to herself, it still couldn't give her back June in December.

The scenario is not science fiction: There IS a computer in your future—your own computer. Maybe not next week or even next year. But it's a good bet that a small computer system like the one described above will be a familiar fixture in your home by the early 1980s.

216

SOURCE: *Tulsa World,* March 19, 1978. Reprinted by permission.

As capable as those million-dollar giants of 10 years ago, it probably won't cost much more, or look much different, than the tv and stereo in your living room now.

Your own computer.

If you're skeptical, consider this: The computer in your future is already available. You can walk into an electronics store, and, for about $600, order a system consisting of a video screen, typewriter keyboard, cassette recorder and a breadbox-sized computer.

By plugging it into a standard socket and following a few simple directions, you can: balance your checkbook, keep track of your debts (or credits, if you're lucky), teach your kids math and foreign languages, play games, store recipes and adjust the proportions, as well as remind yourself who's coming to dinner.

And, says Andre Rozwadowski, owner of a N.Y. computer shop called Computer Microsystems, these simple systems presently available "are really just expensive toys, compared to what will soon be possible."

Average consumers will have small computer systems that keep track of their finances—storing and correlating hundreds of financial transactions fed it throughout the year—and provide them with the data to do their taxes at the end of the year.

A program, for example, will be keyed to evaluate and separate transactions into tax deductions, exemptions, income, etc., and in some cases even print out a tax form at the push of a button.

In the future, your computer will control the temperature throughout your home—shutting off heat, for example, to rooms always unoccupied at certain times and not allowing the others to rise above a certain amount—and tell you exactly what your fuel bill is at any moment. Or telephone bill, if the computer is programmed with the phone rates.

This may usher in a new era of consumerism, allowing the user, for the first time, to monitor the utilites' bookkeeping with a convincing degree of accuracy.

The computers also will be connected to and monitor smoke and burglar alarms when you're sleeping or not at home. And when an alarm is activated, the computer will phone the police or fire department and play a tape recording: "Hello, this is the Jones family at 29 Maple Dr. We're not home now and our alarm has been activated. We'd appreciate it if you'd check our house. Thank you."

And to make a house look lived in when a family is on a vacation, their computer will also turn on tv sets, turn on lights and even flush toilets to convince a burglar that someone's at home.

Giant computers in modern office buildings do those things as a matter of routine. For the price of a new car—$5,000 to $10,000—you can already get a computer and the companion devices for some of those sophisticated "applications" for personal use.

But most computer experts agree that unless you have a strong technical background, you'd probably never get off the ground: The "hardware"—the computer and companion devices to carry out those more sophisticated functions—is generally available. But the "software" or "program"—the instructions reminding the computer what to do—is not. So, for the most part, you'd have to set up and program the system yourself.

Not for long, though; not if things keep developing at their present pace.

Nick Barton, co-owner of Byte Shop East, who opened the N.Y. retail computer store in November 1976, said, "When we started, the demand was already growing faster than the available hardware." But the hardware has just about caught up to demand, and so will the software.

Some computer retailers caution against what they see as snake-oil salesmen who promise their machines can do too much. "There is a danger," says Rozwadowski, "of discouraging people by raising their expectations too high, too soon." But they have a hard time containing their own enthusiasm.

"It's still growing by leaps and bounds," said Bob Glassman, an engineer with Schweber Electronics, a manufacturer of components. "In the next few years, there won't be a household that won't have some kind of computer control."

Joseph Abruscati, another Schweber engineer, sees the time when many homes will be equipped with "terminals" hooked up to central data banks, programmed to be electronic encyclopedias for kids and parents.

Let's say you want to write a term paper on sea sponges. Type in the word "sponge" on the screen, press a few buttons and the computer would offer you several categories, including "sea," each with a number next to it.

If you type in the number of "sea," the information on the subject programmed into the electronic encyclopedia would pop up on the screen. Included would be cross-references such as Gulf of Mexico or Diving—just as you would find in a good encyclopedia or textbook.

The information would be copied off the machine onto a printer or, more elaborately, a photocopier. Many libraries and newspapers already have similar systems.

These same terminals could help ease the lives of the handicapped or elderly persons confined to their homes by serving as security, entertainment and communication centers hooked up to a central computer.

For example, one computer could look after hundreds of home-confined elderly persons by automatically calling the home of anyone who forgets to press a button indicating "I'm okay" or "I've taken my medication" within a prearranged time.

There would also be an "emergency" button on the terminal that would tell the central computer to call the doctor or police. The same terminal would enable the invalid—or anybody, for that matter—to call up any number of games or puzzles, ranging from crossword to chess to intricate battles.

It may be fitting that the first retail computer operation was run from the corner of a New York City toy store. For, of the estimated 50,000 micro-computers sold in America since 1975, most have been bought by technically proficient "hobbyists" who use them to devise and play various complicated, challenging games.

(These shouldn't be confused with the "match-wits-with-a-computer" games that have been heavily advertised and featured in toy departments recently. Although the toys are controlled by a micro-processor, they are pre-programmed and the user has no choice but to play what comes.)

But where is the market going from here? Sales to these hobbyists have just about reached the saturation point, say experts. One big area of sale will be to small businesses. Of the 150,000 micro-computers expected to be sold this year—triple the combined sales of the last three years—most will be for small businesses.

"For an investment of $5,000 to $10,000, you can get a computer and programming that will take care of accounts payable and receivable, payroll, general ledger, inventory and other basic applications for a business of up to 50 employees," said Robert Jones, publisher of *Interface Age,* a magazine for computer hobbyists.

"When faced with the choice of spending $10,000 a year or more for another bookkeeper or spending the same amount only once, plus a nominal charge for maintenance, I think businesses will begin choosing computers more and more."

On the home front, low-cost plug-in home computers are available. There is the TRS-80, produced by the Tandy Corp. ($600 at Radio Shack), the PET, by Commodore ($495 at Computer shops) and the APPLE-II, made by Apple Computer Inc. ($1,295 also at shops).

Neighborhood computer stores are regularly springing up, and R.H. Macy's California division and Foley's Department Store in Houston recently broke new ground for mass merchandisers.

According to Frank Brown, of Technical Design Lab in Princeton, N.J., heat and energy conservation will be the main impetus for expansion into the home. "The average homeowner won't buy a computer just to store recipes or remind them of what to do during the day," he said.

"What will make him shell out $1,500 to $3,000 or more will be the savings that could be realized in extremely lower fuel bills. And any computer capable of doing that could also store recipes and play games and do any number of other things."

In the first year of the micro-computer's development, 1975, a half-dozen magazines and some 100 retail stores sprang up across the country to cater to the market. Now there are an estimated 500 to 600 computer stores. Some shops just specialize in the huge number of new technical publications.

There are dozens of how-to books for beginners and experts alike being published each month. There are also at least a dozen slick magazines.

The monthly *Interface Age,* for example, started with 430 subscriptions as a computer club's newsletter, but has since expanded to 53,000 and it is still growing.

And many of these magazines, such as ROM or Personal Computing, are geared to appeal to people with little or no technical background.

33

SMALL COMPUTERS: NEW FASHION IN RETAILING

Executives with inventory problems can profit from taking a look at what fashion retailers are doing. Inventory has traditionally been a problem in this competitive business, complicated by the wide variety of merchandise and the capriciousness of the buying public. The business takes its highest toll on merchandising management of stores selling moderately priced ladies' sportswear aimed at the younger crowd. Buy too much of the wrong thing, and massive markdowns with lost profits are the rule. Under-order on a hot new item and shoppers go somewhere else. Here is how one company neatly solved the problem.

Will Friedman, president of Contempo Casuals, Inc., Van Nuys, California, was feeling the press of these inventory problems, compounded by the logistics of stocking 14 stores spread all over Southern California. He investigated several computerized systems, but found that their maximum-minimum stock level measurements were adequate only for relatively static inventories. They lacked the scope and sophistication needed for his business.

After much searching, he found a combination ideally suited for his business: a Microdata Reality minicomputer and a packaged inventory system. The minicomputer had one of Friedman's first prerequisites: ease of operation. Microdata's computer language is called ENGLISH and can be used by anyone who can read and write English. The machine can actually be learned in minutes.

The system was provided by Jack Hill, head of Retail Oriented Computer Systems (ROCS). The software is sophisticated, but geared up toward making the users job easy. A self-teaching concept was used, so that operating instructions are displayed to the user for each step, making the system virtually error-free.

Keyboard/CRT's are used for inquiry and data entry. All entry is on-line so that data is as up-to-date as possible. Friedman says the system requires no operating manual, no computer department, and no computer room. Everyone on the staff—from the president to the receiving clerk—has access to, and operates, the system: "Training time was actually measured in minutes and seconds. It's so easy to use that everyone here has experimented."

220

SOURCE: Reprinted from the June 1975 issue of *Modern Office Procedures* and copyrighted 1975 by Penton/IPC, subsidiary of Pittway Corporation.

The system provides complete merchandise inventory information, keeping track of goods from purchase to final sale. It keeps records for every piece of merchandise, typically 15,000 items in stock and a like amount on order. The system is used in virtually every phase of merchandising (Figure 33—1).

Among its 100 different functions are:

Management inventory decisions. Management is given detailed sales analysis and forecasting reports. Decisions on what and when to buy can be entered on line.

Purchasing, receiving. The system will automatically generate purchase orders for the items management chooses. The on-line mechanism permits cancellations or delivery data requests to be requested at any time. When the goods are received, the system automatically updates the purchase order file and the warehouse inventory.

Inspection, splitting, accounts payable. Incoming items are inspected and the

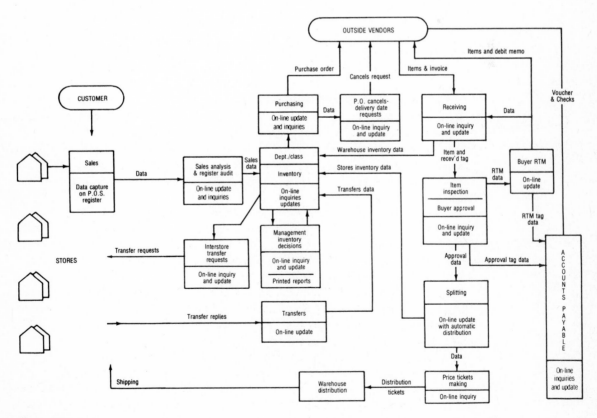

Figure 33-1

system provides for 1) Returning unsatisfactory merchandise to the vendor, 2) Approving a payable item to the accounts payable system which then automatically produces a voucher and check 3) Dividing the incoming order among several stores. In doing this it prints price tickets, prints distribution tickets for the warehouse to expedite shipping the required items to each store, and updating a stores inventory after withdrawing the items from the warehouse inventory.

Sales. All retail sales at the 14 stores are recorded on Sweda point-of-sale registers. Data is captured on tape casettes. This is sent in to the central system daily where it updates the sales and stores inventory files.

PART SIX
DISCUSSION QUESTIONS

1. Discuss some clarifications that could be made in accounting jargon.

2. What is meant by LIFO? How is it different from FIFO?

3. Why have so many companies switched to LIFO?

4. What can be done to improve the data processing department's relations with the rest of the firm?

5. Discuss the reason why the accounting profession is coming under close scrutiny. Are the reasons justified?

6. Discuss the prospects of adding a computer to your home—advantages and disadvantages.

7. Describe the use of computers in retailing.

ADDITIONAL DIMENSIONS

Throughout this book, many of the readings have keynoted the idea that change (some good and some bad) is prevalent in our business system. This section highlights some of the areas where the change in business is really dramatic. International business is undergoing upheavals. Nationalism and the oil cartel of the Middle East are partly responsible. American businesspersons are apprehensive about going into many of these countries with their multinational operations. However, many foreign countries are soliciting American investment money. Jordan is one example. Reading 34, "Where U.S. Firms Are Missing a Bet," illustrates the problem.

Reading 35 shows how small businesses have had to cope with change as they struggle to survive. Changes in our legal system have also affected business. Contract language and small claims court are examples of our changing legal environment, as seen in Readings 36 and 37.

Potential dangers to the future of the United States give rise to the need for solutions to six basic problems that must be worked out to ensure lasting prosperity. The American industrial community is gearing for some dramatic changes.

34

WHERE U.S. FIRMS ARE MISSING A BET

STERLING G. SLAPPEY

Amman, Jordan—On practically every road in this desert kingdom, the German automobile reigns supreme. In fact, the Mercedes-Benz is more common than the camel here.

Experts from Taiwan are setting up a textile plant. The beer is Dutch, and British and Japanese consumer goods are big in the shops.

British and German ship-loading equipment is on the docks at the Red Sea port of Aqaba. Germans built the new railroad from Amman to Aqaba and they are now laying out the new Amman International Airport. The French are developing copper mining.

All this gives an American an eerie feeling here in the country that is the United States' best friend in the Arab world. And, it makes one wonder: "Where are the Yanks?"

It's a pertinent question when you recall that since World War II the U.S. has provided Jordan with $800 million in cash gifts, and in long-term loans at minute interest, for civilian development. Another quarter-billion has gone to the Jordanian army and air force.

The U.S. Department of Commerce recognizes the shortage of effort by Americans in Jordan, as well as elsewhere in the Middle East. In a "Report to U.S. Business," it said: "Billions of dollars in orders will be written over the next few years by the oil-rich states of the Middle East and their neighbors for precisely the kind of products and services in which U.S. companies excel. Unfortunately, a great many of these orders are likely to go by default to British, French, German, Italian or Japanese suppliers, because U.S. companies are slow in reacting."

Prime Minister Zaid Rifai—fluent in English, urbane, and a frequent, welcome visitor to Washington—has his theory on why Americans, who are just about everywhere else in the commercial world, have not come to Jordan in large numbers.

"Capitalists are often cowards," he told NATION'S BUSINESS during a visit in his Amman office. "Often Americans are afraid to come here, partially for political reasons—the fear of another Middle East war." But then he pointed to the Germans, Britons, Swedes, Japanese, Taiwan Chinese and Frenchmen thronging hotels.

Prime Minister Rifai also said one factor keeping Americans from at least matching the

SOURCE: Reprinted by permission from *Nation's Business*, February 1975. Copyright 1975 by Nation's Business, Chamber of Commerce of the United States.

business efforts of other nationalities is "the memory of the internal unrest"—which amounted to a full-scale, but brief, civil war four years ago between radical Palestinians and the Jordanian government.

Chances for more such "unrest" appear to have lessened now, because Jordan's King Hussein went along with the recent decision by other Arab rulers to support formation of a Palestinian nation on the West Bank of the River Jordan, in territory formerly held by the Jordanians and now held by the Israelis.

The Prime Minister, numerous government development executives and heads of Jordanian banks, other private businesses and commercial associations plead for attention from American business and offer large helpings of tax relief and a dozen other major concessions under the "Encouragement of Investment Law of 1972."

It's a law specifying that Jordan is a land of private enterprise where government rarely takes a leading role. In most business, the government has no role whatsoever.

An example of Jordanian private enterprise in Amman is a flourishing market where livestock is bartered, just as it has been for thousands of years. Nearby is a modern computer center, also privately owned, and an American enterprise—a recently established branch of New York's First National City Bank.

"We want all kinds of American participation, not just banks," the Prime Minister said. "We want Americans in on the development of our natural resources. We have over a billion tons of phosphate in the ground and we are nearly doubling production each year. Until recently, we had a shortage of railway equipment and trucks to handle the phosphate, but that is now corrected. We have also large copper deposits.

"We admire American businessmen and we want them in joint ventures with our government or our private enterprises—or the Americans can come in entirely on their own."

Ali T. Dajani, director of the Amman Chamber of Industry, and Dr. Khalil Salem, president of the National Planning Council, both believe the smallness of the Jordanian market—only three million people—makes Americans prefer to go elsewhere to invest.

SIZE IS A FACTOR

Mr. Dajani ran off a list of Jordanian private enterprises looking for American partners, and the amount of money needed in these joint ventures was invariably small by American standards—usually from $500,000 to $1 million.

The companies produce textiles, confections, glass, ceramics, building materials, oil products, paper, cardboard, woolens, agricultural equipment, toothpaste, shaving cream, auto batteries and other items.

"If I had a medium-size American business," Mr. Dajani said in his office in the center of the colorful Old City section of Amman, "I would put up a tire plant here. Local money is ready for a joint venture. The number of cars here goes up fast and Egypt has the nearest tire factory. There is an excellent opportunity to sell tires here and to export them throughout the Arab world.

"Here we do not think only of the Jordanian market. We think of Saudi Arabia, just next door and with all that oil money to spend; we think of Kuwait—very rich—of Syria, Iraq, the sheikhdoms to the east. Jordan has a superb port at Aqaba—it's east of Suez, and the whole of the east coast of Africa can quickly be reached from it.

"A well-equipped printing plant could be profitable, for there is no such thing here now.

We must even have our passports printed in Great Britain. Business partners are waiting here to help erect a printing shop.

"The Arab world can use every bag of cement that can be produced. We have much building. We need big trucks that mix cement while on the way to building sites, such as you find in the West. Did you know that, here in Amman, we still follow the old-fashioned, wasteful, foolish practice of mixing cement by hand in tubs at the building sites?

"Look anywhere and you see construction. Construction workers get from $3 to $12 a day, depending on skills and the job.

"The Middle East is the land of sheep and yet we need millions more animals. We need at least one million extra every year for Moslem pilgrims to take with them to Mecca. Arab states in our neighborhood—the Saudis for example—would take all the meat they can get. Now, much of our meat comes from Bulgaria, of all places. We also eat more poultry every year. American agribusinesses have many opportunities here."

Good labor relations prevail in Jordan—strikes are rare. Pay scales are above those in several Arab countries, but productivity is considerably higher. Only Lebanon has a better literacy rate in the Middle East.

Jordan is often described as an Arab country without oil, but it now appears that this is not true. Prime Minister Rifai declined to give details other than to say that oil very probably is here and that he hopes to enlist American oil exploration companies to help bring it up.

The desire for more American investment and participation is so great, Planning Council President Salem said, that King Hussein is "holding open the door" for American participation in developing a copper industry. The King is popular with Jordanians, except with the radical Palestinians. He mixes well with the people, flies jet fighters, water skis at Aqaba and moves smoothly on the tuxedo-diplomatic circuits of Washington and London. Also, he is effective—when he advocates something, things begin to happen. His prestige is partially responsible for decisions by American hotel companies—Holiday Inns and Sheraton among them—to participate in new hotels here.

FATEFUL PHOSPHATE

Jordan's main export item, phosphate, currently provides revenue unheard of until the past few months. "The price went from a break-even $16 per ton to $65 and it is now heading for $80," Dr. Salem said. "Production will reach eight million tons yearly very soon and this means Jordan has the money to help finance many incoming industries and to meet commitments on loans from abroad. Right now we need $1 billion, which isn't much in these days, and we will get it.

"We have good credit and our dinar is quite sound. We are far ahead of our development program in many instances."

A prime contributor to Jordan's improving economy is the beautiful and fertile Jordan River Valley.

Without the East Ghor Canal to carry water to thousands of farmers, the valley would be desolate, as is most of the country. Americans can take pleasure in the fact that the 60-kilometer-long (37 miles) canal, which is being extended another 18 kilometers toward the Dead Sea, is to their credit. The 16-feet-wide, three-feet-deep cement-trench canal has been financed during the past 12 years largely through American gifts of cash and easy loans.

The Jordan Valley is an open air hothouse hundreds of feet below sea level where a variety of crops are harvested three times yearly. American experts consider its potential to be about equal to that of the Imperial Valley in California.

Another prime contributor to Jordan's economy is the tourist trade.

Though Israel holds the holy city of Jerusalem, which was part of Jordan until the 1967 war, Western tourists pour into Amman for visits, travel to Jerusalem by bus, and then visit Antioch, Bethlehem and Galilee before returning across the Jordan River to Amman. About 150,000 did this in 1974.

Abed Alruhan Abu Rabah, general director of the Ministry of Tourism, said the number of visitors going to holy places increases steadily and scores of business opportunities exist for Americans to take part in providing transport and lodgings for them.

A WEALTH OF HISTORY

Jordan is rich in tourist attractions.

This is a land where Lawrence of Arabia led desert fighters against the Turks. There are Crusader castles, and the ancient, hidden city of Petra. The best-preserved Roman ruins in the world are at Jerash. In the Jordan Valley 10,000 years ago, many archeologists say, man first stopped being a rover and settled in the world's first community.

It's a land of many holy places for Christians, Jews and Moslems. It's the birthplace of scores of Biblical figures. It's where Salome danced and John the Baptist lost his head.

In addition, there are camelback vacations to take in the eastern desert, great wadis (valleys) comparable to the Grand Canyon, and the modern beaches of Aqaba.

Also, there's royalty, always a magnet for tourists. Plus accoutrements of the Moslem world—veiled women, mosques, holy men in dress unlike anywhere else, bedouin camps in the desert.

It all makes for a colorful, different backdrop for investment of Western money and know-how.

There is one jarring note in Jordan's mixture of today with yesterday. When the people are called to prayer, and the whining chant comes down from the minarets of the mosques, it comes not from the throats of muezzins, but from recordings played on phonographs.

And not even the phonographs are American-made. They are German or Japanese.

35

SMALL BUSINESS: THE MADDENING STRUGGLE TO SURVIVE

"I would be nuts to go through this another season," sighs Ben Blanc, president of Calliope, Inc., a Philadelphia manufacturer of children's wear. In the past year his volume has shrunk from $250,000 to $150,000, his material costs have increased 25%, and his labor costs have risen 20%. But pinched by heavy inventories ("I overbought last year when I thought prices were right") and the drop in sales, he has been able to raise his prices only 15%. Blanc complains that only his bigger competitors can survive these days.

"Take Oshkosh B'Gosh, Inc. They can make something that sells for $3.75," he says. "Hell, I can't even start to make it for that." Another big problem is accounts receivable. More than 25% of last year's sales are on collection, a situation Blanc calls "deadly." Says he: "The collection agencies charge you 20% to collect, but my margin is only 16%, so I'm losing money collecting money." Blanc, who has been in business 15 years, concludes: "If we have another bad season, I will shutter down."

Blanc's lament is repeated by small businessmen in virtually every industry in every part of the country. "The small businessman these days is like the guy in Las Vegas who prays, 'Please God, let me break even. I need the money,'" says Oliver O. Ward, head of the Smaller Business Assn. of New England. "Things are tough now, and it looks like they will be tough for a long time coming."

THE TRIBULATIONS OF SMALLNESS

After months of devastating inflation and recession, many of the nation's smaller entrepreneurs are fighting for survival. Squeezed by tight money, rising costs, depressed markets, and uncertain supply sources, they find it tougher to cope with economic adversity than larger, more financially robust competitors. Their problems are compounded by growing government intervention. New occupational safety rules, environmental restrictions, product safety regulations, and increased minimum wages pose costly challenges that are more difficult for the small businessman. Just as significant, the harsh economic climate has created unprecedented barriers for new entrepreneurs eager to enter the marketplace.

SOURCE: Reprinted from the June 30, 1975, issue of *Business Week* by special permission. **231**

These tribulations are vividly pointed up in the steady rise in bankruptcies and the decline in new business incorporations. Dun & Bradstreet's statistics on commercial and industrial failures, which essentially cover small businesses, last year reached a three-year high in numbers—9,915—and a record high in total dollar liabilities. Last March the rate was the highest for any month in eight years. (See Figure 35—1).

Dollar liabilities topped $3 billion for the first time in 1974, and included an unprecedented 427 bankruptcies in the million-dollar category. Increasingly affected are larger businesses, not just store-front "mom-and-pop" operations. Especially hard hit are retailers of general merchandise, building contractors, home furnishings retailers, and building materials dealers. Failures are also up in textile and apparel manufacturing and among transportation equipment producers. New business incorporations slumped to 319,149 last year from a record 329,358 in 1973. Early in 1975 the numbers dropped to the lowest level in four years.

To be sure, economic calamity is not universal among small businessmen. Many continue to thrive, and some even see strategic advantages in their size during a recession. "We can be more flexible, can move more quickly, and concentrate on smaller segments of markets," notes David Bigelow, president of R. C. Bigelow Co., a Norwalk (Conn.)-based specialty foods outfit that grosses about $10 million.

Bigelow's most successful product is a spiced tea, Constant Comment. General Foods had a competitive brand that was abandoned. Now Bigelow is battling GF again in spiced- and fruit-flavored instant coffees. This time, Bigelow concedes, General Foods has "flattened us out a bit."

Nevertheless, Bigelow is bullish about the future of small business. "I feel the large corporations are failing in this country, leaving opportunities for small specialty companies,"

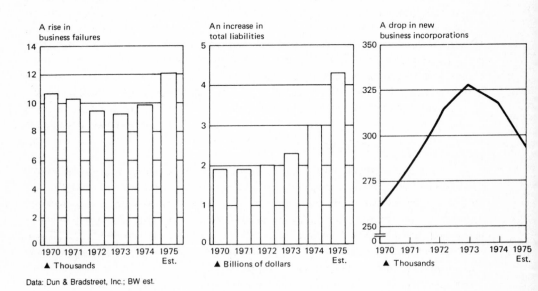

Data: Dun & Bradstreet, Inc.; BW est.

Figure 35-1 The Recession's Impact on Small Business

he says. "Big manufacturers are making such bad products. The big, discount-type retail operators run stores where no one gives a damn about the customer. So there are opportunities for small businessmen. But it takes a strong individual to handle them."

HOW SMALL IS SMALL?

Getting an exact fix on the life and times of small business is complicated by the question of definition. The official definition—employed by the Small Business Administration on loans—ranges all over the lot. In manufacturing, it is based on numbers of employees and the industry. Apparel and textile companies are regarded as "small" if they have no more than 250 employees. For producers of aircraft and ammunition, the number is 1,500. In the service industries, the criterion is dollar volume: a maximum of $5 million for department stores, groceries, and auto dealers, and $1 million for most other retailers; $5 million for general contractors; and $5 million for most wholesalers. To reflect inflation, SBA is now revising the sales figures upward by as much as 90%.

The problems of size, however, are not limited to companies that fit neatly into the government's "small business" pigeonholes. Scores of companies with sales running into nine figures—"second-tier" corporations in industries dominated by billion-dollar giants—suffer the same kind of disadvantages in a recession. Their difficulties in raising capital, lining up stable supply sources, and remaining competitively strong are likely to result in growing concentration of market shares among the giant companies.

The cost and availability of capital head the list of small business problems. Financing a small business is like a line from Gilbert & Sullivan, quips Oliver Ward. "The small businessman tries his sisters and his cousins and his aunts." Raising money to launch or expand a small enterprise is never easy. But business conditions, the collapse of the new equity market, and a possible nationwide capital drought have made it tougher than ever.

"Small businessmen aren't thinking in terms of growth," asserts Timothy Hay, president of First Small Business Investment of California. "They're thinking in terms of survival—getting their houses in order rather than increasing their commitments."

James M. McCarl, president of Perfection Furniture Co. of Claremont, N.C., who now performs janitorial chores in his own plant to cut overhead costs, says that "December and January were the two worst months I have seen in my 20 years in the furniture business. If you look at our balance sheet and P&L statement, if it didn't curl your hair, it would turn it white." He now operates his plant only four days a week, and with other executives, helps clean up on Fridays.

But things are looking up, says McCarl, with the entrepreneur's incurable optimism. "Business has gone from horrible to terrible." Long range, he believes, "the things we are trying to do will eventually turn this company around unless the economy just stays sour." For example, he is offering customers three weeks delivery on his medium-priced, special-order upholstered furniture. "A competitor asked me how I could do it, and I told him it wasn't hard at all with a two-week backlog," he says. "The slump taught me to take every adversity, and try to turn it into an opportunity."

McCarl's bankers helped with a loan extension, but other small businessmen paint a different picture of bank largesse. "The banks don't cooperate as they do with big firms," complains Edwin H. Stern, who operates a suburban Atlanta gift shop. "We pay higher interest rates, and credit is not as easily available."

Financial problems are by no means limited to gift shops, however. Sierracin Corp. of Sylmar, Calif., a $23-million producer of coatings, heating devices, and other highly specialized products, is sandwiched "between billion-dollar customers and billion-dollar vendors," says its president, John P. Endicott. "Many of our vendors will not give us fixed prices for any length of time, and some are strictly on price at time of delivery. At the other end, we have to give our customers firm commitments for much longer than our vendors are willing to give us."

Partly because of his track record with two other ventures, Endicott has been in the enviable position of having a good line of credit and not needing to tap it. Part of his success is sticking to product lines requiring narrow, intense skills, says Endicott, who proves the theory that entrepreneurs succeed less with pure invention than with perseverance.

THE SEARCH FOR FINANCING

Still another headache for small business is its inability to increase prices. Says Richard M. Bailey, an economist at the University of California at Berkeley: "Volume is more steady" for small than for large manufacturers, but "small business may have problems raising prices in inflationary times because it's closer to the consumer, and too substantial price rises might cut them out."

Premix, Inc., of North Kingsville, Ohio, is a case in point. President George H. Kaull started his reinforced plastics business with two partners on borrowed capital of $22,400. Fifteen years later, he does $20-million in sales and declares that "inflation and recession have played hell with us."

Kaull says polyester resin soared from 18¢ per lb. to 48¢ in one year, and some raw ingredients for his plastics went up 500%. "But the small supplier has a particularly difficult time passing inflationary costs on to his big customers," says Kaull. "A little guy making knobs for windshield wipers doesn't really know how to go to Ford and tell them that prices are going to have to go up 12½%. When Ford says absolutely no, the little guy often can't tell them to take their business elsewhere. He's caught in a tighter bind than a large corporation."

Kaull is equally bitter about increased government regulation. "OSHA [Occupational Safety & Health Administration] will probably destroy more businesses than lack of financing will," he says. "When OSHA regulations slipped through Congress, there was no coherent body that scrutinized what the effects would be. OSHA is the glaring example of how uncoordinated our government activity can be, and how punitive they can be on small business in a very unintentional manner. If OSHA had passed 10 years earlier, our company wouldn't exist."

Nicholas G. Polydoris, president of ENM Corp., a Chicago manufacturer of electrical counters, says his company has swallowed $100,000 in inventory on occasion when a big customer asked him to take it back. "We could sue, but the customer will remember you down the pike," says Polydoris, who in the meantime has to pacify his own banker's complaints about ENM's high inventories.

"You don't run the business on profit, you run on survival," says Polydoris, who last year netted $375,000 on sales of $7.5-million. Sales are off 15% from last year, and ENM has reduced employment mostly by laying off part-time workers.

Flexibility and tenacity are key ingredients in any small company's success. "The average

small businessman has no investments outside of his own business, doesn't read business
journals, doesn't understand the economy, and tends to guess wrong," says Henry Warren,
head of SBA's management services section. Warren adds, however, that "one of the
interesting things about small business is that it is very adaptable."

A classic example is Certron Corp., an Anaheim (Calif.) producer of blank cassette
cartridges and precision computer parts. "There was simply no financing available for us,"
says Edwin R. Gamson, Certron's president, about a $600,000 operating loss reported last
year when the oil crisis sent plastics prices soaring. "We stayed alive by trimming operations
and keeping on a positive cash basis. The banks have been extremely cooperative with us,
except in giving us money."

After its big suppliers, Du Pont and Monsanto, could not fill company orders during the
shortage, Certron had to turn elsewhere for 50% of its materials. "Black market was out
of the question," Gamson says. "Their prices were out of sight." So Gamson turned to the
major airlines, purchasing their used plastic dishes, eating utensils, and cocktail glasses.
"With help from the health department we learned to clean them, grind them up, and use
them over again," he explains. "We also bought used Kodak Instamatic film cartridges from
film processors."

Certron had been selling cassette cartridges to Ford Motor Co. in several different colors,
but adding the new materials gave the batches a muddy color. Undaunted, Gamson added
black to disguise the polyglot antecedents. "And we convinced Ford they would have any
color they wanted as long as it was black," he says with a grin.

Byron L. Godbersen, president of Midwest Industries, Inc., of Ida Grove, Iowa, a manufacturer of farm and marine equipment, solves his financial problems by dealing solely with a
factoring firm. Midwest's sales have grown from $600,000 in 1964 to $15.5-million last year,
on which it netted more than 6%. To compete with the giants in its field, which offer
promotions in the fall on spring items at reduced terms, Midwest sells its invoices to William
Iselin & Co., of New York, for ready cash, permitting it to offer customers the same financial
terms as its competition.

Other companies, such as Houston-based Big State Pest Control, report that business
is still booming, but profits are not sufficient to provide for future expansion. "This company
could be two or three times this size if we could get an attractive long-term loan," complains
William J. Spitz, who launched the company 25 years ago with a $400 loan. "But we're not
big enough to go to insurance companies and other long-term lenders."

Kaull of Premix is even more critical. "Discrimination is practiced in small business
financing by financial institutions," he asserts. "It's called 'sound banking practice.' " Loans
are smaller, terms shorter, and interest rates higher. A 16% to 18% interest rate on
short-term loans was not unusual last year. "Small businesses normally can't withstand that
type of interest expense when they invest in new equipment," Kaull complains. "They can't
get the return on it to justify that interest. Either they can't grow or they don't survive."

WHY BANKS ARE RELUCTANT

For their part, most bankers insist that their basic lending policies are the same for all
businesses regardless of size: They make loans only on the reasonable assurance that they
are going to be paid back. But small businesses, which almost inevitably are woefully

undercapitalized, do have a harder time than their bigger corporate brethren in convincing banks that they can repay.

For one thing, says Leonard O'Connor at the First National Bank of Boston, most small-business borrowing is term business ranging from 12 months to as long as 10 years, compared with the more common 90-day loans to larger corporations. And that, he explains, makes the small-business loan more risky at the outset. "We look at the cash flow of a small business to see if it will support monthly loan payments," says O'Connor. "In making a loan to a major corporation, we look at the balance sheet and assets and liabilities." In addition, his bank also probes for secondary sources of repayment that the small businessman might have—property, equipment, and even the personal assets of the owners.

Even so, many banks—especially those serving more limited local communities—actively cultivate small-business financing. Such business actually may be more profitable; sharp-pencil treasurers of large corporations can shop around for cut-rate banking deals. But as Luther L. Hodges, Jr., chairman of North Carolina National Bank, explains, the small firm often "has no other credit source" than his local bank.

Kenneth R. Keck, head of Chicago's Harris Trust & Savings Bank's small-business section, claims that "the banking community has become much more interested in small business in the past few years. People who thought that companies like the Penn Central were safe because they were big found out otherwise, and some banks also were badly burned on foreign commitments. Small businesses, other than the mom-and-pop ones, which are basically inefficient, are more stable because they don't have access to other money markets as do big ones."

Government loans are sometimes available, but a problem is that they make it easy for small businesses to fail by building in onerous debt loads, contends Brian Haslett, director of development for the Institute of New Enterprise Development (INED), a private consulting organization funded by both the government and foundations. To help remedy that situation, INED, which is based in Belmont, Mass., has launched a series of screening workshops from Appalachia to Salt Lake City to uncover promising new ventures. Those with the potential to become million-dollar enterprises within two years are recommended to local community development corporations, which can supply badly needed equity capital.

Traditionally, private venture capital companies have been the vehicle for raising seed money for new businesses. But tight money and the current economic slump have drastically shifted their method of operation. Venture capitalists take positions in fledgling companies, nurturing them until the enterprise can be taken public. But while $1.4-billion was raised for companies with less than $5-million sales in the equity markets during 1969 at the peak of the "hot issue" craze, such public financing now has dried up.

Undaunted by the scarcity of money, L. L. Durr, an Indianapolis engineer who has successfully run his own businesses before, started Interdyne, Inc., which designs and produces purification and recycling systems, in early 1974, with four partners and $100,000 equity. "I prefer a tough economic period to start a business," says Durr. "It eliminates the blue-suede-shoe boys, and customers are convinced you probably will last. The major reason most new firms fail is that management doesn't understand its true costs. They see a manufacturing cost of $10 per product, overhead of $5, add 10%, and think they are making money. But you must take the manufacturing cost and multiply it by six. You have to take all you can get, all the market will bear."

He also cautions entrepreneurs to put up as little as possible of their own money. "You never spend it as wisely as someone else's," says Durr, who in addition to each partner's $25,000 equity, sold $150,000 convertible debentures, borrowed $50,000 from the SBA, and arranged a credit line of $250,000. "Starting a new business these days is no game for amateurs," says Durr, who concedes that his object is capital gains. "We're ready for sale, and have talked to a big technology company, although I'd prefer to go public in a couple of years."

While men such as Durr charge ahead, businesses in fields like construction and retailing are barely hanging on. About 85% of the firms in construction are classed as small, and Frank E. Carroll, president of Deck Industries, in Rolling Meadows, a Chicago suburb, admits, "I'm just not generating any new business." An MIT alumnus who grosses $5-million annually in roofing, Carroll has watched his receivables drop from $1.1-million on Jan. 1 to less than $500,000 on Apr. 30. "It's pretty sad," says Carroll. "I'll probably survive because I've been able to build up a bit of momentum. But those new projects just are not coming in, and my backlog is disappearing." Unless things change quickly, says Carroll, "most small contractors are going to go under. They don't have a backlog, and they don't have the financial resources to stay afloat."

Many retailers face an equally gloomy and frightening future. "There is no question that the small retailer is taking the brunt of the recession," says Barbara Cole, director of New York University's Institute of Retail Management. "The industry today is dominated by large conglomerates that have the resources to ride out the bad times, but the small merchant just doesn't have the same access to capital funds, research, or the management needed to pull him through."

Merrill Douglass, an assistant professor at Emory University's Business School, says: "A typical cycle for a lot of retailers who are only marginally profitable to begin with and have very limited credit of their own is this: Profits disappear and then they got no credit. Inventory starts to decrease, they lack the merchandise they need to sell, and the cycle is downward."

COMING UP FIGHTING

Hard times notwithstanding, most small businessmen stubbornly cling to their way of life. "I'm just as much a businessman as the president of Lockheed or AT&T," says Carl I. Marias, a carpet dealer in West Los Angeles. "We've carved out a niche where price is only a secondary consideration to service and quality." Marias, whose company had sales of $700,000 last year, complains that government paperwork takes up 25% of his firm's time, but says: "I like being a little businessman. We can watch every dime a lot better than the big guys."

Robert G. Cheeseboro, a black engineer, is equally enthusiastic, despite seemingly unbeatable odds. His company makes phonograph record players for use in cars and other moving vehicles, and is located only blocks from the scene of the Watts race riots of 1965, the year before he went into business. Cheeseboro never has turned a profit and he now is suing his bank for breach of contract over a loan he failed to get. Yet, Cheeseboro says, "after Watergate and the recession, it seems that the little guy, no matter how beleaguered, is the only one who isn't jaded. We feel as if we are all that's left of creativity and dogged determination. Up until now, we were always the ones who didn't know what we were doing. Now, we can look out at the giants—the same examples we were supposed to admire—and see them with massive problems. The recession has killed the mystique of big business for the small businessman."

Cheeseboro's exuberance is not shared by Jack Meister, who started his own company, Integrated Electronics Corp. of Rockaway, N.J., in 1961, and built it into a highly profitable manufacturer of electrical parts for the auto industry. With Detroit in a slump, Meister's volume is down sharply. Still, he says, "the recession is a blessing in disguise because it makes you clinically analyze your methods. With stringent economies, we have been able to drop our break-even point from $65,000 billing a week to $35,000."

He did this in one week—laying off 25 of his 175 employees, cutting his own salary, and canceling purchase orders. "Our major problem," he says, "has been conserving working capital. And this has been difficult because as the economy changed, we were getting into inventory excesses. In the past, we would carry liberal inventories to meet customer needs. We could afford to carry surpluses. Now we play it close to the vest because of cutbacks in orders. We have to roll with the punches real quick to stay alive."

Now in his late 40s, Meister, an engineer who holds several patents, has become disillusioned despite his success. He wants to go public or sell out. "The rewards are not as great as I anticipated," he complains. "Running your own business takes too much out of you. The difference in the rewards for being in my own business as against working in my own profession has become too small in terms of the personal input that is necessary. It's becoming increasingly rough to be a success in small business. But the country will lose a lot if we lose this entrepreneurship, which big business can't always match."

But the entrepreneurial spirit continues to flourish even while the small business community struggles to survive. Karl H. Vesper, a University of Washington business professor, notes that "the last four years have seen a rapid upswing by the business schools. The demand is by students who want to do their own thing." Prior to 1969, according to a survey made by Vesper, only eight of 631 business schools offered courses on starting new businesses; last year there were 59 and 12 more have plans to begin such courses.

Charles W. Hofer, an assistant professor at Northwestern University, thinks the interest of students in small business is consistent with their search for identity and doubts about institutional bigness. "The typical entrepreneur is acting out what he likes to do," says Hofer. "It's part of the new life style that MBAS are definitely more interested in starting their own businesses."

Concludes Vesper: "Students are continually telling me they didn't realize they could start their own company. This is especially surprising to the revolutionaries who thought the only way they could have an enterprise was to take it away from someone else."

36

WHEREAS . . .

PAUL C. HOOD

How would you like to buy a TV set and find you had to call the salesman for instructions each time you wanted to change the channel? That, explains an insurance executive, is the plight of an insurance customer who can't understand his policy.

Few laymen can. Policyholders have grumbled for years about the obscure fine print. After frustrating efforts lead to bogging down somewhere between "the party of the second part" and the "whereins" and "aforesaids," the customer chucks the policy into a drawer and hopes for the best.

Now the aforesaid customer can take heart. Plain English is finding its way into insurance policies. Several companies have simplified contracts in use and many others are struggling to rewrite the old complex language. Auto policies were the first to change, and now a personal-liability catastrophe policy is out in streamlined form.

This newest entry, from the St. Paul Fire and Marine Insurance Co., uses the talents of Dr. Rudolf Flesch, the foremost advocate of simplicity in writing. For more than 25 years Flesch has been chipping away at obscure writing in the press and in business communications. The onetime Viennese lawyer turned educational researcher devised a readability scale to judge the complexity of writing.

Flesch's scale considers the length of words, the length of sentences, the number of "personal" words (such as names and pronouns) and "personal" sentences (such as quotations and conversational sentences). By charting the count on graphs he arrives at an index figure, ranging from 1 to 100.

The original St. Paul liability policy fell off the scale at -15 (the "sheer verbal jungle level" common to such documents as the Internal Revenue Code). Applying his techniques, Flesch raised the index to 60 in the revised policy. That's the level of several mass-circulation magazines.

USING EXAMPLES

Sentences were chopped into readable length. The policyholder became "you" and the company "we." And sprinkled throughout the policy are key definitions and examples to define the policy's coverage: "Your baby sitter falls down your slippery, uncarpeted stairs and suffers permanent injuries. A jury awards her $150,000. Your homeowners policy has a limit of $100,000 for each occurence. We'll pay the remaining $50,000."

"We completely reorganized the policy as opposed to others who have just cleaned up the language a little bit," says Alan Siegel of Siegel & Gale, the communications consulting company that drew Flesch into the project.

Blended with the new language are typographical tricks and attractive layout to underscore the readability of the new policy. Catchy headings top each section, the smallest type is 12 point (this article is printed in 9-point type), and contrasting color highlights the examples.

Flesch considers simplification a true art form, and votes for colloquial expressions—even slang—if necessary to convey an idea. "You should learn to forget the false rules of prissy or overformal English implanted in your nervous system by your teachers and textbooks ever since you entered first grade," he stresses in his book, *The Art of Readable Writing.*

He feels that the insurance contract he has written puts a business agreement in its simplest terms: "I promise to do this and you promise to do that."

The rise of consumerism and a growing skepticism of big business has inspired the insurance industry's plunge into rewriting old policies. Insurance men insist it's a myth, but the idea persists that policies give the customer something in the large print and take it away in the fine print. To squelch the idea that their jargon is a deliberate effort to baffle customers, the industry is overhauling its policies.

HARRIS SURVEY RESULTS

Sentry Insurance of Steven's Point, Wis., led the way after a Louis Harris survey last year underscored public skepticism. Three out of four interviewed said they relied on agents to interpret their policies rather than read the policies themselves; only 11 per cent admitted to consulting the policy.

Taking a cue from the survey, Sentry worked over its auto policies and had a simplified version ready early this year. "We didn't intend to write a children's primer," explains Don Reutershan, executive vice president. "We were writing for a responsible adult audience."

The new Sentry policy has been accepted by regulatory officials in nearly 40 states, and Reutershan says customer response had been favorable.

AWAITING LEGALISTS' REACTION

Nationwide Insurance Co. of Columbus, Ohio, joined the trend toward simplified policies in January by introducing a plain-English auto policy for Pennsylvania customers. Now that the shakedown period is over, filings are planned in five Midwestern states this month, with more due later.

"We're still going to have to wait and see what the legal community is going to do with the new policy," says John Doulin, who headed Nationwide's rewriting effort. "There's a feeling of security in the old language, and insurance men feel comfortable with it. I don't know why, because we're still going to court over it."

It's the fear of legal tangles that has perpetuated the legalistic prose. In repeated court cases a body of law has been formed that brings fairly uniform interpretation of the standardized phraseology. Any variation from the stock terms, many fear, will lead to new rounds of costly legal attacks.

But with the consumer fires burning, official attitudes are changing. At the instigation of Joe F. Christie, chairman of the Texas Board of Insurance, the Texas Legislature has just passed a bill to require that all health and accident policies written in the state be accompanied by a readable statement of the policy's coverage.

"The need for readable health and accident policies is real," said Gov. Dolph Briscoe in endorsing the move. "It is not so much a problem of outright deception, but a problem of the consumer's inability to understand the jargon that attorneys and insurance companies are so fond of using to fill up the pages of insurance coverage."

DELAY ON LIFE INSURANCE

Because of special legal fears, life insurance may be the last to fall in line. However, at least one major company is attempting to use the plain-talk approach in rewriting its policies.

To Siegel, the job is only partially done when policies themselves are refined. Related application forms and other communications also must change, he insists. "In some cases billing notices are confusing," he explains, "and customer correspondence is put together with total disregard for the mentality of the layman who doesn't understand the procedures."

Before tackling the insurance project, Siegel & Gale used the same simple-English techniques in producing a consumer-loan note for First National City Bank of New York. And in the works are other business applications: product warranties, buyer-instruction booklets, service contracts, and employe-benefits booklets.

There's nothing altruistic about the new emphasis on straight talk—it's just good business, advocates believe. Says Waverly G. Smith, St. Paul Fire and Marine president: "The more consumers know before they buy insurance, the more we save on the cost of adjustments, complaints, and explanatory correspondence."

37

SMALL CLAIMS COURT*

PAULETTE S. EANEMAN,
MICHAEL LIPMAN, and
NANCY ZUPANEC

... The small claims court provides an inexpensive and informal way for individuals, businesses, corporations and governmental agencies to settle disagreements. The first such court was London's Small Debt Court. It was started in 1605. Small claims courts appeared in the United States in the early 1900's—in Ohio in 1913, in Massachusetts in 1920, in California in 1921. Today over half of all the civil claims filed in California each year are small claims.

Briefly, this is now the small claims court operates:

YOU CAN SUE FOR MONEY ONLY

You can't ask the court to issue a "writ"—an order to force someone to do or not to do something. For example, the small claims court judge can't order your neighbor to top a tall tree that's blocking your ocean view. But he may order your neighbor to pay you the $150 he promised toward repairing the fence separating your yards. The one exception to this rule involves landlord-tenant cases. In certain instances—described in detail later—the small claims court may order a tenant to pay his back rent and also to move out of his apartment. This is called an unlawful detainer action.

CLAIMS CAN BE LOWERED

Say your auto body shop repairs Hal's sports car. You charge him $550 for the work, but he never pays you. How can you file a claim for $550 in small claims court, which has a

*Editor's Note: This reading has been excepted from *Small Claims Court,* a publication of the Conference of California Judges. The Procedures discussed here are those used in California. Similar procedures are used in other states. Check with a local County Clerk or attorney for up-to-date regulations in other areas.

$500 limit? You have two alternatives: You can take Hal to a justice or municipal court if you want, but you may end up hiring an attorney who will charge a couple of hundred dollars to represent you. Or you can reduce your claim to $500 and represent yourself in a small claims court. This way you won't have to pay an attorney, so whatever amount the judge awards you is yours.

CLAIMS CAN BE CONSOLIDATED, NOT SPLIT

You are a dentist and Alyce Pierson owes you $30 for x-rays and teeth cleaning, $15 for a cavity you filled last year, and $25 for one you filled last month. You can add up all these smaller claims and sue Alyce for $70 in small claims court. But if instead Alyce owes you $650 for a bridge you made her, you can't sue her once for $500 and once for $150. If you sue her for $500 in small claims court, you must forget the remaining $150 forever. The alternative is to hire an attorney and sue for the full amount in your county's justice or municipal court.

PROCEDURE IS INFORMAL

Attorneys are not allowed to represent people in small claims court. But they may appear if they are parties—the plaintiff or defendant—in a small claims case. If you sue or are sued by someone, you must speak for yourself. There are no juries. You present your case to the judge and he makes the decision. In addition, there's no formal questioning and cross-examination. Usually the judge asks you to tell your side of the dispute in your own words. He may ask you questions to be sure he understands your case. Formal rules of evidence are not used. The judge can listen to any witness you bring with you. If he wants, he can listen to hearsay testimony—statments someone makes to the witness about something the witness himself didn't hear or see. The judge can also examine any document you supply —including copies of documents, rather than the originals. It's up to him.

KINDS OF CASES

Although the small claims court is limited to disputes involving money, it handles many kinds of cases. These are examples of the six most common disputes which find their way into the "people's court."

Automobile Accidents

Often disputes between individuals involve auto accidents. Jack Thomas rear-ends your car as you sit at the corner waiting for the light to change. Unfortunately Jack doesn't have insurance to pay for the necessary repairs to your car. Or for the stitches to sew up the cuts on your forehead. Or for your broken eyeglasses. Or for the time you missed from work because you couldn't see to do your job. Or for the taxis you had to take while your car was being repaired. You can sue Jack Thomas for any of these claims in small claims court.

Of course, you'll have to prove your case. You bring in witnesses who saw the accident. For example, your wife who was riding with you at the time might testify for you. Or a stranger who saw Jack bang into your car. The stranger's testimony will probably carry more weight with the judge than your wife's, since he won't have a stake in the outcome of the case. If the stranger won't come to court voluntarily, the court clerk will show you how to prepare a subpoena to force him to come. It's also smart to bring photos to show the judge how your car looked after the accident. And how you looked after the accident. You should also bring in your broken glasses. Bring estimates of how much it will cost to repair your car and glasses and any other property damaged in the accident. Also bring receipts for repairs already made and copies of any medical bills.

Sale of Goods

Many small claims cases involve the sale of goods. The merchant who is still waiting for payment of the suit or stereo he sold you may sue you in small claims court. On the other hand, perhaps you have the complaint. You bought an electric blender; when you took it home it sprayed food all over the kitchen. You return it to the store. If the merchant says you broke the blender yourself and won't refund your money, you can take him to small claims court.

Suppose a merchant sues for an unpaid bill. He'll bring his records with him to prove to the judge that you still owe him $80 for a brown, two-button Supercrease suit. If you go to court as a consumer, be sure to bring along a sales slip showing how much you paid for the item in question, a copy of the guarantee, and possibly the item itself. It's also helpful to have a witness who can testify you didn't abuse or break the product.

Sales of Services

By far the majority of small claims cases involve disputes over the sale of services. These suits are generally filed by governmental agencies and corporations. For example, a governmental agency—like the county hospital—may sue a patient who doesn't pay his bill. Or the county roads department may sue a driver who runs down a stop sign or light standard and refuses to pay for it.

Businesses and corporations often sue in small claims court for services they provided and for which they didn't get paid. For example, you and your partners run Neat and Tidy, Inc., a yard-cleaning business. You spend a week digging out Mr. Watson's back lot, which is filled with weeds and beer cans. If Mr. Watson refuses to pay you for your work, you can take him to small claims court.

On the other hand, if Mr. Watson pays you in advance to remove the weeds and cans from his lot and you do only half the job, he can take you to small claims court for services not properly performed.

You'll both want to bring any written agreements you signed, canceled checks, and maybe even a "before" and "after" photograph of the yard.

Contracts

A contract is an oral or written agreement between two parties. Individuals, businesses, corporations, and governmental agencies all make contracts. And when one party doesn't live up to its promises, the other party may go to small claims court.

Contract disputes generally happen when: (1) one party promises to do something for the other party, and then doesn't do it, or doesn't do it properly; or (2) the party receiving the goods or services doesn't pay for them.

An example: Steven Boyd signs a written contract with Sanitee Septic Tank Service to clean out his septic tank twice a year for a set fee. Mr. Boyd pays the fee in advance. Sanitee cleans the tank once. Eighteen months later the company's men still haven't returned for the second cleaning. Mr. Boyd, his contract in hand, takes Sanitee to small claims court and asks for his money back.

Most important in any contract dispute is the document itself, if one exists. The judge will certainly want to read it and see just what each person promised. If the contract was oral, the judge will listen to what the parties promised each other verbally.

Loaned Money

Loaned money disputes usually involve two people. Your old pal Dave Albany hits you up for $50. "I'll pay you back next month," he says. That's the last you see of Dave. After repeated requests for the money, you take your former friend to small claims court.

If Dave signed an IOU, bring it along. If he didn't, you might produce a witness who overheard Dave promise to pay back the money. Or your check for $50, with Dave's endorsement on it. Dave may be down and out, in which case you'll probably have trouble collecting the $50—even if the judge tells Dave to pay. If you can't collect, you can at least write off the loan on your federal income tax report as a "business loss."

On the other hand, perhaps you're sued for money borrowed; but you know you've already paid it back. In that case, be sure to have some proof with you. A canceled check is best; a friend who saw you pay back the money may also be helpful.

Back Rent

Landlords often use small claims to collect back rent from slow-paying tenants. In an unlawful detainer action, a landlord can also—under certain circumstances—get the tenant moved out. This means if you have a month-to-month lease on an apartment or house and you haven't paid the rent that's due, the landlord may serve you with a three-day notice asking you to pay up or get out. If you don't the court may order you to do so.

What if you withheld rent because your apartment was in poor condition? Perhaps your bathroom ceiling was falling in and your radiator didn't work. Or your plumbing constantly backed up and cockroaches lived under your bed. In such a case, you won't necessarily be forced to pay up and move out. The law says your landlord is responsible for keeping your apartment in satisfactory condition. If he doesn't, the court may deny his unlawful detainer claim.

Perhaps the problem with your apartment isn't so serious. Your kitchen window is broken and you ask the landlord to fix it. He doesn't, and after a reasonable time you pay to have it fixed yourself. The cost is $58, so you subtract that amount from your month's rent. Can your landlord sue you in small claims court for the $58? The law says a tenant is allowed to withhold up to one month's rent once a year to pay for necessary repairs to an apartment or house—unless he gave up that right when he signed his lease or rental agreement.

On the other hand, tenants frequently use the small claims court to sue their landlords over cleaning and security deposits. In such cases, the tenant asks for the return of his deposit, which he claims the landlord wrongfully refused to refund.

In any landlord-tenant dispute, the landlord will bring to court the rental agreement and a copy of your payment record. If you question the amount owed, bring your canceled checks. Also bring receipts for materials and labor if you claim to have made necessary repairs on the property. "Before" and "after" photographs of the premises are helpful, too. . . .

SMALL CLAIMS COURT TOMORROW

We've described how the small claims court operates and the kinds of cases it handles. However, it's important to know that some court rules and procedures may change in the near future as we attempt to update and improve the small claims process.

Our system of justice is far from perfect. The Legislature—by passing, amending and repealing laws—and the courts—by interpreting and reinterpreting these laws— are continually trying to improve our system.

It's not surprising, then, that the small claims court might need some improvement. Its founders saw the court as an inexpensive and informal means of settling disputes involving small amounts of money. The legislators and judges who devised the system felt it would be used by John Q. Public—the average citizen—who sues his neighbor when the neighbor backs his car into John's fence and refuses to pay for the damages. Today's small claims court handles many individual disputes, but it also hears a vast number of cases which some people feel might best be handled another way. . . .

THE PROFESSIONAL LITIGANT

Since corporations and governmental agencies appear in small claims court more often than individuals, their representatives may gain the advantage of confidence and experience. The creditor who has a large and constant volume of claims uses the court on a weekly or monthly basis, often filing several claims at once. The representative of the corporation or governmental agency—even though not an attorney—knows the ropes in small claims court and has an advantage over the individual who appears only once. In fact, the officer who represents the corporation may have some legal training and certainly has access to the corporation's attorneys. On the other hand, the individual who goes to small claims court for the first time may be frightened and unfamiliar with legal language and procedures. The judge will do his best to help the individual present his case. But once the person is in court, it's too late to tell him what witnesses or documents he should have brought with him.

To help minimize a corporation's advantage, some court reformers would like to prohibit the filing of "group" claims and limit the number of times any one business or agency could appear in small claims court in a given time period. Other reformers feel that attorneys should be allowed to represent both the plaintiff and defendant in a small claims suit. But if lawyers were permitted, their opponents argue, the informal, inexpensive people's court would be replaced by an adversary system at great cost to litigants and taxpayers.

An alternative to the use of lawyers would be some form of paraprofessional representation for the uninformed or low-income litigant. Some people suggest a trained court employee who would meet with the litigant to explain how the small claims court operates. This employee would help the litigant prepare his claim, telling him what witnesses and papers to bring to court. Still others propose the use of trained law school students as people's advocates. Attorneys might oppose these suggestions, however, since they have strict rules about "unauthorized practice of the law."

COLLECTION DIFFICULTIES

Another criticism of the small claims court involves collection of the money the judge awards the winner. Many people think that once they win in small claims court, they will receive their money instantly. Unfortunately, this isn't true. It's up to the person who wins the judgment ot collect it. The court will assist him with a writ of execution. But collecting a small claims court judgment may take time and effort on the winner's part. And some people don't have the time and know-how to collect. Besides, the person who owes you three months back rent may be unemployed and unable to pay anyway.

Every judge who sits in small claims court is aware of the problems we've mentioned, and he does his best to see that both sides receive a fair hearing and a fair decision. But if the judge doesn't agree with some aspects of the system, he can't change them on his own. Our lawmakers must do that—after careful consideration to make sure reforms are actually improvements. The Legislature and courts are currently reviewing the small claims structure to see how it can best be improved. Their goal is to offer the highest standard of justice possible to all of us using the court.

38

SIX DANGERS IN AMERICA'S FUTURE

The latest from Federal Reserve Board Chairman Arthur F. Burns:

The U.S. must solve six problems if it is to have lasting prosperity.

In testimony before the Joint Economic Committee of Congress, Mr. Burns pointed to these persistent weaknesses as standing in the way of achieving a steady rate of economic growth once this recession is over.

PROBLEM NO. 1

Corporation debt, which was only about half as large as stockholders' investments in the nation's business in 1950, is today roughly equal to those investments.

A great deal of the additional debt is of short-term variety, which comes due in a matter of months and therefore needs to be refinanced over and over. Mr. Burns declared:

"The liquidity position of nonfinancial businesses has thus been weakened."

A slumping stock market in 1973 and 1974 was one of the reasons for that pile up of debt. It was difficult, if not impossible, for many companies to raise funds through the sale of new shares of stock. That left them with no alternative to heavy borrowing.

PROBLEM NO. 2

A decline in the earnings of the corporations in "real" terms contributed to the increase in debt by depriving the companies of funds needed for new supplies, construction and equipment.

While corporations generally reported higher profits in 1974, Mr. Burns said this apparent increase came from a rise in the value of inventories as a result of inflation. When this "illusory" element is eliminated, he estimated, the companies' earnings actually went down 20 per cent last year and were smaller than they had been 8 to 10 years ago.

Profits were also distorted by the fact that industry is charging for the use of plant and **249** equipment on the basis of prices paid for them years ago, instead of at the much higher prices that will have to be paid for replacements when the present equipment wears out or becomes obsolete.

Adjust for that factor, Mr. Burns said, and profits were actually not even large enough to cover the dividends being paid to stockholders—let alone to provide for building up the business.

PROBLEM NO. 3

The double-digit inflation of the past year. The Federal Reserve Chairman explained:

"There can be little doubt that inflation is the principal cause of the decline in economic activity in which we now find ourselves. . . . Because of its capricious incidence on income and wealth, inflation has caused disillusionment and discontent among our citizens. And because of its distorting effects on business decisions, inflation has brought into question the liquidity of some major business and financial institutions."

On that score, Mr. Burns was taking issue with George Meany, head of the AFL-CIO, and also with some economists who say the Federal Reserve brought on the recession by keeping money and credit too tight for too long.

Mr. Burns takes the position that the Federal Reserve had to clamp down on the growth of the money supply and let interest rates soar to record levels to check inflation, which he traces in large measure to two of the six problems in his list.

PROBLEM NO. 4

Shrinking gains in productivity—what is otherwise known as output per man-hour—in recent years. Gains here reflect the technological improvements that can be brought about through new machines and methods and the increasing education of the labor force.

The trouble is, Mr. Burns suggested, that industry has not had the incentives needed to invest enough in new plant and equipment or in advanced research. And, at the same time, productivity has been hampered by unfavorable changes in "the attitude of the labor force and some laxity in management."

Said the Federal Reserve Chairman:

"Workers nowadays are well trained, but many of them work with less energy than they should, and absenteeism has become a more serious problem."

PROBLEM NO. 5

The mounting tax burden. Mr. Burns pointed out:

"Taxes have progressively reduced the rewards for working, while Government at the same time has increased the share of the national output going to persons who are not productively employed. Twenty-five years ago, a typical worker with three dependents gave up 1 per cent of his gross weekly earnings in federal income and Social Security taxes. Since then, that fraction has risen steadily and reached 13 per cent in 1974."

Mr. Burns contended that the mounting tax burden has taken away some of the worker's incentive and thus tends to reduce productivity. And he blamed the rise in taxes largely on the way federal outlays for "public welfare, Social Security benefits, unemployment insurance, and other public assistance" have grown. These payments, he estimated, have increased about twice as fast as wages and salaries. He warned:

"A society as affluent as ours can ill afford to neglect the poor, the elderly, the unemployed or other disadvantaged persons, but neither can it afford to neglect the fundamental precept that there must be adequate rewards to stimulate individual effort."

PROBLEM NO. 6

The decline of the U.S. dollar in world markets. On that score, the FRB chief declared:

"A substantially greater degree of exchange-rate stability will not be achieved until underlying economic and financial conditions have been put in better order."

What ought to be done? Mr. Burns divided his prescription into short- and long-range remedies.

For the immediate future, he stressed the need to "cushion" the recession with a temporary income-tax cut for individuals, tax relief for business, and "an adequate expansion in supplies of money and bank credit."

For the longer run, he said, Congress must get a firmer grip on federal spending, especially on the so-called transfer payments to people receiving direct assistance of one sort or another from the Government.

Better profits for business and greater incentives for investment also will be needed, Mr. Burns said.

"Above all," he concluded, "ways must be found to bring an end to inflation."

39

THE "FUTURE SHOCK" MAN SEES MORE DRASTIC CHANGES AHEAD

Interview With Alvin Toffler, Author

Q Mr. Toffler, what's in store for the industrial nations of the West?

A A long period of nonserenity. It's a mistake to look at our present situation and see it simply as one more economic recession. Industrial society is going through a profound breakdown and transformation. What's happening now will affect our economy for a generation or more.

All industrial societies share certain common characteristics: mass production, mass distribution, mass education, the nuclear family. They all rely on big science and big organizations. They all share a materialist value system. You find these traits in Russia, the U.S., Sweden, Japan. And, when you look closely, you find each of these is breaking down or moving into crisis. If our problems were only economic, they would be a lot less dangerous.

That's why I use the term "eco-spasm" to describe what's happening today. It's not boom or bust, or recession or "stagflation." It's an economic shake-up in the midst of an ecological crisis, technological and political upsets, and revolutionary changes in family structure, values, sexual attitudes, military and geopolitical power balances.

Q "Eco-spasm" sounds like a cataclysm. Are you suggesting it is inevitable?

A Not inevitable. But it's idiotic to think our troubles will be over if we can get the unemployment rate down, or if we can reduce inflation a few points. The trouble is only beginning.

Q Are you talking about violence—perhaps even revolution?

A We can't rule that out. You have the potential for violence when there is large-scale unemployment side by side with prosperity, or when change is so rapid that the uncertainty and unpredictability in society becomes unbearable.

If we do get violence in this country, it won't only be the rich and the poor at one another's throats—it will break out between age groups, regions, ethnic coalitions, maybe even the sexes. I think we can avoid bloodshed, but it will require tremendous changes.

251

Q What kinds of changes?

A We'll have to scrap our obsolete ideologies—the old political labels like "left wing" or "right wing." And we'll have to recognize that there is no such thing as economics in a vacuum. There is no "economic fix" for our problems. Every time we try to fix something with economics alone, we make matters worse in our communities, our ecology, our family life, our global relations. What's needed is a whole new way of looking at the "eco-spasm."

Conventional wisdom tells us that industrial society will last forever. The assumption is that we can adjust a few levers or twist a few economic dials and somehow the inflation will vanish, the Arabs will fold their tents and recycle their money, and then everything will go on as it did before.

That's an "Alice in Wonderland" fantasy. There's no going back.

Q Isn't "the end of industrialism" a return to the past?

A No. The death or decline of industrial society doesn't mean a return to old-fashioned agriculture. It means a radical shift forward to a wholly new stage of technology, very advanced yet very small-scale, resource-thrifty and human.

It means a shift toward more human services, too. It means social acceptance of new family arrangements, a variety of them, not simply the traditional nuclear family. It means new, antibureaucratic forms of organization. It means a new ecological consciousness and the decline of the nation-state, among many other things. That's not going backward. And until these long-term changes are carried out, no long-term economic stability is possible.

Q Obviously, you don't believe that the economic measures being taken today will solve the current problems—

A Of course not.

We're still trapped in obsolete thinking. We're acting as if the U.S. were still a classical industrial country, instead of a country breaking new ground in the advance toward superindustrialism.

Let me give you an example:

In traditional industrial societies, a boom or a bust spread more or less uniformly over the whole economy. In a superindustrial society, the economy and the society itself is extremely heterogeneous, varied, diverse. It's no longer a "mass society" but a society broken into constantly changing mini-economies, mini-cultures and mini-markets. That's why, in an "eco-spasm," the conditions vary wildly from one city or region to the next, from one industry or social group to the next.

This makes the usual kind of national economic policies almost worthless. It means that when you turn the spigot in the Federal Reserve Bank, you may cure one problem in Detroit, but you intensify or create another one in Birmingham, Alabama, or Fargo, North Dakota.

A single, nationwide dose of credit or tax relief—or the reverse—is like giving Adrenalin or barbiturates to every patient in the hospital, regardless of whether he has a broken leg, a heart attack, a brain tumor or hypertrophic gastritis.

Q Are you saying that no national policies can work?

A I wouldn't go that far. But we have got to shift the emphasis away from the search for nationwide panaceas.

The nation-state is not going to be nearly as important during the superindustrial era. A lot more problems have to be solved at the transnational level, and a lot more will have to be handled down below the national level. That's one reason why we will need totally new approaches to planning.

Q What kind of planning? Planning by whom?

A In the next six months, I think we are going to see a powerful push for centralized economic planning at the national level in this country. The lobbying has already begun, and it's not just unions or liberal economists that are clamoring for it. Increasingly, big business is, too.

Top industrialists and Wall Street financiers are discovering that if Government planning is bad, lack of it is even worse. Sophisticated managers have seen that capitalist countries like France and Japan haven't fallen into the arms of the Kremlin just because they engage in economic planning.

Certainly, it's time we recognized that we can't continue to live from crisis to crisis. The time has come to discard our irrational fears, but not our *rational* fears.

The issue isn't planning or no planning. The real issue is what kind of planning do we want. And here there *is* reason to worry, because centralized, national economic planning, as most of its advocates conceive of it, is just as obsolete as nonplanning.

Q What do you mean by obsolete?

A It is steeped in assumptions that no longer make sense. First, the very notion of economic planning perpetuates the separation of economics from social, political, ecological, cultural, psychological and other forces that are destabilizing the economy itself.

Secónd, as I've suggested a moment ago, the emerging new society is extremely diversified, demassified. What we need is not a single, great master plan in the White House. Nothing could be more unworkable. What's needed is a *process* for generating, changing and regenerating plans at the regional, local and community level, and in every industry and nonprofit sector.

Then there's your question about who is to do it. Traditional planning is dominated by experts and bureaucrats. It's based on the idea that ordinary lay citizens are dumb and passive. It's elitist and subject to capture by powerful interests.

Q But what is the alternative?

A The alternative is "anticipatory democracy." When you plan at the centralized level, you increase the magnitude of potential error. Unless you have feedback coming in from millions of ordinary people whose lives are affected, and unless those millions of ordinary people can alter the plans, you not only create the conditions for "friendly fascism" but the possibilities of massive disaster as well—economic and social dislocations on a scale hitherto unknown.

That's why we had better start paying attention to some experiments now being carried out at the State and community level in many parts of the country.

A few years back, for example, the Governor of Hawaii created something named Hawaii 2000. Hundreds of ordinary citizens—housewifes, students, doctors, executives, truck drivers and teachers—met with experts to discuss issues like: What should the urban-rural mix be in Hawaii in the year 2000? How much tourism ought to be permitted? How should schools be redesigned to prepare kids for the future? What kind of health or transport systems do we want 30 years from now?

The results were so exciting, it is being repeated on the county and township level. In Iowa last year, a grass-roots program called Iowa 2000 brought from 35,000 to 50,000 citizens together in from 1,500 to 1,800 meetings, and came up with ideas that are now being considered by the State's politicians.

In Washington State, the process has been tied much more closely into the State's planning agency. Literally thousands of citizens have participated in drawing up goals for the future of the State. They've written scenarios to see how those goals might be achieved and what new problems would be created. They have systematically studied the "cross impacts" among goals to see how each one would affect the others, and put together a number of policy alternatives for the State. They have presented these on television in ways that permitted viewers to vote on them, and even opinion-polled the general public to compare the attitudes of nonparticipants with those who did participate in the over-all program. Out of this have come proposals for the State legislature.

There are also interesting experiments with planning and citizen goal-setting in hundreds of cities. None of these are, as yet, the whole answer to democratic planning. But they suggest all sorts of possibilities that have not yet been explored.

That's why I think that, with luck, we *can* not only avoid the "eco-spasm," but take advantage of new opportunities as they arise. It won't be easy. But I think we have a fighting chance. If we invent some new tools, we'll improve our chances of avoiding bloodshed.

Anticipatory democracy—decentralized, democratized attention to the future, rather than traditional economic planning—may be the most important tool of all.

PART SEVEN
DISCUSSION QUESTIONS

1. What do you think of Jordan as a potential export market for many U.S. products?

2. How can U.S. manufacturers hope to compete against Japanese auto makers in the Pacific?

3. Outline the major problems faced by small businesses.

4. What is your impression of the new contract language described in the article entitled "Whereas . . ."?

5. Describe the benefits and/or drawbacks you see with small claims courts.

6. Do Arthur Burns and Alvin Toffler agree or disagree on the future? Comment.

APPENDIX

Selections for Additional Reading

PART I BUSINESS AND ITS ENVIRONMENT

"The Realization of Our American Dream," *The Office,* January 1978.

"Where New Small Businesses Go Wrong," *Changing Times,* December 1976.

"Is the Ethics of Business Changing?" *Harvard Business Review,* January 1977.

"What Do Corporations Do?" *The New Republic,* May 21, 1977.

PART II MANAGEMENT OF THE ENTERPRISE

"Schools for Entrepreneurs," *Free Enterprise,* April 1978.

"What First-Line Managers Must Know," *The Office,* January 1978.

"Understanding Today's Young Executive," *Nation's Business,* September 1977.

"The Social Responsibility of People in Business," *Nation's Business,* April 1977.

PART III MANAGEMENT OF HUMAN RESOURCES AND PRODUCTION

"The Changing Role of the Administrator," *The Office,* January 1978.

"Mobile Managers—Well Paid and Discontent," *Harvard Business Review,* September 1977.

"Merit Money: More Firms Link Pay to Job Performance," *Wall Street Journal,* March 7, 1977.

"Productivity: How to Beat Inflation and Boost Earnings," *Nation's Business,* July 1975.

"The Watchdog," *Wall Street Journal,* December 12, 1975.

"Productivity: Patterns and Perspectives," *Financial Executive,* April 1977.

"Costly Conversion: Industry Shifts to Coal as Government Forces Conservation," *Wall Street Journal,* August 15, 1977.

"A Decade of Physical Distribution," *Handling and Shipping,* June 1977.

PART IV MARKETING MANAGEMENT

"Pricing Strategy in an Inflation Economy," *Business Week,* April 6, 1974.

"P & G Uses Pampers Story to Teach the Consumer about Marketing," *Advertising Age,* April 4, 1977.

"Seagram Antes $40 Million," *Business Week,* August 22, 1977.

PART V FINANCING THE ENTERPRISE 257

"How to Use Tax Shelters the Way the Rich Do," *Family Circle,* October 18, 1977.

"The Teenage Tycoon Who Turns Old Coins into $100,000 A Year," *Free Enterprise,* April 1978.

"Junk Bonds: Wall Street Lays a Golden Egg," *Money,* May 1978.

"Come Now, Dow Jones," *Money,* May 1978.

"Financing a New Business," *Money,* May 1978.

"Annual Overhaul: Zero-Base Budgeting Used by Many Firms," *Wall Street Journal,* March 14, 1977.

"The Great Fiscal Illusion," *Forbes,* October 15, 1975.

"The Controller: Inflation Gives Him More Clout with Management," *Business Week,* August 15, 1977.

PART VI QUANTITATIVE TOOLS OF MANAGEMENT

"Computers' Marriage to Communication to Yield Big Benefits—If It Ever Occurs," *Wall Street Journal,* November 2, 1977.

"Living: Pushbutton Power," *Time,* February 20, 1978.

"Computers in Developing Nations: A Cautionary Tale," *Personal Computing,* February 1978.

"Computers That Use Plain English Permit Vast New Applications," *Wall Street Journal,* March 27, 1978.

PART VII ADDITIONAL DIMENSIONS

"Careers for the 1980's: 10 of the Best—and 10 of the Worst," *Money,* November 1977.

"Job Meccas For the 80's," *Money,* May 1978.

"Worry for World Business: How to Compete with Japan," *U.S. News & World Report,* September 26, 1977.

"Detroit Finds New Routes Across the Pacific," *Fortune,* October 1973.

"Where U.S. Firms Are Missing A Bet," *Nation's Business,* February 1975.

"Building Business with Africa," *Dun's Review,* May 1977.

"When We'll Start Running Out of Oil," *Fortune,* October 1977.

"Work in the Year 2001," *The Futurist,* February 1977.

"Write a Résumé That Gets the Job," *Changing Times,* July 1975.

"Managing Your Time by Managing Yourself," *Nation's Business,* April 1977.

"Franchising Comes of Age," *Dun's Review,* August 1977.

"How to Be Your Own Boss without Having a Fool for an Employer," *Money,* June 1977.